NEW MERMAIDS

General editor: Brian Gibbons
Professor of English Literature, University of Münster

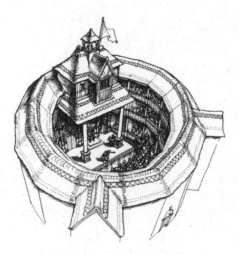

Reconstruction of an Elizabethan Theatre
by C. Walter Hodges

NEW MERMAIDS

The Alchemist

All for Love

Arden of Faversham

Bartholmew Fair

The Beaux' Stratagem

The Changeling

A Chaste Maid in Cheapside

The Country Wife

The Critic

Dr Faustus

The Duchess of Malfi

The Dutch Courtesan

Eastward Ho!

Edward the Second

Epicoene or The Silent Woman

Every Man In His Humour

Gammer Gurton's Needle

An Ideal Husband

The Importance of Being Earnest

The Jew of Malta

The Knight of the Burning Pestle

Lady Windermere's Fan

Love for Love

The Malcontent

The Man of Mode

Marriage A-la-Mode

A New Way to Pay Old Debts

The Old Wife's Tale

The Playboy of the Western World

The Provoked Wife

The Recruiting Officer

The Relapse

The Revenger's Tragedy

The Rivals

The Roaring Girl

The Rover

The School for Scandal

She Stoops to Conquer

The Shoemaker's Holiday

The Spanish Tragedy

Tamburlaine

Three Late Medieval Morality Plays

    Mankind

    Everyman

    Mundus et Infans

'Tis Pity She's a Whore

Volpone

The Way of the World

The White Devil

The Witch

The Witch of Edmonton

A Woman Killed with Kindness

A Woman of No Importance

Women Beware Women

NEW MERMAIDS

JOHN WEBSTER

THE WHITE DEVIL

edited by Christina Luckyj

Associate Professor, Dalhousie University

A & C Black • London
WW Norton • New York

Second edition 1996
Reprinted 1998, 2001
Reprinted with new cover 2003
A & C Black Publishers Limited
37 Soho Square
London W1D 3QZ
www.acblack.com

ISBN 0-7136-6793-1

First New Mermaid edition 1966

Published in the United States of America by
W. W. Norton & Company Inc.
500 Fifth Avenue, New York, NY 10110

ISBN 0-393-90078-9

CIP catalogue records for this book are available
from the British Library and the Library of Congress

Printed in Great Britain by
Bookmarque Ltd, Croydon, Surrey

CONTENTS

Acknowledgements   vi
Abbreviations   viii
Introduction   ix
   The Author   ix
   Sources   xi
   The Play   xiv
   Note on the Text   xxix
Further Reading   xxxi
THE WHITE DEVIL   1
   Dramatis Personae   3
   To the Reader   5
   Text   7

ACKNOWLEDGEMENTS

I am deeply indebted to previous editors of *The White Devil*, especially to Elizabeth Brennan and John Russell Brown, who provided me with sound text and commentary to revise, augment and above all rely on. I am also extremely grateful to Anthony Hammond, D. C. Gunby and David Carnegie for generously allowing me to read their new Cambridge edition of Webster in proof. The present edition is deeply enriched by their painstaking scholarship. At New Mermaids, my immediate debts are to Professor Brian Gibbons for his encouragement and good sense, Anne Watts for her patience and efficiency, and Margaret Parker for her excellent copy-editing of this text. With the aid of a Research and Development Fund grant from my own university, I was able to employ three graduate research assistants: Tanya Caldwell, Dawn Henwood and Derrick Higginbotham, each of whom contributed something invaluable to the commentary. My colleagues Ronald Huebert and John Baxter supported my work. It is impossible to imagine my love of Webster without thinking of those who instilled and nurtured it: Alexander Leggatt and Sheldon Zitner. My deepest thanks go to my husband, Keith Lawson, who uncomplainingly tended babies and read drafts, sometimes at the same time. All errors are, of course, my own.

FOR KEITH

ABBREVIATIONS

Boklund   Gunnar Boklund, *The Sources of 'The White Devil'* (Cambridge, Mass.: Harvard University Press, 1957)

Brown   John Russell Brown, ed., *The White Devil* (The Revels Plays, London: Methuen, 1960)

Dent   R. W. Dent, *John Webster's Borrowing* (Berkeley and Los Angeles: University of California Press, 1960)

Lucas   F. L. Lucas, ed., *The Complete Works of John Webster* I (London: Chatto and Windus, 1927)

NCW   (The New Cambridge Webster) D. C. Gunby, David Carnegie and Anthony Hammond, eds., *The Works of John Webster* I (Cambridge: Cambridge University Press, 1995)

OED   J. A. Simpson and E. S. C. Weiner, general eds., *The Oxford English Dictionary*, 2nd ed. (Oxford: Clarendon, 1989)

Pettie   George Pettie, trans., *The Civile Conversation of M. Steeven Guazzo* (1581; London: Constable and New York: Alfred A. Knopf, 1925)

Shakespeare *The Riverside Shakespeare*, ed. G. Blakemore Evans (Boston: Houghton Mifflin, 1974)

s.d.   stage direction

s.p.   speech prefix

Tilley   Morris Palmer Tilley, *A Dictionary of the Proverbs in England in the Sixteenth and Seventeenth Centuries* (Ann Arbor: University of Michigan Press, 1950)

Quotations are taken from the following New Mermaid texts: *A Chaste Maid in Cheapside*, ed. Alan Brissenden (1968); *Dr Faustus*, ed. Roma Gill (1989); *The Revenger's Tragedy*, ed. Brian Gibbons (1990); *The Duchess of Malfi*, ed. Elizabeth M. Brennan (1993).

INTRODUCTION

THE AUTHOR

UNLIKE *The White Devil*'s bitter, impecunious Flamineo, John Webster came from the prosperous middle class. Born in 1578 or 1579 (about fifteen years after Shakespeare) to a wealthy coachmaker whose business – the making, hiring and selling of an increasingly fashionable mode of transport – elevated him to the 'status of a Renaissance Henry Ford or Walter Chrysler',[1] Webster grew up in the noisy, smelly, densely populated parish of St Sepulchre, near Smithfield, the hub of London's thriving manufacturing trade. Since his father supplied everything from carts for transporting whores and condemned criminals to vehicles for civic pageants and lavish coaches for the nobility, the young Webster might well have rubbed elbows with a wide spectrum of London society, including theatre professionals. As his father was a freeman of the Merchant Taylors' Company, Webster probably attended the famous Merchant Taylors' School (which boasted Thomas Kyd and Edmund Spenser among its former pupils). That school's rigorous and broad curriculum would have given him a foundation in the classics and an esteem for the vernacular championed by its first headmaster, Richard Mulcaster. Later, possibly after a brief stint as an actor,[2] Webster probably passed on to the New Inn and then to the Middle Temple, one of the Inns of Court, where his legal education became not only the inspiration for his many courtroom scenes but also a means of acquiring all the rhetorical skills, tastes and connections that were necessary to get ahead in Jacobean London. There, in this already privileged group of wealthy young men, 'one and all aspired to some connection with Whitehall'.[3]

Thus, even if Webster did not share Flamineo's ruined fortunes, he mirrored his creation's ambition. Unlike his younger brother Edward, Webster showed little interest in the family

[1] Charles R. Forker, *The Skull Beneath the Skin: The Achievement of John Webster* (Southern Illinois University Press, 1986), p. 4. I am indebted to Forker's book for its exhaustive study of Webster's life and work.
[2] Forker discusses the 'extremely tenuous' evidence for Webster's involvement with Robert Browne's troupe of English actors in Germany in 1596 (*Skull*, p. 5).
[3] M. C. Bradbrook, *John Webster: Citizen and Dramatist* (Weidenfeld and Nicholson, 1980), p. 29

trade; indeed, he probably purchased his status in the Merchant Taylors' (to which he was entitled by patrimony) chiefly to allow himself the glory of serving as their official poet – an ambition that was realized in 1624 when Webster was commissioned to design the festivities for the investiture of Sir John Gore, a Merchant Taylor, as Lord Mayor of London; his *Monuments of Honour* was the most lavish and expensive pageant of the age. Even Webster's early career reveals his aspirations. After an apprenticeship as one of Philip Henslowe's journeyman dramatists, collaborating with others such as Thomas Dekker, Anthony Munday, Thomas Middleton, Henry Chettle, Thomas Heywood and Michael Drayton on the plays *Caesar's Fall, Christmas Comes but Once a Year* (both lost), and *Lady Jane* (which survives only in a condensed reconstruction as *The Famous History of Sir Thomas Wyatt*, 1607), Webster went on in 1604 to write an Induction and other additions for *The Malcontent*, by John Marston, fellow Middle Templar and 'a prominent member of the intellectual avant-garde',[4] for performance by the King's Men at the Globe. In 1604 and 1605 Webster collaborated with Dekker again on two racy citizen comedies, *Westward Ho!* and *Northward Ho!*, for the fashionable, private children's company, Paul's Boys. After these theatrical successes, Webster seems to have stopped writing for a time – whether because of the frequent closure of the theatres due to plague, or his own hasty marriage in 1605/6 to Sara Peniall, who at the age of sixteen was seven months pregnant with the first of their several children. Not until 1612 did *The White Devil* appear, first performed at the Red Bull, where it failed to please. In the Preface to the published text, Webster strikes a pose of swaggering self-assurance: he not only scorns the 'ignorant asses' who failed to give his play its due, he also claims kinship with the learned dramatists Chapman and Jonson. During the year 1612, Webster wrote both *The Duchess of Malfi* for the King's Men and *A Monumental Column*, an elegy for the death of Prince Henry dedicated to the king's favourite, Sir Robert Carr. We can imagine that he felt he was transcending his origins as 'the Play-wright, Cart-wright'[5] of Cow Lane, West Smithfield. In fact, his confidence was unwarranted. Although he continued to write (thirty-two new characters for the sixth edition of Sir Thomas Overbury's *Characters* in 1615; *Guise*, a lost play, the date of which is unknown; *The Devil's Law-Case*, a tragicomedy, in 1617) and to collaborate (with Dekker, William

[4] Forker, *Skull*, p. 75
[5] The satirical description of Webster is Henry Fitzgeffrey's from *Notes from Blackfriars, Satyres and Satyricall Epigrams* (1617), and is quoted in full in ibid., pp. 58–9.

Rowley and John Ford on *The Late Murder of the Son upon the Mother, or Keep the Widow Waking*, 1624, now lost; perhaps with Middleton on *Anything for a Quiet Life*, 1620/1, and *The Fair Maid of the Inn*, 1626; with Rowley and perhaps Heywood on *A Cure for a Cuckold*, 1624/5, and *Appius and Virginia*, 1627?), Webster never equalled the tragic mastery of his first two independent plays. He probably died in the 1630s.

SOURCES

Webster had a restless and voracious intelligence: even more than his contemporaries, he mined the writings of other men for words, phrases and incidents which he then reshaped into his own art. He read widely in Renaissance literature (usually in English translation); *The White Devil* contains verbal borrowings from Montaigne (in Florio's translation), William Alexander's *The Alexandrean Tragedy* (1607), Stefano Guazzo's *Civil Conversation* (trans. George Pettie 1581), Nicolas de Montreux's *Honour's Academy* (trans. R. Tofte 1610), Richard Stanyhurst's *Description of Ireland* in Holinshed's *Chronicles* and Antonio de Guevara's *Dial of Princes* (trans. Thomas North 1557), to mention only a few. For incidents such as Brachiano's macabre death scene (V.iii.137–48), he was indebted to Erasmus' colloquy *Funus*; for the papal election in IV.iii, to H. Bignon's *A Treatise of the Election of Popes* (trans. 1605); for Cornelia's distraction after Marcello's death (V.ii.36–41; V.iv.64ff.), to Shakespeare's *King Lear* and *Hamlet*. Though a modern audience may recognize only the latter debt, originally a good deal of the play's intellectual pleasure may have depended on the audience's appreciation of Webster's ingenious adaptation of existing materials. His Preface indicates his desire to be read by the light of his fellow dramatists, and his play is marked by the sententiousness of Chapman, the biting satire of Marston, the shocking reversals of Beaumont and Fletcher, the citizen comedy of Dekker and the dark irony of Middleton, not to mention the moral intensity of Shakespeare. Thus to discover precise sources for Webster's drama is impossible, and perhaps undesirable, since its uniqueness lies in its fusion of disparate materials into a brilliant, eclectic whole.

It is, however, possible to locate sources for the story on which Webster bases *The White Devil*. Gunnar Boklund, in an exhaustive study of the play's sources,[6] has counted 109 manuscript versions and 6 published accounts of the notorious scan-

[6] *The Sources of 'The White Devil'* (Harvard University Press, 1957)

dal, and identified two or three texts as the probable origins of Webster's play: first, *A Letter Lately Written from Rome, by an Italian Gentleman* (trans. Florio 1585); second, an Italian source (now lost) for a German newsletter written for the Fugger banking house (extant in manuscript); and third, another source more difficult to identify (perhaps Cesare Campana's *Delle Historie del Mondo*, 1596, and the early sixteenth-century Italian pamphlet *Il miserabil e compassionevol caso*). A conflation of these sources can give us some idea of what Webster probably believed of the affair (which is often quite distinct from historical fact).[7]

The story as Webster probably knew it began in 1580, when Paolo Giordano, Duke of Bracciano, husband (of twenty-two years) to Isabella de' Medici and father to Giovanni, met Vittoria Accoramboni, a beautiful gentlewoman married to a nephew of Cardinal Montalto. He fell in love with her, but she virtuously refused him. With the aid of her brother Marcello, he then had her husband killed (at Monte Cavallo in Rome), but she again refused him. He then killed his own wife, and finally Vittoria submitted to him. His brother-in-law, Cardinal Medici, along with the Orsinis, entreated the Pope not to allow their kinsman to marry someone of so base a fortune. Cardinal Montalto desired to avenge his innocent nephew. Though Vittoria was apprehended on her way to Paolo Giordano's house in the country and confined in a nunnery, and later in Castel Sant'Angelo, Paolo Giordano set her free and married her. When Montalto was elected Pope Sixtus V, he advised Paolo Giordano to leave Rome. The couple went to Padua, where they kept a magnificent court. Two months later Paolo Giordano died, and there was suspicion of poison. His will left his young widow a large property. She was urged to put aside the will, but she refused. Fifty armed men then stormed her house at Padua and shot her brother Flaminio. A kinsman to her husband, Lodovico Orsini (who by age 34 had killed forty men, for which he had been forced to leave Rome), stabbed Vittoria at prayer. After this murder, his house was bombarded by cannon until he surrendered, dagger in hand. Once he had confessed that he had committed the deed at the command of great

---

[7] Historically, Isabella was strangled by her husband for carrying on an adulterous affair before he even set eyes on Vittoria. Later, after Bracciano had Vittoria's husband (Francesco Peretti) murdered, he twice married her secretly and subsequently left her at the Pope's command, the second time prompting her to attempt suicide. Bracciano died of natural causes in 1585. Lodovico Orsino took no personal part in the murders of Vittoria and her brother. Webster was probably ignorant of these facts.

princes, he spoke only once more: 'sed manet altamente
repostum' ('it shall be treasured up in the depths of my mind':
cf. II.i.262). Afterwards he was privately strangled, while his
accomplices were first riven asunder with red-hot tongs, then
killed with a hammer and finally quartered.

This story, while it clearly contained enough lust and murder
to fire Webster's imagination, was for dramatic purposes loose
and sketchy. The changes Webster makes are designed to give
his play dramatic momentum and structural unity: he develops
characters like Lodovico and Francisco into full-scale, strongly
motivated avengers present from the play's beginning. This also
allows him to create patterns of parallel and contrast among
different characters: Francisco is implicitly compared both with
Brachiano, another murderous great man,[8] and with Flamineo,
another Machiavellian schemer and social commentator, as the
latter also stands in clear relation to Lodovico, his double
(especially clear in III.iii). Analogies in turn suggest distinctions: while all are villains, they are driven by different impulses.
Unlike the sources, where action originates simply in Paolo
Giordano's vicious murders, in the play the interventions of
family members (Cornelia, Francisco, Monticelso) actually
seem to initiate events. Webster also chooses to problematize
and complicate the simple story he inherits. Brachiano mistreats
his saintly wife (characterless in Webster's source), then
becomes merely a bystander at her murder. Thus Webster mit-
igates, even as he suggests, his villainy. Similarly, if the sources
suggest Vittoria to be a woman of conventional, if flexible,
virtue, the play daringly implicates her in adultery and murder
while at the same time vindicating her – because she is a frustrated wife to a foolish, impotent husband, then an outraged
victim of masculine hypocrisy in two trial scenes (III.ii and
IV.ii) that are wholly Webster's invention. Finally, Webster
conflates the two brothers from the sources, the evil Marcello
and the innocent Flaminio, to create *The White Devil*'s Flamineo, whose incessant, sceptical commentary, brutal fratricide
and dawning self-awareness are all Webster's inventions. Characters like Marcello, Cornelia and Giovanni (expanded from a
mere hint in the sources to mete out final justice) are added to
the play as exponents of an often tyrannical moral code.

---

[8] Francisco himself, when disguised as Mulinassar, draws attention to the analogy
between himself and Brachiano: 'What difference is between the Duke and I?' he
muses. 'No more than between two bricks; all made of one clay' (V.i.106–8). And,
as Brachiano dominates the play's first half, stage-managing the action with the aid
of Flamineo, so Francisco dominates the second half, with Flamineo as his constant
companion.

THE PLAY

Tragic mode

Webster's play does not fit easily into traditional tragic modes. At first glance, *The White Devil* appears to be a revenge tragedy, which pits justified revengers against their villainous enemies. These revengers, however, are deeply implicated in the corrupt world around them. Lodovico has already committed 'certain murders' (I.i.31) he considers 'flea-bitings' (I.i.32), and Monticelso vows to 'stake a brother's life' (II.i.392) to gain revenge – even before the murders of Camillo and Isabella are committed. After the murder of Isabella is discovered, Francisco summons the conventional props of the revenger only to dismiss them. Face to face with Isabella's ghost, he cries:

> Remove this object,
> Out of my brain with't: what have I to do
> With tombs, or death-beds, funerals, or tears,
> That have to meditate upon revenge?   (IV.i.111–14)

In fact, Francisco's revenge is fuelled by his 'wit' (IV.i.130); he parodies Brachiano by writing Vittoria a love letter and later arranges disguises which allow for elaborate verbal jokes (e.g. V.iii.38–9). As a revenger, he is close to the witty detachment of Vindice in *The Revenger's Tragedy* (1607). 'My tragedy must have some idle mirth in't' (IV.i.118), he declares. But, unlike Vindice, Francisco is not the hero of this play; neither his satiric perspective nor his rough justice can delimit the real heroes, who inhabit the world of *de casibus* rather than revenge tragedy.

De casibus tragedy in its simplest form is indebted to 'the medieval idea that tragedy is a fall from greatness resulting from the instability of all sublunary affairs'.[9] At the moment of death (which defines all Webster's characters), Brachiano attributes his fall, not to the 'unction ... sent from the great Duke of Florence' (V.iii.28), but to his exalted position:

> O thou soft natural death, that art joint-twin
> To sweetest slumber: no rough-bearded comet
> Stares on thy mild departure: the dull owl
> Beats not against thy casement: the hoarse wolf
> Scents not thy carrion. Pity winds thy corse,
> Whilst horror waits on princes.   (V.iii.30–5)

As Brachiano has reached the pinnacle of earthly success, with his marriage to Vittoria, he is flung down by Fortune, that 'right

---

[9] Madeleine Doran, *Endeavors of Art: A Study of Form in Elizabethan Drama* (University of Wisconsin Press, 1954), p. 118

whore' (I.i.4). He can meditate on the instability of earthly power:

> I that have given life to offending slaves
> And wretched murderers, have I not power
> To lengthen mine own a twelvemonth? (V.iii.24–6)

Lee Bliss remarks: 'Far as his plays seem from the "old-fashioned" heroic tradition explored by Chapman and Shakespeare, Webster does in fact play out that dying mode'.[10] That 'dying mode' is, however, reshaped and revitalized by Webster's insistently social critique – a critique that is expressed largely through his other tragic characters, Flamineo and Vittoria.

Flamineo

Flamineo, a scurrilous pander and cynical malcontent, at first seems more suited to the role of comic manipulator than that of tragic hero. During the first four acts of *The White Devil*, his actions, including his murder of Camillo (in II.ii) are defined by his position as Brachiano's 'secretary'; in Act V, however, Flamineo begins to emerge as a tragic figure who can say 'at myself I will begin and end' (V.vi.256). The first sign of his new autonomy is his murder of his brother, Marcello, in an episode frequently condemned as superfluous by critics.[11] An outraged response to his family's moralistic attacks on his mistress, Zanche, Flamineo's fratricide finally stirs his 'compassion' (V.iv.112) for others and illuminates 'the maze of conscience' (V.iv.118) within himself. This glimpse of a complex interior life is more powerful for its understatement, and is followed by the appearance of Brachiano's ghost with its *memento mori* (V.iv.131). Flamineo's defiant cry 'I do dare my fate / To do its worst' (V.iv.139–40) links him with Shakespeare's tragic heroes: so Romeo, learning of the death of Juliet, cries 'Then I defy you, stars!' (V.i.24); so Hamlet, sensing his own death, says 'we defy augury' (V.ii.219). Like them, and like Brachiano, Flamineo conceives of himself as locked in a struggle, not with unworthy human opponents, but with Fate.

---

[10] Lee Bliss, *The World's Perspective: John Webster and the Jacobean Drama* (Harvester, 1983), p. 59

[11] See, for example, Harold Jenkins ('The Tragedy of Revenge in Shakespeare and Webster', *Shakespeare Survey* 14 (1961)), who deplores Webster's 'fatal tendency to complication' in *The White Devil* and contrasts it with *The Duchess of Malfi*, in which 'there is now no ghost, no mad wailing mother, no good brother to be killed by a bad' (p. 53). See also Larry S. Champion ('Webster's *The White Devil* and the Jacobean Tragic Perspective', *Texas Studies in Literature and Language* 16 (1974)), who contends that 'Marcello's murder and Cornelia's madness are never effectively integrated into the major action' (p. 457).

With Flamineo, however, Webster fuses the old-fashioned *de casibus* idea of tragedy (as human will confronting implacable destiny) with a more modern, Jacobean notion of human will confronting a corrupt society (a notion inherited from revenge tragedy). The two ideas are interlinked from the beginning of the play: Lodovico rails against both Fortune, that 'right whore' (I.i.4), and Fortune's worldly representatives, his 'great enemies' (I.i.7). Similarly, describing his act of murder as his 'misfortune' (V.ii.47), Flamineo recalls those Shakespearean heroes who feel themselves instruments of Fate even as they commit violent deeds: so Romeo, after killing Tybalt, cries, 'O, I am fortune's fool!' (III.i.136). Yet Flamineo's sense of suffering recalls Vindice's rather than Romeo's because it is rooted in a particular *economic* condition. As Flamineo cries to his mother in Act I:

> My father proved himself a gentleman,
> Sold all's land, and like a fortunate fellow
> Died ere the money was spent. You brought me up,
> At Padua I confess, where I protest,
> For want of means (the university judge me)
> I have been fain to heel my tutor's stockings
> At least seven years. (I.ii.315–21)

In Renaissance Europe, downward social mobility and court sycophancy for well-born and educated young men like Flamineo bred dangerous discontent. For Webster Flamineo's struggle for 'preferment' is not vulgar social climbing but a desperate bid for a place in an increasingly corrupt and mobile society. 'We think caged birds sing, when indeed they cry' (V.iv.120), observes Flamineo of himself; the cage which he inhabits is at once the court and his own tortured mind. His final speech contains an indictment of 'great men' like Brachiano:

> Let all that belong to great men remember th'old wives' tradition, to be like the lions i'th'Tower on Candlemas day, to mourn if the sun shine for fear of the pitiful remainder of winter to come.
>
> (V.vi.263–6)

The lesson, characteristically (for Webster) couched in animal analogies, is one of bitter resignation – resignation not to cruel destiny, but to corrupt and powerful men.

Vittoria

The subtitle of the 1612 quarto of *The White Devil* is *The Tragedy of Paulo Giordano Ursini, Duke of Brachiano, with the Life and Death of Vittoria Corombona the famous Venetian Curtizan*;

the ornamental title at the opening of Act I is *The Tragedy of Paulo Giordano Ursini Duke of Brachiano, and Vittoria Corombona*. While both titles may have been the work of the printer, their differing perspectives on Vittoria – as ancillary, or as central to the play's tragic vision – may reveal contemporary confusion about her role. Brachiano is the aristocratic, masculine hero of a familiar form of tragedy, and Flamineo straddles old and new, but Vittoria stands in uneasy relation to the traditional mode. With Brachiano, Webster is conservative, with Flamineo he is cautiously innovative; with Vittoria, however, Webster stands on the edge of a radical experiment. In *The White Devil*, as in Shakespeare's *Antony and Cleopatra* (1606/7), the male hero dies first, and the female character survives to enact the play's tragic climax. Unlike Cleopatra, however, who dies crying 'O Antony!' (V.ii.312), Vittoria mentions Brachiano only when she is feigning martyrdom (V.vi.81–4) and implicitly accuses him with her last breath:

> O happy they that never saw the court,
> 'Nor ever knew great man but by report'.   (V.vi.259–60)

Brachiano is the hero of his own tragedy, but he appears to be the villain in Vittoria's. He seduces her only to abandon her partway through her trial,[12] and later turns on her in private. If Flamineo is disadvantaged because of his class, Vittoria is doubly oppressed – both as a member of the fallen gentry and as a woman.

The White Devil was written at a time when controversy about the nature of woman had reached fever pitch. While attacks on women and defences of their virtue had been popular since antiquity, they proliferated during the Renaissance, when 'the English middle class had a distinct taste for this fare'.[13] Like many of his contemporaries (such as Tourneur), Webster writes some of the terms of the debate into his play: Vittoria is both a god and a wolf (IV.ii.89–90) to Brachiano. Unlike most contemporary dramatists and pamphleteers, however, Webster

---

[12] In a critical review of the 1991 National Theatre *White Devil*, Paul Taylor points out that 'Prowse does not make enough of her desertion by her adulterous paramour (played by Quilley as a shallow, childish sensualist). Because the vulnerability of her position here is underemphasised, her behaviour risks coming across as simple brazenness' (*Independent*, 20 June 1991).

[13] Katherine Usher Henderson and Barbara F. McManus, eds., *Half Humankind: Contexts and Texts of the Controversy about Women in England, 1540–1640* (University of Illinois Press, 1985), p. 3. This book discusses the history and range of the controversy, and provides significant excerpts. For a more extended discussion, see Linda Woodbridge, *Women and the English Renaissance: Literature and the Nature of Womankind, 1540–1620* (University of Illinois Press, 1984).

does not simply endorse misogyny, but probes its social and economic causes.

Vittoria's arraignment

Misogyny is a major force in *The White Devil*. From Lodovico's opening speech, in which he deflects blame from his 'great enemies' (I.i.7) onto a feminine Fortune, that 'right whore' (I.i.4), and a devouring she-wolf (I.i.8–9), to Flamineo's caution – 'Trust a woman? Never, never' (V.vi.158) – the men in the play constantly devalue woman as inherently evil and destructive to men. The antifeminist rhetoric clearly reaches its peak during the arraignment of Vittoria, when Monticelso invokes Eve as the cause of man's fall from grace, and suggests that 'Were there a second paradise to loose / This devil would betray it' (III.ii.70–1). The prosecutors are not without justification, moreover: Vittoria is implicated, however obliquely, in the murders of Camillo and Isabella when she recounts a dream in which – at least according to Flamineo – she instructs Brachiano to 'make away his Duchess and her husband' (I.ii.256). The arraignment has been interpreted in different ways: on the one hand celebrated as 'one of the great moments of the English stage',[14] on the other condemned by some critics as 'an artistic insincerity – a lie in the poet's heart',[15] an example of Webster's 'emphasis ... on vivid sympathetic insights at the expense of ethical coherence',[16] or – more recently – as an illustration of the unstable and discontinuous position of women in early modern culture.[17]

The arraignment is carefully positioned in a series of more and less formal trial scenes (I.i, II.i, III.ii, IV.ii, V.vi) which illuminate it by parallel and contrast. Brachiano's informal trial is juxtaposed with Vittoria's much more formal one in III.ii to reveal not only a glaring double standard but also a significant relation between gender and genre. Whereas Francisco and Monticelso courteously invite Brachiano to sit (II.i.20; III.ii.4), they order Vittoria to 'stand to the table' (III.ii.8). And although

---

[14] Jack Landau, 'Elizabethan Art in a Mickey Spillane Setting', *Theatre Arts* 39 (1955); reprinted in R. V. Holdsworth, ed., *Webster: 'The White Devil' and 'The Duchess of Malfi': A Casebook* (Macmillan, 1975), p. 234

[15] Ian Jack, 'The Case of John Webster', *Scrutiny* 16 (1949); reprinted in *John Webster: A Critical Anthology*, ed. G. K. and S. K. Hunter (Penguin, 1969), p. 162

[16] Doran, *Endeavors of Art*, p. 355

[17] Catherine Belsey asserts that 'only Vittoria seems to have no place, intelligible to the audience as single and continuous, from which to speak, to be recognized' and perceives this as an illustration of the fact that 'in the family as in the state women had no single, unified, fixed position from which to speak' (*The Subject of Tragedy: Identity and Difference in Renaissance Drama* (Methuen, 1985), pp. 163, 160).

we have seen Brachiano both arrange and oversee the murders of Camillo and Isabella (II.i.312–19; II.ii), it is Vittoria who is apprehended and tried – for her sexuality rather than for her uncertain role in the murders. Monticelso defines Brachiano's as a classic *de casibus* tragedy, lamenting his fall from 'High gifts of learning' and an 'awful throne' (II.i.30–1) to an 'insatiate bed' (II.i.32); he is an eagle 'that should gaze upon the sun' (II.i.49). By contrast, Vittoria can only 'fall' from appearance to reality: 'You see my lords what goodly fruit she seems', cries Monticelso. 'I will but touch her and you straight shall see / She'll fall to soot and ashes' (III.ii.63, 66–7). If Brachiano may 'to wilful shipwreck loose good fame' (II.i.41), Vittoria *is* a shipwreck 'in calmest weather' (III.ii.83). But Webster undermines the misogynist stereotypes by hinting at their social and economic base. Flamineo himself conflates woman's looseness with contemporary social unrest:

> These politic enclosures for paltry mutton makes more rebellion in the flesh than all the provocative electuaries doctors have uttered since last Jubilee.   (I.ii.94–6)

Woman's 'lust', far from being innate, is a frustrated response to being oppressed that is analogous to the social rebellion produced by economic hardship. During the trial, the Cardinal significantly ties Vittoria's poverty to her sexuality when he describes her as 'a hard penny-worth, the ware being so light' (III.ii.242).

Throughout her trial, Vittoria 'personate[s] masculine virtue' (III.ii.136) so well that one is almost tempted to accept her account of the 'frosty answer' (III.ii.202) she gave to Brachiano's importunities. But the audience knows otherwise: Brachiano's initial gesture, spreading a gown on the floor (III.ii.3 s.d.), recalls their earlier embraces upon cushions (I.ii.202 s.d.), and Flamineo's shocked aside (III.ii.265) reminds us of his role as pander. In the next act, we hear Vittoria acknowledge herself as Brachiano's 'whore' (IV.ii.142) and cry bitterly:

> I do wish
> That I could make you full executor
> To all my sins–   (IV.ii.121–3)

Thus Vittoria's 'masculine virtue' in the trial is effective but duplicitous. Most critics assume that this makes Vittoria the 'white devil' of the title, or reveals Webster's moral irresponsibility. It may equally, however, illuminate the impossible position of the female character in tragedy. To become authors of their own choices women must *act* in both senses of the word –

take action and play a (male) role (as Vittoria and Isabella both do) – which can make them targets of misogyny.

Webster, however, never makes it easy for his audience to sympathize with Vittoria. We are never given access to Vittoria's 'real', inner self, to her motives or feelings, as we are made privy to Brachiano's and Flamineo's. Is her dream intended to instigate murder? Does she love Brachiano or merely exploit him? Is she 'at . . . prayers' (V.vi.1) when the final scene opens and, if so, why? Vittoria is constantly withdrawn by Webster from our knowledge – most obviously at IV.ii.188, when she retires into a silence which may be quiet triumph, wordless contempt or mute devastation. By refusing to provide a full portrait of Vittoria, Webster challenges our conventional moral judgements and focuses attention on oppressive social forces which make her evasions necessary.

Isabella and Zanche

That Webster is interested in women as an exploited group with innate heroic potential is evident from his treatment of other women in the play. Isabella, for example, as Vittoria's rival and victim might be expected to show up the latter's villainy; instead, Webster's artful dramatic construction places the two women in parallel relation. Because Webster chooses to suppress knowledge that Isabella has been murdered until after Vittoria's trial, Vittoria's victimization by masculine authority in III.ii is juxtaposed with Isabella's treatment by those who 'wrapped her in a cruel fold of lead' (III.ii.333). Vittoria's ambiguity – she engages in adultery in I.ii, yet hurls defiance at her accusers in III.ii – is mirrored in Isabella's, who is both a 'piteous' martyr (II.i.223) and a 'foolish, mad, / And jealous woman' (263–4). Though Isabella is supposedly playing a part in her rejection of Brachiano (II.i.224), like Vittoria she finds a convincing voice in the male role she adopts. Both women are identified with the dangerous female 'fury' (II.i.244; III.ii.278) in their rage. Isabella's lament could well speak for Vittoria:

> O that I were a man, or that I had power
> To execute my apprehended wishes,   (II.i.242–3)

Vittoria is condemned by her mother, frustrated by her impotent husband, arraigned by hypocritical judges, accused and betrayed by her own lover, and finally murdered. Zanche, Vittoria's black servant, re-enacts her mistress's career in simplified form in the last act: she is put off by Flamineo, attacked by Cornelia and Marcello and finally killed. Vittoria and Zanche,

tried together in III.ii, die side by side at the end. Webster finds
in Vittoria an expression of the plight of her gender.

The White Devil first hints at the possibility of an alternative
female heroism during the arraignment. Vittoria pointedly
invokes matrilineage when she asserts her own high birth:

> You raise a blood as noble in this cheek
> As ever was your mother's. (III.ii.54–5)

When the trial ends, Vittoria identifies herself with the female
emblem of blind Justice (III.ii.274) – an affirmative rival to the
blind and fickle female Fortune often railed at by the men. The
final scene begins with Flamineo giving full vent to his misogyny, as he successfully exposes the women's heroic vows of
self-sacrifice (V.vi.80–97) as mere 'feminine arguments' (l.67)
which are abandoned as soon as they can 'tread upon' him
(V.vi.117 s.d.). When the real murderers arrive Vittoria strikes
the pose of masculine virtue so familiar from the trial scene:

> Yes, I shall welcome death
> As princes do some great ambassadors:
> I'll meet thy weapon halfway. (V.vi.217–19)

When Lodovico expresses surprise at her lack of fear, however,
Vittoria reformulates her heroism:

> O thou art deceived, I am too true a woman:
> Conceit can never kill me. (V.vi.221–2)

Here Webster stakes everything on the abilities of the boy actor
playing Vittoria, for she grounds her defiance, not in masculine
heroism, but in female biology: 'conceit' contains a complex
pun on 'conception'. Women's capacity to conceive life is
extended by Flamineo when he says admiringly to Vittoria, in
a reversal of his earlier misogyny:

> I love thee now. If woman do breed man
> She ought to teach him manhood: (V.vi.240–1)

The White Devil on the modern stage

From a modern perspective, *The White Devil* may seem a
strange and disorienting play composed of disparate elements.
Its characters can speak with bold directness, prosy informality
or formal sententiousness. Its scenes range from formal and
ceremonial (like the papal election in IV.iii) to intense and
intimate (like Brachiano's and Vittoria's quarrel in IV.ii);
indeed, much of the play's power is derived from abrupt, ironic
juxtaposition of private and public moments. Webster also uses
many pre-Shakespearean stage conventions – such as the dumb
shows of II.ii and the ghosts of IV.i and V.iv – alongside more

innovative staging. Again, the mixture is purposeful since Webster often strives for a distancing effect only to engage his audience more fully in the surrounding drama.[18] Such stylistic eclecticism, however, poses problems for modern theatre professionals. As Peter Thomson points out, 'we must expect the "impure" confusion of convention and realism to reach the point of crisis for anyone who tries to act in his plays'.[19] Moreover, *The White Devil*, though set in sixteenth-century Italy, is peppered with allusions to contemporary England; Webster intended his play to involve his Jacobean audience. To be true to Webster, a modern director must approach the play not as a museum piece but as a drama to engage today's audiences directly. Though no single production of *The White Devil* has been entirely successful in doing so, three British productions since 1969 have illuminated different aspects of this difficult play.

The curtain opened on the 1969 National Theatre *White Devil* at the Old Vic to reveal a massive wall of giant blocks of crumbling yellow stone, gliding apart to show ledges and alleyways along which brilliantly costumed actors scuttled like so many exotic insects. Designed by the Italian film director Fellini's frequent collaborator Piero Gherardi, this production appeared to adopt Rupert Brooke's description of Webster's drama as 'full of the feverish and ghastly turmoil of a nest of maggots'.[20] Geraldine McEwan as Vittoria first appeared in a towering wig and enormous, sweeping ruff, 'her frail body and naked back enveloped by a cobra-hood, her face evil with the mixed satiety and appetite, leer and snigger, coquetry and indecency, of the consummate whore'.[21] If Gherardi's designs dwarfed the actors and constricted their movement, Frank Dunlop's direction conspired to detach the audience from the play and reduce it to an exhibition of high camp. Vittoria, for example, who cast off her white cloak at the opening of the trial to reveal a red dress beneath, was simply a hypocritical whore in 'a world where selfishness and immediate satisfaction drench out tragedy and suffering'.[22] Although critical response was gen-

---

[18] The best example of this is at II.ii.49–51, where Brachiano's confident detachment is suddenly undermined when the conjuror warns that they must escape from the 'armed men' of the dumb show, who are coming to Vittoria's house to arrest her.

[19] Peter Thomson, 'Webster and the Actor' in *John Webster*, ed. Brian Morris (Ernest Benn, 1970), p. 32

[20] From *John Webster and the Elizabethan Drama* (1916); reprinted in *John Webster: A Critical Anthology*, p. 94

[21] John Barber, 'Triumph for Designer in Jacobean Tragedy', *Daily Telegraph*, 14 November 1969

[22] Helen Dawson, '*The White Devil*: Old Vic', *Plays and Players* 17.4 (January 1970), 39

erally negative, the dumb shows were strikingly effective: Isabella's 'mimed death – the duchess sinking within her stiff,
white, lacy draperies, convulsed silently and briefly like an
insect trapped inside a muslin net – has a masque-like, formal
beauty'.[23] The production, which conceived of Webster's characters as dehumanized creatures moving about in an abstract
ballet of cruelty, here unexpectedly captured something of
Webster's peculiar horror.

The production of *The White Devil* mounted by Michael
Lindsay-Hogg seven years later at the same theatre was a direct
response to – even a challenge to – the earlier one. Irving
Wardle suggests that the 1969 production's mistake was 'to
identify the characters as Them. This time, at least, they are
supposed to be Us'.[24] Thus the simple set, equipped with a
pair of swing-doors downstage, suggested the deserted foyer of
a grand hotel, and the actors wore casual modern clothes, sometimes topped off with dressing gowns. The dramatist Edward
Bond (author of *Saved* and *Lear*), who prepared the acting edition, turned Machiavellian acts of revenge into modern surgical
operations. By emphasizing the play's brutal realism, however,
the production exhibited 'puritanical disapproval' quite at odds
with Webster's own 'complex and evasive' moral judgements.[25]
Playing Webster's characters as seedy, jaded moderns or fan-
tastic, fragile insects illuminated a double bind in staging *The
White Devil*: emphasizing realism may mask the greatness of
which Webster's characters are capable, while heightening their
exoticism may remove them into a world estranged from our
own.

The most significant difference between the two Old Vic productions lay in the interpretation of Vittoria. In contrast to Geraldine McEwan's coquettish whore, Glenda Jackson played her
in 1976 as a bold feminist whose acute intelligence teaches her
only the conditions of her own oppression.

> When she flinched with her whole body against Monticelso's abuse of
> the legal process, it was out of shocked recognition of his hatred of her
> sex; and when she majestically stood her ground, calmly showing him
> the degree to which he traduced his office as judge, she was defending
> more than her own self.[26]

This Vittoria was not only the Cardinal's victim but also Brach-

[23] Hilary Spurling, 'Devil Incarnate', *Spectator*, 22 November 1969, 722

[24] Irving Wardle, '*The White Devil*: Old Vic', *The Times*, 13 July 1976

[25] Robert Cushman, *Observer*, London, 18 July 1976

[26] Richard Allen Cave, '*The White Devil*' and '*The Duchess of Malfi*': *Text and Performance* (Macmillan, 1988), p. 55. Cave's impressions of the 1976 production are far
more positive in general than those of most of the reviewers.

iano's and Flamineo's; in the final scene she exultantly trampled on the latter as 'the embodiment of all things male that she had come to loathe'.[27] Even if she could not 'reconcile the character's separate aspects',[28] this Vittoria could expose the conflicts in her situation as a woman.

Philip Prowse, a designer-turned-director of the Glasgow Citizens' Theatre, who had directed *The Duchess of Malfi* for the National Theatre in 1985, returned to the National to direct *The White Devil* in 1991. So devoted to striking visual effects that he once notoriously remarked that 'the words of an author are no more important than the work of an usherette',[29] Prowse created a monumental set for the Olivier Theatre's vast acting space to suggest the claustrophobic grandeur of Renaissance Italy.

> Beneath a vast curved brick wall are huge tombs and altars, some topped by cobwebbed crosses, one by the shell of a model basilica . . . The effect is of a half-built crypt, or half-ruined mausoleum, a place to remind us of T. S. Eliot's view that Webster was 'much possessed by death and saw the skull beneath the skin'.[30]

Bells tolled, candles flickered and thunder rumbled as sinister, cowled monks and ghosts (including the murdered Camillo and Isabella) prowled the marble floor. This too was an extreme case of designer's theatre, which too often dwarfed the actors onstage. Paul Taylor remarks that 'the trouble with all this kitschy overkill is that it presents the decor of death while failing to impart any sense of its horrifying finality'.[31] Not only did this production thus diminish the real impact of the horror it wished to create, it also failed to capture the characters' exuberant appetites for life and sex.

Prowse opted to translate into theatrical and contemporary terms the play's social inequalities: he cast Vittoria and her family as black. 'The effect is electric', wrote one reviewer:

> When Vittoria is charged with the murder of her husband, it is a black family that is slumped in chains in the court alongside her. To the Cardinal and the Duke of Florence, Brachiano's liaison becomes a visible form of class treachery.[32]

Reviewers admired Josette Simon's Vittoria. 'She paints a compelling, languorously tragic portrait',[33] comments one reviewer:

---

[27] Ibid., p. 56   [28] Wardle, *The Times*, 13 July 1976

[29] Charles Spencer, *Daily Telegraph*, 20 June 1991

[30] Benedict Nightingale, *The Times*, 19 June 1991   [31] *Independent*, 20 June 1991

[32] Kirsty Milne, 'Rank Disorder', *New Statesman and Society*, June 1991

[33] Michael Coveney, *Observer*, 23 June 1991

Josette Simon as Vittoria and Denis Quilley as Brachiano in the Royal National Theatre production of 1991 (photo: Donald Cooper © Photostage)

She can shut her gilded eyelids and sensuously purr when male hands are on her. Yet whether she is facing accusing potentates, a suspicious lover, or even her murderer, there is something fine, proud and wonderfully defiant about her. She stands, looks, silently commands, and is herself: a gemlike flame in Prowse and Webster's funereal world.[34]

In contrast to Jackson's 1976 embittered Vittoria, Simon sought to reconcile the character's sensuality with her feminist defiance but did not conceal her guilt. Her subtle and complex performance clearly stood out in an otherwise heavy-handed production.

Modern professional productions have emphasized *The White Devil*'s elements of formal spectacle (in the dumb shows, arraignment and papal election) by staging it on a proscenium stage with elaborate sets in a large auditorium. By contrast, semi-professional studio productions of the play have sometimes succeeded better in capturing its intimate, human drama. In the 1983 York Graduate Theatre Company production in Toronto, for example, the dumb shows of II.ii seemed almost naturalistic, and Isabella's drawing of the curtain to reveal Brachiano's picture was clearly mirrored later when the same curtain was drawn to reveal Brachiano in his bed (V.iii). While characters did strike poses (Brachiano mourning Isabella's death, or Flamineo feigning madness in III.ii, for example), the loneliness and despair underlying them filled the intimate theatre space. The 1994 Ursa Major Theatre Company production in London played up the delicious sensuality of the main characters as desperate pleasures in a world ridden with 'weary disappointment'.[35] *The White Devil*'s still, small moments must counterpoint the play's pageantry if Webster's play is to engage its audience deeply.

The White Devil at the Red Bull

On a winter's day (probably in February) in 1612, *The White Devil* opened at the Red Bull Theatre on St John's Street in Clerkenwell, north of the city of London. The Red Bull and its neighbour, the Fortune, were citizen playhouses where the common fare tended to be 'heroic and spectacular'[36] in contrast to the subtler, romantic repertory of the rival Bankside theatres such as the Globe. Despite their heavier use of spectacle, however, Red Bull plays were performed on a stage structurally

---

[34] Benedict Nightingale, *The Times*, 19 June 1991
[35] The phrase comes from the programme notes for the production.
[36] Andrew Gurr, *The Shakespearean Stage, 1574–1642*, 2nd ed. (Cambridge University Press, 1980), p. 14

much like that of the Globe or the Swan.[37] Like the DeWitt drawing of the Swan, the Red Bull had a large, bare platform stage (about 12 metres across) with trap below and 'heavens' above (supported by posts and protecting the stage from the weather); actors entered through two doors from the tiring house, and possibly also through a central curtained 'discovery space';[38] and a balcony above the stage provided a limited area for playing. The stage projected into the middle of the unroofed yard and was surrounded by tiers of galleries. Thus the two distinctive qualities of the Red Bull Theatre, like all Elizabethan theatres, were its simplicity and its close contact with the audience. With no painted scenery of an illusionistic kind, Elizabethan stagecraft emphasized the actors and their formal groupings, dramatic exits and entrances and visual contrasts and parallels; thronged about with spectators in broad daylight, the actors could either address them in asides or ignore them in a theatre which drew equally on the non-naturalistic staging of the morality play and the 'true imitation of life' (V.vi.304) commended by Webster.

Stage action ranges from Flamineo's private whisper in Brachiano's ear (I.ii.6) to the procession of the ambassadors (IV.iii.5–17), demanding close, intimate engagement or detached appreciation from the audience. The audience is often required to attend to more than one thing at a time: in II.i, for example, Francisco, Camillo and Marcello whisper together about their new commission while Flamineo and Brachiano hire Dr Julio as their assassin (ll. 282–322). Moreover, almost nothing in *The White Devil* happens without an onstage audience commenting on it. Occasionally this engagement becomes overt, as when Marcello directs the audience to 'Mark this strange encounter' (III.iii.65) or when Flamineo pre-empts criticism of his 'tale' by acknowledging that it 'may appear to some ridiculous / Thus to talk knave and madman' (IV.ii.239–40). Indeed, the Red Bull, a theatre in which (unlike the Globe) 'apprentices and small tradesmen . . . might sit on the stage with the air of grandeur affected by the gallants who patronized the

---

[37] George F. Reynolds, *The Staging of Elizabethan Plays at the Red Bull Theater 1605–1625* (Modern Language Association, 1940), p. 188

[38] Although no discovery space is shown in the DeWitt sketch, Gurr concludes that 'there was certainly some sort of enclosed space at the back of the stage, which could be pressed into use for the Globe plays' (*The Shakespearean Stage*, p. 137). Reynolds discusses the evidence for the Red Bull and concludes that 'a curtained space was available on the Red Bull stage' (*Staging of Elizabethan Plays*, p. 162), though he believes it may not have been a permanent feature.

more stylish theatres',[39] may have encouraged an especially close actor-audience relationship.

The simplicity of the Elizabethan stage heightened its symbolic potential. The formal stage picture of I.ii, for example, with Brachiano and Vittoria framed by Flamineo on the one hand and Cornelia on the other, draws on (and complicates) the conventional pattern of the morality play, where Vice and Virtue solicit the human soul. Without the distraction of backdrops or sets, visual contrasts and parallels emerge with greater clarity: Brachiano and Vittoria probably kiss to seal their union (I.ii.213), while Brachiano and Isabella kiss to seal their divorce (II.i.252); Isabella kisses Brachiano's poisoned mouth in the portrait and dies (II.ii.23 s.d.), while Brachiano's beaver (mouthpiece) is poisoned to kill him (V.ii.77 s.d.); Brachiano shows love for Vittoria by kissing her (IV.ii.190) and by not kissing her (V.iii.27).[40] As Antonelli and Gasparo frame Lodovico in I.i like a 'well . . . with two buckets' (I.i.29), so Francisco and Monticelso confront Brachiano in II.i, and the visual parallels suggest significant distinctions between a hardened villain and a passionate lover.

The actors would have provided a parade of lavish costumes.[41] Apparel is a visual sign of power in *The White Devil*, from the Cardinal's ecclesiastical scarlet to the ambassadors' magnificent robes as 'knights / Of several orders' (IV.iii.6–7). This is a world in which clothes do make the man, as Francisco points out with reference to Giovanni's suit of armour: 'a good habit makes a child a man, / Whereas a bad one makes a man a beast' (II.i.137–8). Flamineo expresses frustration at finding himself 'not a suit the richer' (I.ii.325) after his sojourn at court; Vittoria, on the other hand, as Brachiano's mistress can wear 'cloth of tissue' (II.i.55) and (probably) a sumptuous gown that advertises her 'scorn and impudence' (III.ii.122) at the trial. Yet the play is also constantly undermining appearances: Vittoria points out that charity is seldom found in scarlet (III.ii.71–2), while Flamineo notes that Camillo's outer garb

[39] Louis B. Wright, *Middle-Class Culture in Elizabethan England* (University of North Carolina Press, 1935), p. 611. Reynolds concurs that 'seats on the stage were counted among the regular sources of income' (*Staging of Elizabethan Plays*, pp. 8–9).

[40] Peter Thomson explores kissing as a 'figure in action' in the play ('Webster and the Actor', pp. 39–41); David Gunby extends this analysis in his Critical Introduction to *The White Devil* (NCW, pp. 61–3).

[41] Gurr points out that 'the impresarios and players invested much more money in apparel than in properties' (*The Shakespearean Stage*, p. 178); he prints a long list of sumptuous costumes from Henslowe's *Diary* for 1598. David Carnegie comments extensively on costume in the play in his Theatrical Introduction to the Cambridge edition (NCW, pp. 87–91).

of a 'politician' is really 'an ass in's foot-cloth' (I.ii.49–51). The proliferation of disguises in the final act further emphasizes the deceptiveness of appearances. Thus the play makes use of the company's large stock of lavish costumes to further its own biting satire.

Webster acknowledges in his preface to the reader that the Red Bull patrons did not provide a 'full and understanding auditory' for *The White Devil* at its first performance. One can only guess at the reasons. While Gurr blames the 'overcast wintry weather',[42] one may also imagine the cause to have been Webster's radical experimentation with gender and genre, as well as his unorthodox moral complexities. The Red Bull players were well known for a broad acting style (inherited from Edward Alleyn's playing of Marlowe).[43] The Red Bull was clearly the wrong theatre for a play as subtle and complex as *The White Devil*. Wisely, Webster chose rival playhouses for the staging of *The Duchess of Malfi*: the Globe and its indoor venue, the Blackfriars. It has been noticed that studio theatre performance suits *The Duchess of Malfi*;[44] the professional theatre would do well to consider more intimate venues for *The White Devil*.

NOTE ON THE TEXT

The White Devil was first printed in 1612 by Nicholas Okes, and is free from major textual obscurity. I have taken as my copy text the authoritative first quarto (British Museum shelfmark C.34. e.18). Press corrections have been supplied from John Russell Brown's list ('The Printing of John Webster's Plays (II)', *Studies in Bibliography* 8 (1956), 113–17); substantive press variants indicate that Webster himself may have been involved in proofreading and correcting. Recently, Anthony Hammond has distinguished three main compositors, whom he calls A, B and N, the latter (who set B1r–E4v) being the least experienced and most prone both to commit error and to follow his copy in matters of punctuation.[45]

The manuscript which Webster supplied to the printer was

---

[42] Andrew Gurr, *Playgoing in Shakespeare's London* (Cambridge University Press, 1987) p. 36

[43] See Gurr, *The Shakespearean Stage*, pp. 110–11.

[44] One thinks here of the success of *The Duchess of Malfi* at the Royal Exchange, Manchester, in 1980, or at the Swan, Stratford-upon-Avon, and the Pit, Barbican, in 1990.

[45] Anthony Hammond, '*The White Devil* in Nicholas Okes's Shop', *Studies in Bibliography* 39 (1986), 135–76

probably based on his 'foul papers' rather than on a text adapted for use in the theatre, judging from the irregular speech headings, misplaced entries and complete absence of act and scene divisions in the copy, as well as the truculent attitude he adopts in the preface towards the playhouse. As his afterword commending the players indicates, Webster was acutely sensitive to performance; indeed, he attempted to supplement the necessarily incomplete experience of a *reader* of the play by adding a number of stage directions to the second part of the text, perhaps while the first part was already being set by the printer. In the published text, these added stage directions occur in the margins after F3v. Since they are not different in kind from other stage directions, which the compositors usually squeezed into available text space, they are treated as accidental features of the printer's copy, and both marginal and other stage directions are incorporated into the text at appropriate points in the dialogue, though all changes to their position are recorded in the notes.

I have modernized spelling (unless the original spelling allowed for a play on words), eliminated both capitalized nouns and italicized proper names, regularized speech prefixes and expanded elisions such as final syllable apostrophes. Because there is reason to doubt compositorial consistency (Brown lxx), I have used quotation marks for all gnomic pointing in the copy (normally indicated by either italics or inverted commas). I have added the customary act and scene divisions in square brackets. In accordance with the policy of this series, I have followed the lineation of the copy text except when verse is obviously set as prose to save space, in which case the change is indicated in the notes. Blank verse lines are staggered when they are shared by two or more speakers. The light punctuation of Q has been followed wherever possible, though it has been necessary in some cases to add commas, semi-colons and dashes to capture, without arresting, Webster's fluid language.

FURTHER READING

Berry, Ralph. *The Art of John Webster* (Oxford: Clarendon,1972)

Bliss, Lee. *The World's Perspective: John Webster and the Jacobean Drama* (Sussex: Harvester, 1983)

Boklund, Gunnar. *The Sources of 'The White Devil'* (Cambridge, Mass.: Harvard University Press, 1957)

Bradbrook, M. C. *John Webster: Citizen and Dramatist* (London: Weidenfeld and Nicolson, 1980)

Bromley, Laura G. 'The Rhetoric of Feminine Identity in *The White Devil*' in *In Another Country: Feminist Perspectives on Renaissance Drama*, ed. Dorothea Kehler and Susan Baker (Metuchen, N.J.: Scarecrow, 1991), pp. 50–70

Bruster, Douglas. *Quoting Shakespeare: Form and Culture in Early Modern Drama* (Lincoln, NE, 2000)

Cave, Richard Allen. *'The White Devil' and 'The Duchess of Malfi': Text and Performance* (London: Macmillan, 1988)

Champion, Larry S. 'Webster's *The White Devil* and the Jacobean Tragic Perspective', *Texas Studies in Literature and Language* 16 (1974), pp. 447–62

Dollimore, Jonathan. *Radical Tragedy: Religion and Power in the Drama of Shakespeare and his Contemporaries* (Sussex: Harvester, 1984)

Ewbank, Inga-Stina. 'Webster's Realism, or, "A Cunning Piece Wrought Perspective" ' in *John Webster*, ed. Brian Morris (London: Ernest Benn, 1970), pp. 157–78

Forker, Charles R. *The Skull Beneath the Skin: The Achievement of John Webster* (Carbondale: Southern Illinois University Press, 1986)

Goldberg, Dena ' "By Report": The Spectator as Voyeur in Webster's *The White Devil*', in *English Literary Renaissance* 17.1 (1987), pp. 67–84

Gunby, D. C., David Carnegie, and Anthony Hammond, eds. *The Works of John Webster* I (Cambridge: Cambridge University Press, 1995)

Jenkins, Harold. 'The Tragedy of Revenge in Shakespeare and Webster', *Shakespeare Survey* 14 (1961), pp. 45–55

Jones, Ann Rosalind. 'Italians and Others: *The White Devil* (1612)' in *Staging the Renaissance: Reinterpretations of Elizabethan and Jacobean Drama* (New York: Routledge, 1991)

Luckyj, Christina. *A Winter's Snake: Dramatic Form in the Tragedies of John Webster* (Athens: University of Georgia Press, 1989)

Luckyj, Christina. 'Gender, Rhetoric and Performance in John Webster's *The White Devil*' in *Enacting Gender on the English Renaissance Stage*, ed. Viviana Comensoli and Anne Russell (Urbana: University of Illinois Press, 1998)

McLeod, Susan H. *Dramatic Imagery in the Plays of John Webster*, Jacobean Drama Studies 68 (Salzburg: Universität Salzburg, 1977)

Mulryne, J. R. 'Webster and the Uses of Tragicomedy' in *John Webster*, ed. Brian Morris (London: Ernest Benn, 1970), pp. 133–55

Pearson, Jacqueline. *Tragedy and Tragicomedy in the Plays of John Webster* (Manchester: Manchester University Press, 1980)

Stevenson, Sheryl. ' "As Differing as Two Adamants": Sexual Difference in *The White Devil*' in *Sexuality and Politics in Renaissance Drama*, ed. Carole Levin and Karen Robertson (Lewiston: Edwin Mellen, 1991), pp. 159–74

Thomson, Peter. 'Webster and the Actor' in *John Webster*, ed. Brian Morris (London: Ernest Benn, 1970), pp. 23–44

Weil, Judith . '*The White Devil* and Old Wives' Tales', *Modern Language Review* 94.2 (April 1999), pp. 328-40

1612 title page:

non inferiora secutus 'Engaged in no less noble service' (Virgil, *Æneid*, vi, 170): 'The words should perhaps be rendered - "following no ignoble there" or "a theme not less noble than my rivals or predecessors have treated".' (Lucas, *Webster*, i, 194)

THE
WHITE DIVEL,

OR,

The Tragedy of *Paulo Giordano Ursini*, Duke of *Brachiano*,

With

The Life and Death of Vittoria
Corombona the famous
Venetian Curtizan.

Acted by the Queenes Maiesties Seruants.

Written by IOHN WEBSTER.

Non inferiora secutus.

LONDON,
Printed by *N.O.* for *Thomas Archer*, and are to be sold
at his Shop in Popes head Pallace, neere the
Royall Exchange. 1612.

[DRAMATIS PERSONAE]

[MONTICELSO, a Cardinal; afterwards Pope PAUL IV

FRANCISCO DE' MEDICI, Duke of Florence; in the fifth act disguised for a Moor, under the name of MULINASSAR

BRACHIANO, otherwise PAULO GIORDANO URSINI, Duke of Brachiano; husband to Isabella and in love with Vittoria

GIOVANNI, his son, by Isabella

LODOVICO or LODOWICK, an Italian Count, but decayed

ANTONELLI and GASPARO, his friends, and dependents of the Duke of Florence

CAMILLO, husband to Vittoria

HORTENSIO, one of Brachiano's officers

MARCELLO, an attendant of the Duke of Florence, and brother to Vittoria

FLAMINEO, his brother; secretary to Brachiano

CARDINAL OF ARRAGON

DOCTOR JULIO, a conjuror

*CHRISTOPHERO, his assistant

*GUID-ANTONIO

*FERNESE

*JACQUES, a Moor, servant to Giovanni

ISABELLA, sister to Francisco de' Medici, and wife to Brachiano

VITTORIA COROMBONA, a Venetian Lady, first married to Camillo, afterwards to Brachiano

CORNELIA, mother to Vittoria, Flamineo and Marcello

ZANCHE, a Moor; servant to Vittoria

MATRON of the House of Convertites

CARLO

PEDRO

AMBASSADORS	CHANCELLOR
PHYSICIANS	REGISTER
COURTIERS	PAGE
LAWYERS	ARMOURER
OFFICERS	CONJUROR
ATTENDANTS	CONCLAVIST]

*non-speaking parts or 'ghost characters'

3

TO THE READER

In publishing this tragedy, I do but challenge to myself that liberty, which other men have ta'en before me; not that I affect praise by it, for, *nos haec novimus esse nihil,* only since it was acted, in so dull a time of winter, presented in so open and black a theatre, that it wanted (that 5 which is the only grace and setting out of a tragedy) a full and understanding auditory: and that since that time I have noted, most of the people that come to that playhouse, resemble those ignorant asses (who visiting stationers' shops, their use is not to enquire for good books, 10 but new books) I present it to the general view with this confidence:

> *Nec rhoncos metues, maligniorum,*
> *Nec scombris tunicas, dabis molestas.*

If it be objected this is no true dramatic poem, I shall 15 easily confess it, – *non potes in nugas dicere plura meas: ipse ego quam dixi,* – willingly, and not ignorantly, in this kind have I faulted: for should a man present to such an auditory, the most sententious tragedy that ever was written, observing all the critical laws, as height of style, and grav- 20 ity of person; enrich it with the sententious *Chorus,* and

---

1 *challenge* claim

3 *nos ... nihil* 'We know these things are nothing' (Martial XIII, 2); Webster probably borrowed this quotation and that at ll. 17–18 from Dekker's preface to *Satiromastix* (1602).

5 *open ... theatre* The Red Bull, the playhouse in which *The White Devil* was first performed in February or March 1612, was unroofed and thus open to the weather, which may have been quite 'black', or overcast on the occasion.

7 *understanding auditory* i.e. an appreciative audience (possibly in contrast to those simply 'standing under' the stage, in the yard); like his contemporaries, Webster commends the ear, not the eye (cf. his character of 'An Excellent Actor': 'Sit in a full theatre, and you will think you see so many lines drawn from the circumference of so many ears, while the actor is the centre.')

13–14 *Nec ... molestas* 'You [the poet's book] will not fear the sneers of the malicious, nor supply wrappers for mackerel' (Martial IV, 86).

16–17 *non ... dixi* 'You cannot say more against my trifles than I have said myself' (Martial XIII, 2).

17–18 *willingly ... faulted* Thus Webster aligns his play not with the compressive simplicity of classical theatre but with the episodic multiplicity of native English drama.

19 *sententious* full of maxims and *sententiae,* as in the tragedies of Seneca

5

as it were lifen death, in the passionate and weighty *Nuntius:* yet after all this divine rapture, *O dura messorum ilia*, the breath that comes from the uncapable multitude is able to poison it, and ere it be acted, let the author resolve   25 to fix to every scene, this of Horace,

> *Haec hodie porcis comedenda relinques.*

To those who report I was a long time in finishing this tragedy, I confess I do not write with a goose-quill, winged with two feathers, and if they will needs make it my fault,   30 I must answer them with that of Euripides to Alcestides, a tragic writer: Alcestides objecting that Euripides had only in three days composed three verses, whereas himself had written three hundred: 'Thou tell'st truth', (quoth he), 'but here's the difference: thine shall only be read for   35 three days, whereas mine shall continue three ages'.

Detraction is the sworn friend to ignorance: for mine own part I have ever truly cherished my good opinion of other men's worthy labours, especially of that full and heightened style of Master Chapman, the laboured and   40 understanding works of Master Jonson: the no less worthy composures of the both worthily excellent Master Beaumont, and Master Fletcher: and lastly (without wrong last to be named) the right happy and copious industry of Master Shakespeare, Master Dekker, and Master Hey-   45 wood, wishing what I write may be read by their light: protesting, that, in the strength of mine own judgement, I know them so worthy, that though I rest silent in my own work, yet to most of theirs I dare (without flattery) fix that of Martial: 50

> *non norunt, haec monumenta mori.*

22-3 *lifen . . . Nuntius* i.e. make death come alive in the report of the passionate and serious messenger

23 *O . . . ilia* 'O strong stomachs of harvesters' (Horace, *Epodes* III, 4; alluding to peasants' love of garlic)

27 *Haec . . . relinques* 'What you leave will go today to feed the pigs' (Horace, *Epistles* I, vii, 19)

28-30 *I . . . feathers* Webster published nothing between 1605 and 1612, when *The White Devil* appeared; he may indeed have laboured over his first independent dramatic effort.

32-6 In the original story (told by Valerius Maximus), the poet Alcestis writes a hundred verses in three days; Webster probably borrowed his version from L. Lloyd, *Linceus Spectacles* (1607).

41 *understanding* intellectual

51 *non . . . mori* 'These monuments do not know death' (Martial X, ii, 12; comparing literature with ruined tombs).

THE TRAGEDY OF PAULO GIORDANO URSINI DUKE OF BRACHIANO, and VITTORIA COROMBONA

[Act I, Scene i]

Enter Count LODOVICO, ANTONELLI *and* GASPARO

LODOVICO
  Banished?
ANTONELLI It grieved me much to hear the sentence.
LODOVICO
  Ha, ha, O Democritus, thy gods
  That govern the whole world: courtly reward,
  And punishment. Fortune's a right whore:
  If she give ought, she deals it in small parcels,　　　　　5
  That she may take away all at one swoop.
  This 'tis to have great enemies, God quite them.
  Your wolf no longer seems to be a wolf
  Than when she's hungry.
GASPARO　　　　　　　　　　You term those enemies
  Are men of princely rank.
LODOVICO　　　　　　　　　　O I pray for them.　　　　10
  The violent thunder is adored by those
  Are pashed in pieces by it.
ANTONELLI　　　　　　　　Come my lord,
  You are justly doomed; look but a little back
  Into your former life: you have in three years
  Ruined the noblest earldom –

---

0 s.d. The three men may enter and react together to a previous offstage sentence,
  or (probably more effective theatrically) Antonelli and Gasparo may enter to
  hand Lodovico his decree of banishment, visually re-enacting the confrontation
  between social forces and the anarchic individual. Not only does Webster
  choose to open and close the play with Lodovico, he also sets him up as an
  analogue to the desperate Brachiano of I.ii.
1–4 ed. (Banisht ... to / heare ... sentence / LODO ... Gods / That ... re- / ward
  ... whore Q – lineation altered to make room for ornamental first letter)
2 *Democritus, thy gods* Webster is here borrowing from Guevara's *Diall of Princes*
  (trans. North 1557), which attributes to Pliny and Democritus the view that
  'there were two gods, which governed the universal world: ... reward and
  punishment'.
5 *parcels* portions
6 *swoop* stroke
7 *quite* requite　　　　　12 *pashed* dashed

7

GASPARO   Your followers   15
　　Have swallowed you like mummia, and being sick
　　With such unnatural and horrid physic
　　Vomit you up i'th'kennel –
ANTONELLI   All the damnable degrees
　　Of drinkings have you staggered through. One citizen
　　Is lord of two fair manors, called you master   20
　　Only for caviar.
GASPARO   Those noblemen
　　Which were invited to your prodigal feasts,
　　Wherein the phoenix scarce could scape your throats,
　　Laugh at your misery, as fore-deeming you
　　An idle meteor which, drawn forth the earth,   25
　　Would be soon lost i'th'air.
ANTONELLI   Jest upon you
　　And say you were begotten in an earthquake,
　　You have ruined such fair lordships.
LODOVICO   Very good,
　　This well goes with two buckets, I must tend
　　The pouring out of either.
GASPARO   Worse than these,   30
　　You have acted certain murders here in Rome,
　　Bloody and full of horror.
LODOVICO   'Las they were flea-bitings:
　　Why took they not my head then?
GASPARO   O my lord
　　The law doth sometimes mediate, thinks it good
　　Not ever to steep violent sins in blood.   35
　　This gentle penance may both end your crimes
　　And in the example better these bad times.

16 *mummia* a medicine made from dead flesh, difficult to swallow but thought to
　　produce excellent results
18 *kennel* gutter
19 *you* (you, you Q)
19–21 i.e. a citizen, though richer than you, was prepared to humble himself in
　　order to get your gifts
23 *phoenix* legendary bird and rare delicacy. Since only one phoenix lived at one
　　time, the new bird rose from the ashes of the old.
25 *idle* worthless
　　meteor a luminous body seen temporarily in the sky and supposed to emerge
　　from a lower region or corrupt source; an evil omen
29–30 *This . . . either* Lodovico uses the image of two buckets alternately drawing
　　from a common well to caricature the alternation of Antonelli's and Gasparo's
　　attacks as mechanical and composed of mere proverbs. The image may be rein-
　　forced visually, with Antonelli and Gasparo on either side of Lodovico (NCW
　　I.ii.29–30 n.).
31 *acted* carried out
36 *This gentle penance* i.e. banishment

LODOVICO
  So, but I wonder then some great men scape
  This banishment; there's Paulo Giordano Orsini,
  The Duke of Brachiano, now lives in Rome,   40
  And by close panderism seeks to prostitute
  The honour of Vittoria Corombona:
  Vittoria, she that might have got my pardon
  For one kiss to the Duke.
ANTONELLI   Have a full man within you.
  We see that trees bear no such pleasant fruit   45
  There where they grew first, as where they are new set.
  Perfumes, the more they are chafed, the more they
      render
  Their pleasing scents; and so affliction
  Expresseth virtue fully, whether true,
  Or else adulterate.
LODOVICO   Leave your painted comforts.   50
  I'll make Italian cut-works in their guts
  If ever I return.
GASPARO   O sir.
LODOVICO   I am patient.
  I have seen some ready to be executed
  Give pleasant looks, and money, and grown familiar
  With the knave hangman; so do I, I thank them,   55
  And would account them nobly merciful
  Would they dispatch me quickly.
ANTONELLI   Fare you well,
  We shall find time I doubt not to repeal
  Your banishment.   *Sennet* [*sounds*]
LODOVICO   I am ever bound to you:
  This is the world's alms; pray make use of it;   60
  Great men sell sheep, thus to be cut in pieces,
  When first they have shorn them bare and sold their
      fleeces.

                                        Exeunt

41 *close* secret   44 *Have . . . you* i.e. be the complete and self-sufficient man
46 *they* ed. (the Q)
    new set transplanted   50 *painted* false, artificial
51 *Italian cut-works* openwork embroidery, an Italian fashion
55 *knave* menial servant; base rogue
59 s.d. *Sennet* ed. (Enter Senate Q) a set of notes sounded on the trumpet to
    announce a ceremonial entrance (that of Vittoria, Brachiano and attendants in
    the following scene). The trumpeters may have appeared on the stage.
60 Previous editors have taken 'alms' to refer to the cynical adage that follows, but
    it is possible that Lodovico is giving Gasparo and Antonelli money to repeal
    his banishment, at the same time cynically referring to them as hangmen (l.
    55).
    make use of it earn interest on it (NCW I.i.60 n.)

[Act I, Scene ii]

Enter BRACHIANO, CAMILLO, FLAMINEO, VITTORIA
COROMBONA [*and* GENTLEMEN *with torches*]

BRACHIANO
  Your best of rest.
VITTORIA   Unto my lord the Duke
  The best of welcome. More lights, attend the Duke.
                    [*Exeunt* VITTORIA *and* CAMILLO]
BRACHIANO
  Flamineo.
FLAMINEO   My lord.
BRACHIANO   Quite lost Flamineo.
FLAMINEO
  Pursue your noble wishes, I am prompt
  As lightning to your service, O my lord!   5
  (*Whispers*) The fair Vittoria, my happy sister
  Shall give you present audience. [*Aloud*] Gentlemen,
  Let the caroche go on, and 'tis his pleasure
  You put out all your torches and depart.
                    [*Exeunt* GENTLEMEN *with torches*]
BRACHIANO
  Are we so happy?
FLAMINEO   Can't be otherwise?   10
  Observed you not tonight, my honoured lord,
  Which way so e'er you went she threw her eyes?
  I have dealt already with her chamber-maid
  Zanche the Moor, and she is wondrous proud
  To be the agent for so high a spirit.   15
BRACHIANO
  We are happy above thought, because 'bove merit.
FLAMINEO
  'Bove merit! We may now talk freely: 'bove merit; what
  is't you doubt? Her coyness, that's but the superficies
  of lust most women have. Yet why should ladies blush

0–9 Vittoria passes over the stage in a blaze of light (cf. III.ii.294). In a typical
  stroke of dramaturgy, Webster first crowds and illuminates the stage only to
  empty and (imaginatively, in an outdoor theatre) darken it: a public, ceremonial
  world quickly gives way to the private intensity of Brachiano's illicit passion.
6 s.d. (*Whispers*) ed. (whisper r. margin opposite l. 7 in Q)
8 *caroche* luxurious coach for town use
15 i.e. help you because of your outstanding desire and high rank
17 *talk freely* As Flamineo relaxes with Brachiano on a stage now cleared of observers, his speech acquires the metrical looseness of prose.

to hear that named, which they do not fear to handle? 20
O they are politic; they know our desire is increased by
the difficulty of enjoying, whereas satiety is a blunt,
weary and drowsy passion. If the buttery-hatch at court
stood continually open there would be nothing so passionate crowding, nor hot suit after the beverage. 25

BRACHIANO

O but her jealous husband –

FLAMINEO

Hang him, a gilder that hath his brains perished with
quicksilver is not more cold in the liver. The great barriers moulted not more feathers than he hath shed hairs
by the confession of his doctor. An Irish gamester that 30
will play himself naked, and then wage all downward,
at hazard, is not more venturous. So unable to please a
woman that like a Dutch doublet all his back is shrunk
into his breeches.
Shroud you within this closet, good my lord; 35
Some trick now must be thought on to divide
My brother-in-law from his fair bed-fellow.

22 *whereas* ed. (where a Q)

23 *buttery-hatch* the half-door over which were served food and drink from the
buttery

27–8 *gilder . . . liver* Gilders used a mixture of gold and mercury to gild objects,
then later drew off the mercury with heat, thereby inhaling the fumes, causing
mercury poisoning; the symptoms include tremors, insanity and general torpor
(or reduction in body heat). Flamineo compares Camillo to gilders because he
is so lacking in passion. The liver was supposedly the seat of the passions.

28–9 *great barriers . . . hairs* During barriers, a martial tournament fought with short
swords or pikes across a low railing (cf. V.iii), the feathers in the helmets of
combatants would often be struck off. As the challengers at barriers lose
feathers, so Camillo's sexual encounters have given him syphilis, which causes
hair loss and impotence.

30–2 *An Irish gamester . . . venturous* According to Richard Stanyhurst's *Description
of Irelande* in Holinshed's *Chronicles*, some 'wild Irish' would gamble away their
clothes until they were stark naked, then pawn their fingernails, toenails and
even their testicles, which they lost or redeemed at the courtesy of the winner.
The sense here is that Camillo has pawned his virility.

33–4 *Dutch doublet . . . breeches* Like a Dutch doublet, which was close fitting
except for its large breeches, Camillo's 'back' (manhood) has withered or
shrunk.

35 *Shroud you . . . closet* It is unlikely that Brachiano actually disappears from the
audience's view here (or at l. 47), since the effectiveness of Flamineo's cross-talk
would be heightened by Brachiano's visibility. The actor may simply retreat to
a different part of the stage, crouching, perhaps, behind an arras or door; later
in the scene, Cornelia is likewise visible to the audience but invisible to the
other characters. The stage direction for Brachiano's entrance at l. 195 thus
registers his coming forward to centre stage.

BRACHIANO

O should she fail to come!

FLAMINEO

I must not have your lordship thus unwisely amorous;
I myself have loved a lady and pursued her with a great   40
deal of under-age protestation, whom some three or
four gallants that have enjoyed would with all their
hearts have been glad to have been rid of. 'Tis just like
a summer bird-cage in a garden: the birds that are without, despair to get in, and the birds that are within des-   45
pair and are in a consumption for fear they shall never
get out: away, away my lord –

Enter CAMILLO [BRACHIANO *withdraws*]

See, here he comes; this fellow by his apparel
Some men would judge a politician,
But call his wit in question, you shall find it   50
Merely an ass in's foot-cloth. [*To* CAMILLO] How now,
    brother,
What, travailing to bed to your kind wife?

CAMILLO

I assure you brother, no. My voyage lies
More northerly, in a far colder clime;
I do not well remember, I protest,   55
When I last lay with her.

FLAMINEO   Strange you should lose your
    count.

CAMILLO

We never lay together but ere morning
There grew a flaw between us.

FLAMINEO   'T had been your part
To have made up that flaw.

---

41 *under-age protestation* inexperienced or immature declaration of love
48–9 *his apparel . . . politician* Camillo appears dressed in the long robes of a coun-
    sellor of state or an old man (NCW I.ii.47 n.)
51 *foot-cloth* a large and richly ornamented cloth laid over the back of a horse,
    hanging down to the ground on either side, considered a mark of dignity (here,
    adorning an ass)
51–2 ed. (cloath / How . . . wife? Q)
52 *travailing* archaic form of 'travelling', containing both the straightforward sense
    of 'journeying' and the more sardonic sense of 'labouring, exerting yourself'
    (with another disparaging glance at Camillo's futile exertions as a lover)
55–6 ed. (I do not well . . . her / Strange Q)
56 *lose your count* a bawdy pun, again at Camillo's expense. 'Count' was a variant
    spelling of (and probably close in pronunciation to) 'cunt'.

CAMILLO   True, but she loathes
    I should be seen in't.
FLAMINEO   Why sir, what's the matter?   60
CAMILLO
    The Duke your master visits me, I thank him,
    And I perceive how like an earnest bowler
    He very passionately leans that way
    He should have his bowl run.
FLAMINEO   I hope you do not think –
CAMILLO
    That noblemen bowl booty? 'Faith his cheek   65
    Hath a most excellent bias, it would fain
    Jump with my mistress.
FLAMINEO   Will you be an ass
    Despite your Aristotle, or a cuckold
    Contrary to your ephemerides
    Which shows you under what a smiling planet   70
    You were first swaddled?
CAMILLO   Pew wew, sir tell not me
    Of planets nor of ephemerides.
    A man may be made cuckold in the day-time
    When the stars' eyes are out.
FLAMINEO   Sir, God boy you,
    I do commit you to your pitiful pillow   75
    Stuffed with horn-shavings.

59 *flaw* a sudden storm or squall (which would part two ships which 'lay together' after a 'voyage'), or, figuratively, a passionate outburst; also a breach or crack (with a bawdy allusion to the female genitals; cf. *A Chaste Maid in Cheapside* I.i. 29)
59–60 ed. (Trew . . . in't / Why Q)
65 *bowl booty* a term from the game of bowls: to conspire with another player in order to victimize a third player; hence, to play the game falsely so as to gain a desired object. (Camillo suspects Brachiano and Flamineo are conspiring against him to win Vittoria.)
65–7 *his cheek . . . mistress* Camillo goes on to compare Brachiano's cheek (buttock) to the bowl itself, whose off-centre weighting (bias) causes it to run in an oblique line towards the 'mistress', the smaller white ball at which the bowls are aimed.
67 *jump with* lie with. When one bowl touches another one or the 'mistress', it is said to 'kiss' it. Camillo wants to suggest Brachiano's overtly sexual motives.
66–7 ed. (Hath . . . mistress / Will . . . asse Q)
68 *your* ed. (you Q)
    Aristotle philosophical learning
69 *ephemerides* astrological tables showing predicted positions of heavenly bodies on successive days
74 *God boy you* God be with you (ironically dismissive)
76 *horn-shavings* Horns were supposed to grow on the foreheads of men whose wives were unfaithful.

CAMILLO   Brother –
FLAMINEO   God refuse me
  Might I advise you now your only course
  Were to lock up your wife.
CAMILLO   'Twere very good.
FLAMINEO
  Bar her the sight of revels.
CAMILLO   Excellent.
FLAMINEO
  Let her not go to church, but like a hound   80
  In leon at your heels.
CAMILLO   'Twere for her honour.
FLAMINEO
  And so you should be certain in one fortnight,
  Despite her chastity or innocence,
  To be cuckolded, which yet is in suspense:
  This is my counsel and I ask no fee for't.   85
CAMILLO
  Come, you know not where my nightcap wrings me.
FLAMINEO
  Wear it o'th'old fashion, let your large ears come
through, it will be more easy; nay, I will be bitter: bar
your wife of her entertainment: women are more will-
ingly and more gloriously chaste, when they are least   90
restrained of their liberty. It seems you would be a fine
capricious mathematically jealous coxcomb, take the
height of your own horns with a Jacob's staff afore they
are up. These politic enclosures for paltry mutton
makes more rebellion in the flesh than all the provoca-   95
tive electuaries doctors have uttered since last Jubilee.
CAMILLO
  This doth not physic me.

---

81 *leon* leash
86 *my nightcap . . . me* i.e. my nightcap pinches me (because of the cuckold's horns
    sprouting from my forehead)
87 *large ears* ass's ears (cf. l. 51)
93 *Jacob's staff* instrument used for measuring height or distance
94–5 *politic . . . flesh* Flamineo's punning is based on 'mutton', slang for loose
    woman. As the enclosure of common land by rich men leads to peasant upris-
    ings, so putting restraints on loose women leads to their sexual rebellion.
95–6 *provocative electuaries* aphrodisiacs
96 *uttered* issued, supplied
    Jubilee a year (first instituted by the Pope in 1300) of remission from sin by
    papal indulgence through various acts of piety. The 'last Jubilee' before the
    play's performance was 1600.

FLAMINEO

It seems you are jealous. I'll show you the error of it
by a familiar example: I have seen a pair of spectacles
fashioned with such perspective art that, lay down but   100
one twelve pence o'th'board, 'twill appear as if there
were twenty; now should you wear a pair of these spectacles, and see your wife tying her shoe, you would
imagine twenty hands were taking up of your wife's
clothes, and this would put you into a horrible causeless   105
fury.

CAMILLO

The fault there, sir, is not in the eyesight –

FLAMINEO

True, but they that have the yellow jaundice, think all
objects they look on to be yellow. Jealousy is worser,
her fits present to a man, like so many bubbles in a   110
basin of water, twenty several crabbed faces; many
times makes his own shadow his cuckold-maker.

Enter [VITTORIA] COROM[BON]A

See she comes; what reason have you to be jealous of
this creature? What an ignorant ass or flattering knave
might he be counted, that should write sonnets to her   115
eyes, or call her brow the snow of Ida, or ivory of
Corinth, or compare her hair to the blackbird's bill,
when 'tis liker the blackbird's feather. This is all: be
wise; I will make you friends and you shall go to bed
together; marry look you, it shall not be your seeking,   120
do you stand upon that by any means; walk you aloof,
I would not have you seen in't. Sister, my lord attends

---

100 *perspective art* the skill of constructing a picture or figure so as to produce some
     fantastic optical effect. These spectacles were cut into facets so as to multiply
     the image twentyfold.

104 *wife's* ed. (wives Q)

109 *worser* worse

112 s.d. ed. (Enter Coroma l. margin; asterisk after -maker Q)

116 *Ida* sacred mountain near Troy, usually associated with the green groves in
     which Paris lived as a shepherd

116–17 *ivory of Corinth* Corinth was famous for excessive luxury.

117–18 *blackbird's bill . . . feather* The blackbird's bill is yellow, its feathers black; in
     sonneteering convention fair-haired women were considered more beautiful
     than dark-haired women.

119 *friends* lovers

121 *walk . . . aloof* Flamineo removes Camillo to a safe distance. He thus jokes pri-
     vately with Vittoria at Camillo's expense, possibly in stage whispers (cf. I.ii.6).

you in the banqueting-house – [*Aside*] your husband is
wondrous discontented.

VITTORIA

I did nothing to displease him, I carved to him at   125
supper-time.

FLAMINEO

You need not have carved him in faith, they say he is
a capon already. I must now seemingly fall out with you.
[*Aloud*] Shall a gentleman so well descended as Camillo
[*Aside*] a lousy slave that within this twenty years rode   130
with the black-guard in the Duke's carriage 'mongst
spits and dripping-pans –

CAMILLO

Now he begins to tickle her.

FLAMINEO

An excellent scholar – one that hath a head filled with
calves' brains without any sage in them – come crouch-   135
ing in the hams to you for a night's lodging – that hath
an itch in's hams, which like the fire at the glass-house
hath not gone out this seven years – Is he not a courtly
gentleman? – When he wears white satin one would take
him by his black muzzle to be no other creature than a   140
maggot – You are a goodly foil, I confess, well set out –
but covered with a false stone, yon counterfeit diamond.

CAMILLO

He will make her know what is in me.

123–58 I have added dashes to those already in the copy text in order to clarify
     Flamineo's cross-talk. Up to l. 142, Flamineo's jokes depend on remarks which
     Vittoria (and Brachiano) can hear and Camillo cannot; the double meaning of
     l. 144 depends on Camillo's ignorance of Flamineo's asides. After l. 144, since
     Flamineo has promised Vittoria's sexual favours to Brachiano and Camillo, his
     lines apply equally well to both men.
125 *carved* shown great courtesy; made seductive advances – 'by signalling with the
     fingers' (Lucas, p. 209)
127 *carved* castrated
128 *capon* a castrated cock; a eunuch
131 *black-guard* lowest menial servants of a noble household; scullions and
     kitchen-knaves
133 *tickle* excite agreeably, arouse
135 *calves'* . . . *them* Calves' brains unseasoned by the culinary herb sage are a meta-
     phor for the brains of a dolt unseasoned by wisdom.
135–6 *crouching* . . . *hams* in a servile, bowing position
137 *itch in's hams* irritation in the thighs and buttocks
     glass-house the glass factory in which fires were always kept burning; in Webster
     metaphorically associated with sexual organs
141 *foil* setting of a jewel

FLAMINEO

Come, my lord attends you; thou shalt go to bed to my
lord.   145

CAMILLO

Now he comes to't.

FLAMINEO

With a relish as curious as a vintner going to taste new
wine, I am opening your case hard.

CAMILLO

A virtuous brother o' my credit.

FLAMINEO

He will give thee a ring with a philosopher's stone in it.   150

CAMILLO

Indeed I am studying alchemy.

FLAMINEO

Thou shalt lie in a bed stuffed with turtles' feathers,
swoon in perfumed linen like the fellow was smothered
in roses, so perfect shall be thy happiness, that as men
at sea think land and trees and ships go that way they   155
go, so both heaven and earth shall seem to go your
voyage. Shalt meet him, 'tis fixed, with nails of diamonds to inevitable necessity.

VITTORIA

[*Aside*] How shall's rid him hence?

FLAMINEO

[*Aside*] I will put breese in's tail, set him gadding pres-   160
ently. [*To* CAMILLO] I have almost wrought her to it, I
find her coming, but might I advise you now for this
night I would not lie with her, I would cross her humour
to make her more humble.

CAMILLO

Shall I? Shall I?   165

FLAMINEO

It will show in you a supremacy of judgement.

CAMILLO

True, and a mind differing from the tumultuary opinion, for *quae negata grata.*

148 *case* legal case; and punning on the sense, the female genitals
150 *philosopher's stone* miraculous substance sought by alchemists which would turn
    base metals into precious ones, cure disease and prolong life; here also a bawdy
    reference to the testicle (stone)
152 *turtles'* turtle doves', emblems of fidelity in love
159 i.e. how shall we get rid of him?
160 *breese* gadflies   162 *coming* well inclined; sexually receptive
167 *tumultuary* irregular, confused
168 *quae negata grata* what is denied is desired

FLAMINEO
> Right, you are the adamant shall draw her to you,
> though you keep distance off.   170

CAMILLO
> A philosophical reason.

FLAMINEO
> Walk by her o' the nobleman's fashion, and tell her you
> will lie with her at the end of the progress.

CAMILLO
> Vittoria, I cannot be induced or as a man would say
> incited –   175

VITTORIA
> To do what sir?

CAMILLO
> To lie with you tonight; your silkworm useth to fast
> every third day, and the next following spins the better.
> Tomorrow at night I am for you.

VITTORIA
> You'll spin a fair thread, trust to't.   180

FLAMINEO
> But do you hear, I shall have you steal to her chamber
> about midnight.

CAMILLO
> Do you think so? Why look you brother, because you
> shall not think I'll gull you, take the key, lock me into
> the chamber, and say you shall be sure of me.   185

FLAMINEO
> In truth I will, I'll be your jailer once;
> But have you ne'er a false door?

CAMILLO
> A pox on't, as I am a Christian tell me tomorrow how
> scurvily she takes my unkind parting.

FLAMINEO
> I will.   190

CAMILLO
> Didst thou not mark the jest of the silkworm? Good
> night; in faith I will use this trick often.

---

169 *adamant* magnet
171 *philosophical* wise; scientific
173 *progress* a state procession. Camillo might parade himself before Vittoria during
these speeches (NCW I.ii.160 n.).
180 *thread* punning on the sense 'semen'
184 *gull* deceive
189 *scurvily* sourly
191 *mark* ed. (make Q)

FLAMINEO
Do, do, do.

Exit CAMILLO

So now you are safe. Ha ha ha, thou entanglest thyself
in thine own work like a silkworm.   195

[BRACHIANO *comes forward*]

Come sister, darkness hides your blush; women are like
cursed dogs, civility keeps them tied all daytime, but
they are let loose at midnight; then they do most good
or most mischief. My lord, my lord –
BRACHIANO
Give credit: I could wish time would stand still   200
And never end this interview this hour,
But all delight doth itself soon'st devour.

ZANCHE *brings out a carpet, spreads it and lays on it*
two fair cushions

Enter CORNELIA [*listening*]

Let me into your bosom, happy lady,
Pour out instead of eloquence my vows;
Loose me not madam, for if you forgo me   205
I am lost eternally.
VITTORIA
Sir in the way of pity I wish you heart-whole.
BRACHIANO
You are a sweet physician.
VITTORIA
Sure sir a loathed cruelty in ladies
Is as to doctors many funerals: 210
It takes away their credit.

195 s.d. ed. (*Enter Brachiano* Q). See l. 35n. above.
197 *cursed* vicious; (often of women) shrewish
200 *Give credit* i.e. trust me (addressed either to Vittoria or to Flamineo)
202 s.d. The compositor squeezed this stage direction into the text space available
beside Brachiano's speech. While we cannot therefore be certain of the exact
position of the stage direction in the copy, Zanche's actions (and Cornelia's
entrance) are especially significant if they occur as Brachiano addresses Vittoria.
Brachiano's courtly vows are thus immediately counterbalanced by the overtly
sexual nature of the lovers' encounter suggested by the placing of cushions and
also by the presence of an outsider and critic (Cornelia, perhaps wearing a
crucifix). The staging recalls that of the morality play, with Vice (Flamineo and
Zanche) and Virtue (Cornelia) present as observers, probably framing the lovers
on either side.
205 *loose* release; lose (in modern sense)
205–6 ed. (one line in Q)   210–11 ed. (Is . . . credit / Excellent Q)

BRACHIANO   Excellent creature.
We call the cruel fair, what name for you
That are so merciful?   *[Embraces her]*
ZANCHE   See now they close.
FLAMINEO
Most happy union.
CORNELIA
[Aside] My fears are fall'n upon me, O my heart!   215
My son the pander: now I find our house
Sinking to ruin. Earthquakes leave behind,
Where they have tyrannized, iron, or lead, or stone,
But, woe to ruin, violent lust leaves none.
BRACHIANO
What value is this jewel?
VITTORIA   'Tis the ornament   220
Of a weak fortune.
BRACHIANO
In sooth I'll have it; nay I will but change
My jewel for your jewel.
FLAMINEO   Excellent,
His jewel for her jewel; well put in Duke.
BRACHIANO
Nay let me see you wear it.
VITTORIA   Here sir.   225
BRACHIANO
Nay lower, you shall wear my jewel lower.
FLAMINEO
That's better; she must wear his jewel lower.
VITTORIA
To pass away the time I'll tell your Grace
A dream I had last night.
BRACHIANO   Most wishedly.

213 *close* come together
220 *jewel* Brachiano presumably fingers a gem worn by Vittoria, and then offers one
    of his own, as in a formal betrothal ceremony in which tokens were exchanged
    before witnesses; 'jewel' signifies both married chastity or 'maidenhead' and the
    sexual organ – hence the subsequent word-play. Brachiano encourages Vittoria
    to pin his jewel at the base of her dress's V-shaped bodice, over her pudendum
    (NCW I.ii.205–12 n.).
224 *put in* make a claim; also with a sexual innuendo
225 *Here* ed. (Heare Q)
228–53 By recounting her dream, Vittoria physically disengages herself from Brach-
    iano's sexual overtures, perhaps walking about the stage as she imaginatively
    re-enacts it (NCW I.ii.216 n.). When she has finished, Brachiano reasserts con-
    trol by renewing his embrace.

VITTORIA
A foolish idle dream: 230
Methought I walked about the mid of night,
Into a church-yard, where a goodly yew-tree
Spread her large root in ground; under that yew,
As I sat sadly leaning on a grave,
Checkered with cross-sticks, there came stealing in   235
Your Duchess and my husband; one of them
A pick-axe bore, th'other a rusty spade,
And in rough terms they gan to challenge me,
About this yew.
BRACHIANO   That tree.
VITTORIA   This harmless yew.
They told me my intent was to root up   240
That well-grown yew, and plant i'th'stead of it
A withered blackthorn, and for that they vowed
To bury me alive: my husband straight
With pick-axe gan to dig, and your fell Duchess
With shovel, like a fury, voided out   245
The earth and scattered bones. Lord, how methought
I trembled, and yet for all this terror
I could not pray.
FLAMINEO   No, the devil was in your dream.
VITTORIA
When to my rescue there arose, methought,
A whirlwind which let fall a massy arm   250
From that strong plant,
And both were struck dead by that sacred yew
In that base shallow grave that was their due.
FLAMINEO
Excellent devil.
She hath taught him in a dream   255
To make away his Duchess and her husband.
BRACHIANO
[*Embracing* VITTORIA] Sweetly shall I interpret this your
    dream:

---

235 *cross-sticks* May mean any of the following: wooden crosses sticking out of
    graves; the 'chequered pattern of light and shade' created by the overhanging
    branches of the yew tree against the night sky (Brown, I.ii.236 n.); criss-crossed
    osiers protecting the grave; devices used by witches to raise tempests.
241 *yew* traditionally associated with death (cf. IV.iii.121), here an ambiguous
    symbol. Isabella and Camillo would think of 'that well-grown yew' as Camillo
    himself, the deserving husband, or perhaps as Brachiano, still uncorrupted; Vit-
    toria's obvious pun on 'you' (l. 241) and the end of the dream clearly suggest
    Brachiano as the yew.

You are lodged within his arms who shall protect you
From all the fevers of a jealous husband,
From the poor envy of our phlegmatic Duchess;   260
I'll seat you above law and above scandal,
Give to your thoughts the invention of delight
And the fruition; nor shall government
Divide me from you longer than a care
To keep you great: you shall to me at once   265
Be dukedom, health, wife, children, friends, and all.

CORNELIA
[*Approaching them*] Woe to light hearts, they still fore-
run our fall.

FLAMINEO
What fury raised thee up? Away, away –
                                        Exit ZANCHE

CORNELIA
What make you here, my lord, this dead of night?
Never dropped mildew on a flower here,   270
Till now.

FLAMINEO I pray will you go to bed then,
Lest you be blasted?

CORNELIA   O that this fair garden
Had with all poisoned herbs of Thessaly
At first been planted, made a nursery
For witchcraft; rather than a burial plot   275
For both your honours.

VITTORIA [*Kneeling*]   Dearest mother hear me.

CORNELIA
O thou dost make my brow bend to the earth
Sooner than nature. See the curse of children.
In life they keep us frequently in tears,
And in the cold grave leave us in pale fears.   280

---

263 *government* i.e. governing my dukedom
268 *fury* in classical mythology one of the avenging deities, dread goddesses with
snakes twined in their hair
s.d. Flamineo's direction to Zanche provides an early hint of their illicit relationship of which Cornelia later shows open disapproval (V.i.185).
270–1 ed. (one line in Q)
273 *with* ed. (not in Q)
Thessaly the special home of witches and poisonous herbs
275 *than* ed. (not in Q)
276 s.d. Vittoria probably kneels at this point, as she pleads with her mother, whose
'brow bend[s] to the earth'; at l. 292, Cornelia clearly indicates that she kneels
to join Vittoria. Vittoria's kneeling posture – a traditional show of respect for
authority – softens 'the curse of children' of which Cornelia accuses her
daughter.   280 *leave* ed. (leaves Q)

BRACHIANO
  Come, come, I will not hear you.
VITTORIA   Dear my lord.
CORNELIA
  Where is thy Duchess now, adulterous Duke?
  Thou little dreamed'st this night she is come to Rome.
FLAMINEO
  How? Come to Rome!
VITTORIA   The Duchess –
BRACHIANO   She had been
    better –
CORNELIA
  The lives of princes should like dials move,   285
  Whose regular example is so strong,
  They make the times by them go right or wrong.
FLAMINEO
  So, have you done?
CORNELIA   Unfortunate Camillo.
VITTORIA
  I do protest if any chaste denial,
  If anything but blood could have allayed   290
  His long suit to me –
CORNELIA [*Kneeling*]   I will join with thee,
  To the most woeful end e'er mother kneeled,
  If thou dishonour thus thy husband's bed,
  Be thy life short as are the funeral tears
  In great men's.
BRACHIANO   Fie, fie, the woman's mad.   295
CORNELIA
  Be thy act Judas-like, betray in kissing;
  May'st thou be envied during his short breath,
  And pitied like a wretch after his death.
VITTORIA
  O me accursed.   *Exit*
FLAMINEO
  Are you out of your wits? My lord,   300

290 *blood* her reciprocated sexual passion, life itself (Vittoria's own death or Brach-
     iano's suicide) or bloodshed (crimes which Brachiano is prepared to commit
     to win her)
298 *his* ed. (this Q)
299 s.d. *Exit* ed. (Exit Victoria Q)
300 *Are . . . wits?* The copy text does not reveal whether Flamineo's insolent ques-
     tion is addressed to Brachiano or Cornelia. While Flamineo is clearly furious
     with his mother for spoiling the lovers' meeting, he may also be angry with
     Brachiano for not actively preventing Vittoria's departure. The choice is left to
     the actor.

I'll fetch her back again!
BRACHIANO   No, I'll to bed.
Send Doctor Julio to me presently.
Uncharitable woman, thy rash tongue
Hath raised a fearful and prodigious storm.
Be thou the cause of all ensuing harm.   *Exit* 305
FLAMINEO
Now, you that stand so much upon your honour,
Is this a fitting time o' night, think you,
To send a duke home without e'er a man?
I would fain know where lies the mass of wealth
Which you have hoarded for my maintenance,   310
That I may bear my beard out of the level
Of my lord's stirrup.
CORNELIA   What? Because we are poor,
Shall we be vicious?
FLAMINEO   Pray what means have you
To keep me from the galleys, or the gallows?
My father proved himself a gentleman,   315
Sold all's land, and like a fortunate fellow
Died ere the money was spent. You brought me up,
At Padua I confess, where I protest,
For want of means (the university judge me)
I have been fain to heel my tutor's stockings   320
At least seven years. Conspiring with a beard
Made me a graduate, then to this Duke's service;
I visited the court, whence I returned –
More courteous, more lecherous by far,
But not a suit the richer – and shall I,   325
Having a path so open and so free
To my preferment, still retain your milk
In my pale forehead? No, this face of mine
I'll arm and fortify with lusty wine
'Gainst shame and blushing.   330

---

305 s.d. *Exit* ed. (Exit Brachiano Q)
311–12 *bear . . . stirrup* be in a higher position than unmounted foot attendant to
       my lord; hence, rise above my subservient position
315–16 *gentleman . . . land* alluding ironically to a contemporary social evil
321–2 *Conspiring . . . graduate* Flamineo earned his degree, probably by simply
       reaching physical (rather than intellectual) maturity or possibly by conspiring
       with an older man.
324 *courteous* with manners befitting the court of a prince

CORNELIA
  O that I ne'er had borne thee!
FLAMINEO   So would I.
  I would the common'st courtezan in Rome
  Had been my mother rather than thyself.
  Nature is very pitiful to whores
  To give them but few children, yet those children   335
  Plurality of fathers; they are sure
  They shall not want. Go, go,
  Complain unto my great lord cardinal,
  Yet may be he will justify the act.
  Lycurgus wondered much, men would provide   340
  Good stallions for their mares, and yet would suffer
  Their fair wives to be barren.
CORNELIA
  Misery of miseries.   *Exit*
FLAMINEO
  The Duchess come to court, I like not that;
  We are engaged to mischief and must on.   345
  As rivers, to find out the ocean
  Flow with crook bendings beneath forced banks,
  Or as we see, to aspire some mountain's top
  The way ascends not straight but imitates
  The subtle foldings of a winter's snake,   350
  So, who knows policy and her true aspect,
  Shall find her ways winding and indirect.   *Exit*

340–2 *Lycurgus . . . barren* According to Plutarch, Lycurgus advocated that men
  should share their wives with other 'worthy' men, not to fulfil the needs of
  barren women, but to provide the state with citizens from the best possible
  stock.
343 s.d. *Exit* ed. (Exit Cornelia Q)
347 *crook* crooked
  forced artificially made
350 *winter's snake* probably the mythical *amphisbaena*, symbol of the devil, whose
  two heads allowed elaborate serpentine movement and which, unlike most
  snakes, deliberately sought cold temperatures

[Act II, Scene i]

Enter FRANCISCO DE' MEDICI, *Cardinal* MONTICELSO,
MARCELLO, ISABELLA, *young* GIOVANNI, *with*
little JACQUES *the Moor*

FRANCISCO
Have you not seen your husband since you arrived?
ISABELLA
Not yet sir.
FRANCISCO   Surely he is wondrous kind;
If I had such a dove-house as Camillo's
I would set fire on't, were't but to destroy
The pole-cats that haunt to't – [*To* GIOVANNI] my sweet
    cousin –   5
GIOVANNI
Lord uncle, you did promise me a horse
And armour.
FRANCISCO   That I did my pretty cousin;
Marcello see it fitted.
MARCELLO   My lord the Duke is here.
FRANCISCO
Sister away, you must not yet be seen.
ISABELLA
I do beseech you entreat him mildly,   10
Let not your rough tongue
Set us at louder variance; all my wrongs
Are freely pardoned, and I do not doubt
As men to try the precious unicorn's horn
Make of the powder a preservative circle   15
And in it put a spider, so these arms

---

0 s.d.1 *MONTICELSO* ed. (Mountcelso Q)

   s.d.3 *little* JACQUES *the Moor* A mysterious ghost character with no speaking part,
perhaps (as most editors think) a trace in the manuscript of an idea that was
subsequently undeveloped or discarded by Webster; but Webster may have
intended the presence of the silent young Moor among the company to hint at
the sinister potential of apparently virtuous characters such as Monticelso and
Francisco. Aaron, also a Moor, appears but does not speak in the first scene
of Shakespeare's *Titus Andronicus*; his brooding presence casts a shadow over
the apparently virtuous Tamora (later revealed as Aaron's mistress) as she
pleads for her son's life.

3 *such a* ed. (a such Q)

   dove-house a house for doves; here referring ironically to Vittoria, since the dove
was traditionally a symbol of peace and innocence

5 *pole-cats* small, foul-smelling predatory mammals; a term of abuse for a vile
person or a prostitute

14–16 *unicorn's horn ... spider* In this test a spider was encircled by an extremely
rare and expensive powder believed to come from the mythological unicorn's

Shall charm his poison, force it to obeying
And keep him chaste from an infected straying.

FRANCISCO
I wish it may. Be gone.

Exit [ISABELLA]

Enter BRACHIANO *and* FLAMINEO

Void the chamber;
[*Exeunt* FLAMINEO, MARCELLO, GIOVANNI *and* JACQUES]

You are welcome, will you sit? [BRACHIANO *sits*] I pray
    my lord   20
Be you my orator, my heart's too full;
I'll second you anon.

MONTICELSO   Ere I begin
Let me entreat your grace forego all passion
Which may be raised by my free discourse.

BRACHIANO
As silent as i'th'church – you may proceed.   25

MONTICELSO
It is a wonder to your noble friends
That you have as 'twere entered the world
With a free sceptre in your able hand,
And have to th'use of nature well applied
High gifts of learning, should in your prime age   30
Neglect your awful throne, for the soft down
Of an insatiate bed. O my lord,
The drunkard after all his lavish cups
Is dry, and then is sober; so at length
When you awake from this lascivious dream,   35
Repentance then will follow, like the sting
Placed in the adder's tail: wretched are princes
When fortune blasteth but a petty flower
Of their unwieldy crowns; or ravisheth

---

horn, which was thought to be an antidote to poison; if the horn were genuine,
    the spider would remain inside the circle.
19 *Void the chamber* A bold stroke of staging on Webster's part: no sooner is the
    stage crowded with actors than it is suddenly cleared at Francisco's command.
    The stage picture – in which two men chastise a third for unseemly behaviour –
    replicates I.i, in which Gasparo and Antonelli reprimand Lodovico.
31 *awful* awe-inspiring
36–7 *sting . . . tail* While the adder inflicts injury primarily with its mouth or fangs,
    the hindpart of its tail was also supposed to be able to sting. Monticelso may
    be implying that, while Brachiano's affair now primarily injures his public repu-
    tation, he will later badly regret it himself.
38–9 *fortune . . . crowns* Not a mixed metaphor but a cunning play on words:
    'flower' could mean a jewel in a crown; 'crown' could mean a garland of flowers.

But one pearl from their sceptre; but alas!   40
When they to wilful shipwreck loose good fame
All princely titles perish with their name.
BRACHIANO
You have said, my lord, –
MONTICELSO   Enough to give you taste
How far I am from flattering your greatness?
BRACHIANO
Now you that are his second, what say you?   45
Do not like young hawks fetch a course about;
Your game flies fair and for you.
FRANCISCO   Do not fear it:
I'll answer you in your own hawking phrase;
Some eagles that should gaze upon the sun
Seldom soar high, but take their lustful ease,   50
Since they from dunghill birds their prey can seize.
You know Vittoria.
BRACHIANO   Yes.
FRANCISCO   You shift your shirt there
When you retire from tennis.
BRACHIANO   Happily.
FRANCISCO
Her husband is lord of a poor fortune
Yet she wears cloth of tissue.
BRACHIANO   What of this?   55
Will you urge that, my good lord cardinal,
As part of her confession at next shrift,
And know from whence it sails?
FRANCISCO   She is your strumpet.
BRACHIANO
Uncivil sir there's hemlock in thy breath
And that black slander; were she a whore of mine   60

42 *name* good name, reputation
46 *fetch a course about* change direction, turn tail (as young hawks are supposed to
   do when directed to fly at old game)
51 *prey* ed. (pery Q)
   dunghill birds birds (such as ravens, kites and common barnyard fowl) whose
   prey is offal, contrasted to eagles, by popular belief the only bird able to look
   directly at the sun. Francisco is comparing Brachiano to an eagle sluggish
   enough to seize the contemptible, corrupt prey (Vittoria) of an inferior bird
   (Camillo).
52 *shift* change
53 *Happily* perhaps·
55 *cloth of tissue* a rich kind of cloth, often interwoven with gold or silver, that
   sumptuary laws restricted to women of high birth (NCW II.i.55 n.)
59 *hemlock* poison

All thy loud cannons and thy borrowed Switzers,
Thy galleys nor thy sworn confederates
Durst not supplant her.
FRANCISCO   Let's not talk on thunder.
Thou hast a wife, our sister; would I had given
Both her white hands to death, bound and locked fast   65
In her last winding-sheet, when I gave thee
But one.
BRACHIANO Thou hadst given a soul to God then.
FRANCISCO   True:
Thy ghostly father with all's absolution
Shall ne'er do so by thee.
BRACHIANO   Spit thy poison.
FRANCISCO
I shall not need, lust carries her sharp whip   70
At her own girdle; look to't, for our anger
Is making thunder-bolts.
BRACHIANO   Thunder? In faith,
They are but crackers.
FRANCISCO   We'll end this with the cannon.
BRACHIANO
Thou'lt get nought by it but iron in thy wounds,
And gunpowder in thy nostrils.
FRANCISCO   Better that   75
Than change perfumes for plasters.
BRACHIANO   Pity on thee,
'Twere good you'ld show your slaves or men
    condemned
Your new-ploughed forehead. Defiance! And I'll meet
    thee,
Even in a thicket of thy ablest men.

61 *borrowed Switzers* Swiss mercenary soldiers
67 *Thou . . . then* Brachiano is acknowledging Isabella's fitness for the spiritual life.
    Does he mean this as a genuine compliment, or as an ironic comment on her
    unfitness for the real world? The ambiguity aptly prepares an audience for a
    character whose saintly self-sacrifice leads her to deliver vicious harangues.
68 *ghostly* spiritual
73 *crackers* explosive fireworks (as in modern sense); also, boasts or lies
76 *change . . . plasters* i.e. exchange the sweet smells of sensual indulgence for its
    consequences, the bandages to treat venereal disease
78 *new-ploughed* deeply furrowed (with anger)
    forehead . . . thee ed. (fore-head defiance, and I'le meete thee Q) Repunctuation
    is necessary to make sense of the text. 'Defiance!' is a plausible trumpet call to
    mark Brachiano's shift from contempt for Francisco to self-assertion.

MONTICELSO
  My lords, you shall not word it any further   80
  Without a milder limit.
FRANCISCO   Willingly.
BRACHIANO
  Have you proclaimed a triumph that you bait
  A lion thus?
MONTICELSO My lord.
BRACHIANO   I am tame, I am tame sir.
FRANCISCO
  We send unto the Duke for conference
  'Bout levies 'gainst the pirates. My lord Duke   85
  Is not at home. We come ourself in person,
  Still my lord Duke is busied; but we fear
  When Tiber to each prowling passenger
  Discovers flocks of wild ducks, then my lord
  'Bout moulting time, I mean we shall be certain   90
  To find you sure enough and speak with you.
BRACHIANO   Ha?
FRANCISCO
  A mere tale of a tub, my words are idle,
  But to express the sonnet by natural reason,
  When stags grow melancholic you'll find the season.

        Enter GIOVANNI [*in armour*]

MONTICELSO
  No more my lord; here comes a champion   95

80 *word it* argue, dispute
82 *triumph* a public festivity during which, in ancient Rome, lions might be 'baited', or taunted to fight
82–3 ed. (baite a / Lyon thus Q)
88 *prowling* ed. (proling Q)
    prowling passenger peregrine falcon in search of prey
89 *wild ducks* prey for the falcon; prostitutes
90 *moulting time* when birds shed their plumage; when people lose their hair (as a result of venereal disease; cf. I.ii.28–30); i.e. when his hair begins to fall out, Brachiano will discover Vittoria is a prostitute – another dig at Vittoria's reputation (cf. l. 76)
92 *tale of a tub* proverbial, a cock and bull story; and punning on the sweating tub used in treatment of venereal disease
93 *express . . . reason* i.e. explain this little poem by common sense
94 *stags* male deer; cuckolds (like Brachiano if he discovers Vittoria is a prostitute)
    stags . . . melancholic After stags mated, they were supposed to retreat into solitary ditches to lie alone.
    season fit occasion or opportunity (to meet with us)
    s.d. ed. (to r. of l. 93 in Q)
95 *champion* a valiant combatant. Giovanni is now outfitted in the suit of armour

Shall end the difference between you both,
Your son the prince Giovanni. See my lords
What hopes you store in him; this is a casket
For both your crowns, and should be held like dear.
Now is he apt for knowledge; therefore know   100
It is a more direct and even way
To train to virtue those of princely blood
By examples than by precepts: if by examples
Whom should he rather strive to imitate
Than his own father: be his pattern then,   105
Leave him a stock of virtue that may last,
Should fortune rend his sails and split his mast.

BRACHIANO
Your hand boy – [*Shaking his hand*] growing to a
    soldier?

GIOVANNI
Give me a pike.

                  [*One hands him a pike*]

FRANCISCO
What, practising your pike so young, fair coz?   110

GIOVANNI
[*Tossing the pike*] Suppose me one of Homer's frogs, my
    lord,
Tossing my bullrush thus; pray sir tell me
Might not a child of good discretion
Be leader to an army?

FRANCISCO   Yes cousin, a young prince
Of good discretion might.

GIOVANNI   Say you so?   115
Indeed I have heard 'tis fit a general
Should not endanger his own person oft,
So that he make a noise when he's a horseback
Like a Dansk drummer. O 'tis excellent.

Francisco promised him at the beginning of the scene, a living emblem of the
chivalric ideal Brachiano should strive for (identified in Webster's time with
Prince Henry).

106 *stock* line of descent; store, fund

108 *to a* ed. (to Q)

109 *pike* spear-like weapon used by foot soldiers; the penis

111 *Homer's frogs* from *The Battle of Frogs and Mice*, a burlesque epic attributed to
    Homer in which the frogs used bulrushes as pikes

113 *discretion* good judgement, prudence, circumspection, as in Falstaff's 'the better
    part of valour is discretion' (*1 Henry IV* V.iv.119–20). Giovanni's answer (ll.
    116–17) suggests he takes Francisco to be playing on the latter meaning.

119 *Dansk* Danish (famous for martial music, including drums)

He need not fight; methinks his horse as well   120
Might lead an army for him. If I live
I'll charge the French foe, in the very front
Of all my troops, the foremost man.

FRANCISCO   What, what!

GIOVANNI
And will not bid my soldiers up and follow
But bid them follow me.

BRACHIANO   Forward lapwing.   125
He flies with the shell on's head.

FRANCISCO   Pretty cousin.

GIOVANNI
The first year uncle that I go to war
All prisoners that I take I will set free
Without their ransom.

FRANCISCO   Ha, without their ransom?
How then will you reward your soldiers   130
That took those prisoners for you?

GIOVANNI   Thus my lord:
I'll marry them to all the wealthy widows
That falls that year.

FRANCISCO   Why then the next year following
You'll have no men to go with you to war.

GIOVANNI
Why then I'll press the women to the war,   135
And then the men will follow.

MONTICELSO   Witty prince.

FRANCISCO
See, a good habit makes a child a man,
Whereas a bad one makes a man a beast:
Come, you and I are friends.

BRACHIANO   Most wishedly,
Like bones which broke in sunder and well set   140
Knit the more strongly.

FRANCISCO [*Calling offstage*] Call Camillo hither.
You have received the rumour, how Count Lodowick
Is turned a pirate.

BRACHIANO   Yes.

FRANCISCO   We are now preparing
Some ships to fetch him in.

[*Enter* ISABELLA]

Behold your Duchess;

125 *lapwing* proverbial type of precocity, supposed to run (if not to fly) immediately
    after hatching
137 *habit* garment (applied to Giovanni); custom, practice (applied to Brachiano)

We will now leave you and expect from you   145
Nothing but kind entreaty.
BRACHIANO   You have charmed me.
          Exeunt FR[ANCISCO], MON[TICELSO], GIOV[ANNI]
You are in health we see.
ISABELLA   And above health
To see my lord well.
BRACHIANO   So I wonder much,
What amorous whirlwind hurried you to Rome.
ISABELLA
Devotion, my lord.
BRACHIANO   Devotion?   150
Is your soul charged with any grievous sin?
ISABELLA
'Tis burdened with too many, and I think
The oft'ner that we cast our reckonings up,
Our sleeps will be the sounder.
BRACHIANO   Take your chamber!
ISABELLA
Nay my dear lord, I will not have you angry;   155
Doth not my absence from you two months
Merit one kiss?
BRACHIANO   I do not use to kiss.
If that will dispossess your jealousy,
I'll swear it to you.
ISABELLA   O my loved lord,
I do not come to chide; my jealousy,   160
I am to learn what that Italian means;
You are as welcome to these longing arms,
As I to you a virgin.   [*Attempts to embrace him*]
BRACHIANO [*Turning away*] O your breath!
Out upon sweetmeats, and continued physic.
The plague is in them.
ISABELLA   You have oft for these two lips 165
Neglected cassia or the natural sweets

---

146 s.d. ed. (placed opposite ll. 144–5 in Q for lack of text space)
150 *Devotion* loyalty (most likely Isabella's meaning); religious devoutness
    (Brachiano's sense)
152–4 *'Tis . . . sounder* The historical Isabella had a lover, but Webster was probably
    unaware of this (Boklund, p. 118); rather, Isabella's 'devotion' to Brachiano
    includes implicating herself in his transgressions (compare Desdemona's
    'heaven forgive us' in *Othello* IV.ii.87).
161 *am to learn* am yet to learn (am ignorant of)
    Italian i.e. characteristically Italian emotion (jealousy)
166 *cassia* a kind of cinnamon; in poetic usage, a sweet-smelling herb or perfume

Of the spring violet; they are not yet much withered.
My lord I should be merry; these your frowns
Show in a helmet lovely, but on me,
In such a peaceful interview methinks   170
They are too too roughly knit.
BRACHIANO   O dissemblance.
Do you bandy factions 'gainst me? Have you learnt
The trick of impudent baseness to complain
Unto your kindred?
ISABELLA   Never my dear lord.
BRACHIANO
Must I be haunted out, or was't your trick   175
To meet some amorous gallant here in Rome
That must supply our discontinuance?
ISABELLA
I pray sir burst my heart, and in my death
Turn to your ancient pity, though not love.
BRACHIANO
Because your brother is the corpulent Duke,   180
– That is the great Duke – 'Sdeath I shall not shortly
Racket away five hundred crowns at tennis,
But it shall rest upon record: I scorn him
Like a shaved Polack: all his reverent wit
Lies in his wardrobe; he's a discreet fellow   185
When he's made up in his robes of state.
Your brother the great Duke, because h'as galleys,
And now and then ransacks a Turkish fly-boat,
(Now all the hellish Furies take his soul),
First made this match – accursed be the priest   190
That sang the wedding mass, and even my issue.
ISABELLA
O too too far you have cursed.
BRACHIANO   Your hand I'll kiss:
This is the latest ceremony of my love,

171 *too too* ed. (to too Q)
172 *bandy factions* i.e. form conspiracies
175 *haunted out* visited frequently (with perhaps also the sense of 'hunted out':
    chased away)
181–3 *'Sdeath . . . record* i.e. by God's death, soon I shall not be able to lose 500
    crowns wagered at tennis without having it recorded as evidence (probably
    referring to Francisco's charge at ll. 52–3)
183–4 *I scorn . . . Polack* i.e. I scorn him as of no account. Poles, according to Fynes
    Morison, *Itinerary*, 1617, shaved all their heads except the forehead.
188 *fly-boat* pinnace or fast sailing boat
192 *too too* ed. (to too Q)   193 *latest* last
193–8 *This . . . severed* Brachiano's ceremony of 'love' is a parody or inversion of

Henceforth I'll never lie with thee, by this,
This wedding ring: I'll ne'er more lie with thee.   195
And this divorce shall be as truly kept
As if the judge had doomed it: fare you well,
Our sleeps are severed.

ISABELLA   Forbid it the sweet union
Of all things blessed; why, the saints in heaven
Will knit their brows at that.

BRACHIANO   Let not thy love   200
Make thee an unbeliever. This my vow
Shall never on my soul be satisfied
With my repentance: let thy brother rage
Beyond a horrid tempest or sea-fight,
My vow is fixed.

ISABELLA   O my winding sheet,   205
Now shall I need thee shortly; dear my lord,
Let me hear once more what I would not hear:
Never.

BRACHIANO   Never!

ISABELLA
O my unkind lord, may your sins find mercy
As I upon a woeful widowed bed   210
Shall pray for you, if not to turn your eyes
Upon your wretched wife and hopeful son,
Yet that in time you'll fix them upon heaven.

BRACHIANO
No more; go, go, complain to the great Duke.

ISABELLA
No my dear lord, you shall have present witness   215
How I'll work peace between you; I will make
Myself the author of your cursed vow.
I have some cause to do it, you have none;
Conceal it I beseech you, for the weal
Of both your dukedoms, that you wrought the means   220
Of such a separation; let the fault
Remain with my supposed jealousy,
And think with what a piteous and rent heart
I shall perform this sad ensuing part.

---

the wedding rites, when vows and rings are exchanged. In Jacobean England,
one spouse could divorce another from bed and board (*a mensa et thoro*), especially on grounds of adultery (of which Brachiano accuses Isabella at ll. 175–
7). Such divorce did not, however, allow for remarriage.

Enter FRANCISCO, FLAMINEO, MONTICELSO, MARCELLO
[ISABELLA *weeps*]

BRACHIANO
  Well, take your course – my honourable brother.   225
FRANCISCO
  Sister – this is not well my lord – why, sister –
  She merits not this welcome.
BRACHIANO   Welcome, say?
  She hath given a sharp welcome.
FRANCISCO   Are you foolish?
  Come dry your tears; is this a modest course,
  To better what is nought, to rail and weep?   230
  Grow to a reconcilement, or by heaven,
  I'll ne'er more deal between you.
ISABELLA   Sir you shall not,
  No though Vittoria upon that condition
  Would become honest.
FRANCISCO   Was your husband loud,
  Since we departed?
ISABELLA   By my life sir no.   235
  I swear by that I do not care to loose.
  Are all these ruins of my former beauty
  Laid out for a whore's triumph?
FRANCISCO   Do you hear?
  Look upon other women, with what patience
  They suffer these slight wrongs, with what justice   240
  They study to requite them; take that course.
ISABELLA
  O that I were a man, or that I had power
  To execute my apprehended wishes,
  I would whip some with scorpions.
FRANCISCO   What? Turned fury?
ISABELLA
  To dig the strumpet's eyes out, let her lie   245

---

224 s.d. MONTICELSO ed. (Montcelso Q)
    Enter . . . MARCELLO ed. (Enter . . . MARCELLO, CAMILLO Q)
225 *take* . . . *course* Previous editors punctuate so that Brachiano addresses these
    words to Isabella. Without emendation, however, the line may be read as Brach-
    iano's invitation to Francisco to proceed against Isabella.
230 *nought* wicked, immoral
234 *honest* chaste
243 *apprehended* conceived, fully understood
244 *I* . . . *scorpions* Originally a biblical reference (to I Kings 12.11: 'my father hath
    chastised you with whips, but I will chastise you with scorpions'), the phrase
    denotes punishment by a whip made of knotted cords or steel spikes.

Some twenty months a-dying, to cut off
Her nose and lips, pull out her rotten teeth,
Preserve her flesh like mummia, for trophies
Of my just anger! Hell to my affliction
Is mere snow-water. By your favour sir –   250
Brother draw near, and my lord cardinal –
Sir, let me borrow of you but one kiss.

                               [*Kisses* BRACHIANO]

Henceforth I'll never lie with you, by this,
This wedding-ring.
FRANCISCO   How? ne'er more lie with him!
ISABELLA
And this divorce shall be as truly kept   255
As if in thronged court a thousand ears
Had heard it, and a thousand lawyers' hands
Sealed to the separation.
BRACHIANO   Ne'er lie with me?
ISABELLA
Let not my former dotage
Make thee an unbeliever; this my vow   260
Shall never on my soul be satisficd
With my repentance: *manet alta mente repostum.*
FRANCISCO
Now by my birth you are a foolish, mad,
And jealous woman.
BRACHIANO   You see 'tis not my seeking.
FRANCISCO
Was this your circle of pure unicorn's horn,   265

Turned fury Cf. Flamineo's words to Cornelia at I.ii.268; a specific style of acting may have been required.

248 *mummia* Cf. I.i.16n.

251–62 *Brother . . . repentance* Unlike Brachiano, Isabella theatricalizes her 'divorce' by drawing attention to spectators / auditors both onstage and off. His appeal to the authority of a 'judge' (l. 197) becomes her evocation of 'a thousand ears' (the theatre audience). Compare Vittoria's appeal to 'this auditory / Which come to hear my cause' at III.ii.15–16. Here Isabella is both parodying and outdoing Brachiano.

262 *manet alta mente repostum* a common phrase originating in Virgil's description of Juno's smouldering resentments, 'It shall be treasured up in the depths of my mind' (*Aeneid* I, 26) and thus appropriate to Isabella. In the depths of Juno's mind lay hatred both for Paris, who scorned her beauty (in choosing Venus), and for the Trojan race, descendants of Jupiter's union with Electra, Juno's rival.

repostum ed. (repositum Q)

You said should charm your lord? Now horns upon
   thee,
For jealousy deserves them; keep your vow
And take your chamber.

ISABELLA
No sir, I'll presently to Padua,
I will not stay a minute.

MONTICELSO   O good madam.   270

BRACHIANO
'Twere best to let her have her humour,
Some half-day's journey will bring down her stomach,
And then she'll turn in post.

FRANCISCO   To see her come
To my lord cardinal for a dispensation
Of her rash vow will beget excellent laughter.   275

ISABELLA
[*Aside*] 'Unkindness do thy office, poor heart break,
Those are the killing griefs which dare not speak.'

                                           Exit

                Enter CAMILLO

MARCELLO
Camillo's come my lord.

FRANCISCO
Where's the commission?

MARCELLO
'Tis here.   280

FRANCISCO
Give me the signet.

FLAMINEO
[*To* BRACHIANO] My lord, do you mark their whispering;
I will compound a medicine out of their two heads,

---

266 *horns upon thee* normally, those which grow upon a cuckolded husband's fore-
    head; here transferred to Isabella, whose jealousy in Francisco's view has now
    licensed Brachiano's adultery

268 *take . . . chamber* Cf. Brachiano's command at l.154.

268–9 ed. (one line in Q)

272 *stomach* pride, obstinacy; vexation, pique (*OED*)

273 *turn in post* return post-haste

276–7 *Unkindness . . . speak* a common proverb, signalled in the text by inverted
    commas at the left margin. Cf. Seneca, *Hippolytus, or Phaedra* 607: 'Curae leves
    loquuntur, ingentes stupent.'

279–80 ed. (one line in Q)

282–322 At this point Webster shifts to a split stage, a characteristic technique (cf.
    The Duchess of Malfi I.ii.75–133, III.iii), which allows him to highlight visual
    parallels and contrasts between different groups.

stronger than garlic, deadlier than stibium; the cantharides which are scarce seen to stick upon the flesh when   285
they work to the heart, shall not do it with more silence
or invisible cunning.

Enter Doctor [JULIO]

BRACHIANO
About the murder.

FLAMINEO
They are sending him to Naples, but I'll send him to
Candy; [*Seeing the doctor*] here's another property too.   290

BRACHIANO
O the doctor.

FLAMINEO
A poor quack-salving knave, my lord, one that should
have been lashed for's lechery, but that he confessed a
judgement, had an execution laid upon him, and so put
the whip to a *non plus*.   295

DOCTOR
And was cozened, my lord, by an arranter knave than
myself, and made pay all the colourable execution.

FLAMINEO
He will shoot pills into a man's guts, shall make them
have more ventages than a cornet or a lamprey; he will
poison a kiss, and was once minded, for his masterpiece,   300

284 *stibium* metallic antinomy, used as a poison
284–5 *cantharides* the dried beetle *cantharis vesicatoria*, or Spanish Fly, applied
    externally to produce blisters as a counter-irritant (and taken internally as an
    aphrodisiac, among other things), but poisonous if taken in excess
289–90 *to Candy* to Candia (now Crete), whose inhabitants were believed to live
    on poisonous snakes – hence, to death
290 *property* stage accessory (for the 'play' Flamineo and Brachiano are writing);
    instrument, tool
    here's ed. (her's Q)
292 *quack-salving* characteristic of a quack doctor
292–5 *should . . . non plus* i.e. he should have been whipped for lechery, but that he
    claimed to be under a previous sentence (for debt), was taken into custody,
    and in this way rendered the whip ineffectual
296–7 *And . . . execution* The doctor was then tricked by a greater rascal than himself
    (who pretended to be the creditor to whom money was owed), and he was
    forced to pay out everything required by the legal judgement.
297 *colourable execution* supposed judgement
298 *shoot pills* fire bullets in the form of pills
299 *more . . . lamprey* more holes than a cornet (wind instrument) or a lamprey (fish
    with numerous apertures on its head)

because Ireland breeds no poison, to have prepared a
deadly vapour in a Spaniard's fart that should have
poisoned all Dublin.

BRACHIANO
O Saint Anthony's fire!

DOCTOR
Your secretary is merry my lord.   305

FLAMINEO
O thou cursed antipathy to nature; look, his eye's
bloodshed like a needle a chirurgeon stitcheth a wound
with. Let me embrace thee toad, and love thee,
[*Embraces him*] O thou abhominable loathsome gargarism, that will fetch up lungs, lights, heart, and liver by   310
scruples.

BRACHIANO
No more; I must employ thee honest doctor,
You must to Padua and by the way
Use some of your skill for us.

DOCTOR   Sir I shall.

BRACHIANO
But for Camillo?   315

FLAMINEO
He dies this night by such a politic strain
Men shall suppose him by's own engine slain.
But for your Duchess' death –

DOCTOR   I'll make her sure.

BRACHIANO
Small mischiefs are by greater made secure.

FLAMINEO
Remember this you slave; when knaves come to pre-   320

301 *Ireland . . . poison* Ireland was supposed to be free of venomous beasts, because
    of either the properties of the soil or the influence of St Patrick.
302–3 *deadly . . . Dublin* A doubly xenophobic jest: a Spaniard, Don Diego, was
    notorious for breaking wind in St Paul's some time before 1598; the Irish were
    supposed to find such smells particularly offensive.
304 *Saint Anthony's fire* or *ignis sacer* (sacred fire), probably slang for breaking wind
    (Dent, p. 96)
    Anthony's ed. (Anthony Q)
307 *bloodshed* bloodshot
309 *abhominable* The common Renaissance spelling retains the false etymology of
    the word as from the Latin *ab homine*, away from man, inhuman, beastly.
309–10 *gargarism* gargle
310 *lights* another word for lungs
310–11 *by scruples* in very small quantities
313–14 ed. (one line in Q)
316 *politic strain* cunning exigency; apparent accident
317 *engine* device, means

ferment they rise as gallowses are raised i'th'Low
Countries, one upon another's shoulders.

Exeunt [BRACHIANO, FLAMINEO *and Doctor* JULIO]

MONTICELSO
  [*Hands* CAMILLO *a paper*] Here is an emblem nephew,
    pray peruse it.
  'Twas thrown in at your window.
CAMILLO   At my window?
  Here is a stag, my lord, hath shed his horns,   325
  And for the loss of them the poor beast weeps:
  The word *Inopem me copia fecit*.
MONTICELSO   That is:
  Plenty of horns hath made him poor of horns.
CAMILLO
  What should this mean?
MONTICELSO   I'll tell you: 'tis given out
  You are a cuckold.
CAMILLO   Is it given out so?   330
  I had rather such report as that my lord
  Should keep within doors.
FRANCISCO   Have you any children?
CAMILLO
  None my lord.
FRANCISCO   You are the happier:
  I'll tell you a tale.
CAMILLO   Pray my lord.

321-2 *they . . . shoulders* improvised gallows, where one man hoists the other on his
       shoulders before stepping aside to leave the prisoner hanging
322 *another's* ed. (another Q)
323 *emblem* a picture expressing a moral fable or allegory, usually accompanied by
       a written gloss, extremely popular in Renaissance Europe
327 *word* motto
       Inopem . . . fecit 'My plenty makes me poor' (Narcissus complaining to his
       shadow in Ovid, *Metamorphoses* III, 466). Like many of Webster's allegories,
       this one has several possible applications, all hinging on the bawdy double
       meaning of 'horns' as the sign for cuckold and penis, deprivation and potency,
       as well as their ambiguous reference to Camillo and Brachiano. Thus the motto
       could mean that Camillo's obvious status as a cuckold has made him impotent
       (like the weeping stag); or that Brachiano's ample sexual satisfaction with Vitto-
       ria has left Camillo deprived; or even that Brachiano's potency has left him
       sexually spent (cf. Lodge, *Wits Miserie*, *Works* IV, ii, 321–4: 'his horns are not
       yet budded, because he moulted them verie lately, in the lap of an Harlot',
       cited by Dent, p. 99).

FRANCISCO   An old tale.
Upon a time Phoebus the god of light,   335
Or him we call the sun, would need be married.
The gods gave their consent and Mercury
Was sent to voice it to the general world.
But what a piteous cry there straight arose
Amongst smiths, and feltmakers, brewers and cooks,   340
Reapers and butter-women, amongst fishmongers
And thousand other trades, which are annoyed
By his excessive heat! 'Twas lamentable.
They came to Jupiter all in a sweat
And do forbid the bans. A great fat cook   345
Was made their speaker, who entreats of Jove
That Phoebus might be gelded, for if now
When there was but one sun, so many men
Were like to perish by his violent heat,
What should they do if he were married   350
And should beget more, and those children
Make fireworks like their father? So say I,
Only I will apply it to your wife:
Her issue, should not providence prevent it,
Would make both nature, time, and man repent it.   355
MONTICELSO
Look you cousin,
Go change the air for shame. See if your absence
Will blast your cornucopia. Marcello
Is chosen with you joint commissioner
For the relieving our Italian coast   360
From pirates.
MARCELLO   I am much honoured in't.
CAMILLO   But sir,
Ere I return the stag's horns may be sprouted
Greater than these are shed.

334–55 This 'old tale' is borrowed from *The Fables of Esop in English* (1596 ed.). It
    appears first to apply mockingly either to the foolish Camillo or to the 'fiery'
    Brachiano, both of whom should be 'gelded', castrated; Francisco neatly twists
    it to apply to Vittoria at the end.
345 *bans* (banns) of marriage, called in church
352 *fireworks* fiery displays; products of fire or passion (more children); venereal
    disease; devils (NCW II.i.330–50 n.)
357 *Go . . . air* go and leave this place
358 *cornucopia* normally a symbol of fertility, the 'horn of plenty', here ironically
    the 'plenty of horns' that are the cuckold's heraldry
362–3 *stag's . . . shed* Are these 'stag's horns' Camillo's or Brachiano's? Since the
    stag sprouted horns in preparation for mating, Camillo may anticipate Brach-
    iano's greater sexual vigour in his absence; but since the stag commonly repre-
    sented the cuckold, Camillo may simply fear his shameful status will become
    more obvious.

MONTICELSO   Do not fear it,
I'll be your ranger.
CAMILLO   You must watch i'th'nights,
Then's the most danger.
FRANCISCO   Farewell good Marcello.   365
All the best fortunes of a soldier's wish
Bring you o'ship-board.
CAMILLO
Were I not best now I am turned soldier,
Ere that I leave my wife, sell all she hath
And then take leave of her?
MONTICELSO   I expect good from you,   370
Your parting is so merry.
CAMILLO
Merry my lord, o'th'captain's humour right;
I am resolved to be drunk this night.
                              Exit [with MARCELLO]

FRANCISCO
So, 'twas well fitted, now shall we discern
How his wished absence will give violent way   375
To Duke Brachiano's lust.
MONTICELSO   Why that was it;
To what scorned purpose else should we make choice
Of him for a sea-captain, and besides,
Count Lodowick which was rumoured for a pirate,
Is now in Padua.
FRANCISCO   Is't true?
MONTICELSO   Most certain.   380
I have letters from him, which are suppliant
To work his quick repeal from banishment;
He means to address himself for pension
Unto our sister Duchess.
FRANCISCO   O 'twas well.
We shall not want his absence past six days;   385
I fain would have the Duke Brachiano run
Into notorious scandal, for there's nought
In such cursed dotage to repair his name,
Only the deep sense of some deathless shame.
MONTICELSO
It may be objected I am dishonourable   390
To play thus with my kinsman, but I answer,

364 *ranger* gamekeeper
368 *Were I not best* i.e. would not the best thing for me be
384 *sister Duchess* Monticelso is Camillo's uncle, not Isabella's brother. 'Sister' may
       be a title of courtesy, or Webster may have confused Cardinal Monticelso with
       Cardinal de' Medici, Isabella's brother in life.

For my revenge I'd stake a brother's life
That being wronged durst not avenge himself.
FRANCISCO
Come to observe this strumpet.
MONTICELSO   Curse of greatness,
Sure he'll not leave her.
FRANCISCO   There's small pity in't.   395
Like mistletoe on sere elms spent by weather,
Let him cleave to her and both rot together.

Exeunt

[Act II, Scene ii]

Enter BRACHIANO *with one in the habit of a Conjuror*

BRACHIANO
Now sir I claim your promise; 'tis dead midnight,
The time prefixed to show me by your art
How the intended murder of Camillo
And our loathed Duchess grow to action.
CONJUROR
You have won me by your bounty to a deed   5
I do not often practise; some there are,
Which by sophistic tricks aspire that name
Which I would gladly lose, of nigromancer;
As some that use to juggle upon cards,
Seeming to conjure when indeed they cheat;   10
Others that raise up their confederate spirits
'Bout windmills, and endanger their own necks
For making of a squib; and some there are
Will keep a curtal to show juggling tricks
And give out 'tis a spirit: besides these   15

---

396 *Like . . . weather* Cf. III.i.48–9, where Flamineo alludes to the rare medicinal
    qualities of mistletoe, here ironically associated with Brachiano.

  8 *lose* ed. (loose Q)
    nigromancer one who claims to carry on communication with the dead; wizard,
    conjuror (with a suggestion of the 'black art' contained in the prefix nigro-,
    from Latin *niger*, black)

  9 *juggle* play tricks so as to cheat or deceive

 12 *windmills* fanciful schemes or projects

 13 *squib* explosive firework

 13–15 *some . . . spirit* one of many Renaissance references to Mr Banks, who trav-
    elled around England and the Continent with his performing horse, which was
    by 1595 a docked bay gelding, or curtal, named Morocco. Banks trained
    Morocco to perform some marvellous circus tricks, such as dancing, playing
    dead, counting money and responding to elaborate verbal instructions. Far from

Such a whole ream of almanac-makers, figure-flingers,
Fellows indeed that only live by stealth,
Since they do merely lie about stol'n goods,
They'd make men think the devil were fast and loose,
With speaking fustian Latin. Pray sit down,   20
Put on this night-cap sir, 'tis charmed, and now
I'll show you by my strong-commanding art
The circumstance that breaks your Duchess' heart.

A DUMB SHOW

Enter suspiciously, DOCTOR JULIO *and* CHRISTOPHERO; *they draw a
curtain where* BRACHIANO's *picture is, they put on spectacles of glass
which cover their eyes and noses, and then burn perfumes afore the
picture and wash the lips of the picture; that done, quenching the
fire, and putting off their spectacles, they depart laughing. Enter*

---

giving out that his horse was a spirit, however, Banks frequently defended himself against charges of witchcraft – apparently successfully, since despite Jonson's claim that he was burned at Rome as a witch (*Epigrams* no. 133), he
retired to be a vintner in Cheapside.

16 *ream* realm (kingdom); large quantity (of paper)
   figure-flingers casters of horoscopes, pretenders to astrology

17–18 *live . . . goods* possible reference to the casting of horoscopes to find stolen
   goods

19 *fast and loose* a proverbial phrase meaning shifty, unscrupulous: originally, a
   cheating game (in which a string which appeared to be easily made 'fast' or
   tight was in fact 'loose', easily undone)

20 *fustian* inflated, made-up gibberish (cf. Francisco to the lawyer at III.ii.46)

23 *breaks . . . heart* an echo of Isabella's own last words at II.i.276–7

23 s.d. *DUMB SHOW* The first dumb show anticipates Brachiano's own death by a
   poisoned beaver in V.iii (when he fears his kiss will poison Vittoria, l. 27). It
   also recapitulates allegorically the interview between Brachiano and Isabella in
   II.i, by restaging symbolically their kiss of divorce (l. 252). Both these elaborate
   dumb shows allow Webster to represent highly dramatic action while formaliz-
   ing and distancing its emotional impact (especially important in the case of
   Isabella's murder). Each dumb show was probably staged at either side of the
   full stage (not in a discovery space) to maximize the visual spectacle.

23 s.d.1 *suspiciously* in a manner deserving of suspicion
   CHRISTOPHERO like little Jacques the Moor (II.i.0 s.d.) and Guid-Antonio
   (below), a so-called 'ghost character' who appears briefly but delivers no lines.
   Usually explained as evidence of Webster's revision, such characters may also
   suggest Webster's acute theatrical awareness. Not only are silent figures thus
   clearly individualized, they may also have been doubled for significant visual
   effect. For example, Julio and Christophero, the murderers of Isabella, may
   have been doubled with Antonelli and Gasparo, the murderers of Brachiano,
   to emphasize the play's retributive pattern.

   s.d.2 *BRACHIANO's* ed. (Brachian's Q)

ISABELLA *in her nightgown as to bedward, with lights after her,*
Count LODOVICO, GIOVANNI, GUID-ANTONIO *and others waiting on
her; she kneels down as to prayers, then draws the curtain of the
picture, does three reverences to it, and kisses it thrice. She faints
and will not suffer them to come near it; dies. Sorrow expressed in*
GIOVANNI *and in Count* LODOVICO; *she's conveyed out solemnly.*

BRACHIANO
  Excellent, then she's dead.
CONJUROR   She's poisoned
  By the fumed picture: 'twas her custom nightly,   25
  Before she went to bed, to go and visit
  Your picture, and to feed her eyes and lips
  On the dead shadow; Doctor Julio
  Observing this infects it with an oil
  And other poisoned stuff, which presently   30
  Did suffocate her spirits.
BRACHIANO   Methought I saw
  Count Lodowick there.
CONJUROR   He was, and by my art
  I find he did most passionately dote
  Upon your Duchess – now turn another way,
  And view Camillo's far more politic face,   35
  Strike louder music from this charmed ground,
  To yield, as fits the act, a tragic sound.

THE SECOND DUMB SHOW

Enter FLAMINEO, MARCELLO, CAMILLO *with four more as Captains,
they drink healths and dance, a vaulting-horse is brought into the
room,* MARCELLO *and two more whispered out of the room, while*
FLAMINEO *and* CAMILLO *strip themselves into their shirts, as to vault;
compliment who shall begin; as* CAMILLO *is about to vault,* FLAMI-

25 *fumed* exposed to ammonia vapour
28 *dead shadow* lifeless image
35 *face* Q4 emends 'face' to 'fate', which may be correct. However, Q may stand
    if 'politic face' (sagacious visage) is taken to apply ironically to Camillo (cf.
    Flamineo's remark about Camillo at I.ii.48–51).
36 *Strike . . . music* Webster gives no stage direction to indicate what sort of music
    was provided, but it would have been appropriate if it issued from beneath the
    stage (NCW II.ii.36–7 n.).
37 s.d.2 *vaulting-horse* For this detail Webster may have either misunderstood, or
    knowingly literalized, Monte Cavallo, the actual place where Francesco Peretti,
    Camillo's historical counterpart, was murdered. The vaulting horse may also
    furnish an obscene visual joke at Camillo's expense – since 'vaulting' can mean
    'mounting sexually' (as in *Cymbeline* I.vi.134), Camillo's ignominious position
    under the vaulting horse is a visual sign of his sexual inadequacy.

NEO *pitcheth him upon his neck, and with the help of the rest, writhes*
his neck about, seems to see if it be broke, and lays him folded double
as 'twere under the horse; makes shows to call for help. MARCELLO
comes in, laments, sends for the Cardinal and Duke, who come forth
with armed men, wonder at the act, commands the body to be carried
home, apprehends FLAMINEO, MARCELLO, *and the rest, and go as*
'twere to apprehend VITTORIA.

BRACHIANO
  'Twas quaintly done, but yet each circumstance
  I taste not fully.
CONJUROR   O 'twas most apparent,
  You saw them enter charged with their deep healths   40
  To their boon voyage, and to second that,
  Flamineo calls to have a vaulting-horse
  Maintain their sport. The virtuous Marcello
  Is innocently plotted forth the room
  Whilst your eye saw the rest, and can inform you   45
  The engine of all.
[BRACHIANO]   It seems Marcello and Flamineo
  Are both committed.
CONJUROR   Yes, you saw them guarded,
  And now they are come with purpose to apprehend
  Your mistress, fair Vittoria; we are now
  Beneath her roof: 'twere fit we instantly   50
  Make out by some back postern.
BRACHIANO   Noble friend,
  You bind me ever to you; this shall stand
  As the firm seal annexed to my hand.
  It shall enforce a payment.
CONJUROR   Sir I thank you.
                           Exit BRACHIANO
  Both flowers and weeds spring when the sun is warm,   55
  And great men do great good, or else great harm.
                                 Exit

38 *quaintly* skilfully, ingeniously
41 *boon* prosperous (as in 'bon voyage')
46 *engine* means, contrivance
  s.p. *BRACHIANO* ed. (MAR. Q)
47–51 The distanced perspective of the magical dumb shows is suddenly fore-
  shortened; typically in Webster, observers are never safe from involvement in
  the action of the drama, as one perspective can shift into another with dizzying
  rapidity.
52–3 *this . . . hand* i.e. this token (money, a jewel, or simply, a handshake) will
  stand for the seal attached to my signature
54 s.d. ed. (to r. of l. 53 in Q)
56 s.d. *Exit* ed. (Exit Con. Q)

[Act III, Scene i]

Enter FRANCISCO, *and* MONTICELSO, *their*
CHANCELLOR *and* REGISTER

FRANCISCO
   You have dealt discreetly to obtain the presence
   Of all the grave lieger ambassadors
   To hear Vittoria's trial.
MONTICELSO   'Twas not ill,
   For sir you know we have nought but circumstances
   To charge her with, about her husband's death;   5
   Their approbation therefore to the proofs
   Of her black lust, shall make her infamous
   To all our neighbouring kingdoms. I wonder ·
   If Brachiano will be here.
FRANCISCO   O fie,
   'Twere impudence too palpable.   10

                                           [*Exeunt*]

Enter FLAMINEO *and* MARCELLO *guarded, and a* LAWYER

LAWYER
   What, are you in by the week? So; I will try now whether
   thy wit be close prisoner: methinks none should sit upon
   thy sister but old whore-masters.
FLAMINEO
   Or cuckolds, for your cuckold is your most terrible tick-
   ler of lechery: whore-masters would serve, for none are   15
   judges at tilting, but those that have been old tilters.
LAWYER
   My lord Duke and she have been very private.

---

   0 s.d.1 As Francisco and Monticelso converse, their chancellor and register may
      be setting properties in place for the arraignment: a table (III.ii.8), and probably
      one or two raised chairs or 'states' for Monticelso and Francisco (NCW
      III.i.0.1 n.).
      s.d.2 *REGISTER* registrar (scribe or secretary)
   2 *lieger* resident
   9–10 *If . . . fie / 'Twere . . . palpable* ed. (one line in Q)
   11 *in by the week* ensnared, caught
   12 *sit upon* sit in judgement on, with possibly an obscene suggestion of 'sit astride,
      mount'
   14–15 *tickler* chastiser, punisher; also, provoker, inciter (cf. I.ii.94–6, where the
      jealous cuckold promotes his own betrayal)
   16 *tilting* literally, jousting or thrusting as in a tournament; here, with a sexual
      innuendo of thrusting as in copulation
   17 *private* intimate; secretive, secluded

FLAMINEO
    You are a dull ass; 'tis threatened they have been very
    public.
LAWYER
    If it can be proved they have but kissed one another –   20
FLAMINEO
    What then?
LAWYER   My lord cardinal will ferret them.
FLAMINEO
    A cardinal I hope will not catch conies.
LAWYER
    For to sow kisses (mark what I say), to sow kisses, is to
    reap lechery, and I am sure a woman that will endure
    kissing is half won.   25
FLAMINEO
    True, her upper part by that rule; if you will win her
    nether part too, you know what follows.

                    [*Sennet offstage*]

LAWYER
    Hark, the ambassadors are lighted.
FLAMINEO
    [*Aside*] I do put on this feigned garb of mirth
    To gull suspicion.
MARCELLO   O my unfortunate sister!   30
    I would my dagger's point had cleft her heart
    When she first saw Brachiano. You, 'tis said,
    Were made his engine, and his stalking-horse
    To undo my sister.
FLAMINEO   I made a kind of path
    To her and mine own preferment.
MARCELLO   Your ruin.   35
FLAMINEO
    Hum! thou art a soldier,
    Followest the great Duke, feedest his victories,

---

19 *public* open to general observation, conspicuous; also promiscuous (a 'public
    woman' was a prostitute: cf. *Othello* IV.ii.73: 'O thou public commoner')
21 *ferret* literally, to hunt (rabbits, etc.) with ferrets; metaphorically, to hunt down
    or question searchingly
22 *catch conies* literally, catch rabbits (as above); and punning on the senses swindle
    or dupe people; fornicate with women (a 'cony' could be applied to a woman
    either endearingly or indecently)
33 *engine* instrument
    stalking-horse originally, a trained horse used by a fowler to get within easy reach
    of the game without being observed; hence, a person whose participation in an
    action is used to disguise its real design

As witches do their serviceable spirits,
Even with thy prodigal blood. What hast got?
But like the wealth of captains, a poor handful,   40
Which in thy palm thou bear'st, as men hold water –
Seeking to gripe it fast, the frail reward
Steals through thy fingers.
MARCELLO   Sir –
FLAMINEO   Thou hast scarce
    maintenance
To keep thee in fresh chamois.
MARCELLO   Brother –
FLAMINEO   Hear me.
And thus when we have even poured ourselves   45
Into great fights, for their ambition
Or idle spleen, how shall we find reward,
But as we seldom find the mistletoe
Sacred to physic on the builder oak
Without a mandrake by it, so in our quest of gain.   50
Alas the poorest of their forced dislikes
At a limb proffers, but at heart it strikes:
This is lamented doctrine.
MARCELLO   Come, come.
FLAMINEO
When age shall turn thee
White as a blooming hawthorn –
MARCELLO   I'll interrupt you.   55
For love of virtue bear an honest heart,
And stride over every politic respect,
Which where they most advance they most infect.
Were I your father, as I am your brother,

38 *As . . . spirits* Witches were commonly supposed to nourish their spirits or famil-
     iars (usually beasts sent by the devil) with their own milk or blood from super-
     numary teats.
39 *prodigal* wastefully used
44 *chamois* supple leather jerkins worn beneath armour
48 *mistletoe* parasitic European plant sacred to the Druids which, when found
     growing on the oak, was thought to be able to cure illness
49 *on* ed. (: Or Q)
     builder which builds itself up, or is used for building
50 *mandrake* plant with narcotic and medicinal properties whose forked root
     resembles a human form and attracted superstition: it reputedly shrieked when
     pulled out of the ground and grew under the gallows (or the gallows-tree, the
     oak). The mandrake in Webster feeds, like the witch's familiars, on blood (cf.
     III.iii.112–13), and drives men mad (cf. *The Duchess of Malfi* II.v.1–2).
51–2 *Alas . . . strikes* i.e. the most insignificant of their feigned dislikes appears to
     injure only superficially but in fact it wounds deeply and irrecoverably (because
     it results in loss of favour)

I should not be ambitious to leave you   60
A better patrimony.

Enter Savoy [Ambassador]

FLAMINEO   I'll think on't –
The lord ambassadors.

Here there is a passage of the lieger Ambassadors over
the stage severally. Enter French Ambassador

LAWYER
O my sprightly Frenchman, do you know him? He's an
admirable tilter.

FLAMINEO
I saw him at last tilting; he showed like a pewter candle-   65
stick fashioned like a man in armour, holding a tilting
staff in his hand little bigger than a candle of twelve
i'th'pound.

LAWYER
O but he's an excellent horseman.

FLAMINEO
A lame one in his lofty tricks; he sleeps o' horseback   70
like a poulter.

Enter English and Spanish [Ambassadors]

LAWYER
Lo you my Spaniard.

FLAMINEO
He carries his face in's ruff, as I have seen a serving-man
carry glasses in a cypress hat-band, monstrous steady

---

61 s.d. ed. (opposite l. 60 in Q)
61–2 *A better . . . on't / The . . . ambassadors* ed. (one line in Q)
62 s.d.2 *Enter French Ambassador* ed. (Enter French Embassadours Q)
   Though the stage directions are slightly confusing, the procession is probably
led by Savoy, who is followed by the French ambassador, the English ambassador, the Spanish ambassador and two more. This takes its place among pro-
cessions over the stage, by which Webster highlights pivotal events of his drama
(the arraignment, the papal election, the wedding of Brachiano and Vittoria).
Typically, visual spectacle is counterpointed by verbal commentary, and perspectives are always shifting: the ambassadors are now observed, now observers
of the action (cf. IV.iii.4–32).
64 *tilter* Cf. l. 16 above.
70–1 *he . . . poulter* 'lame' could mean 'impotent': i.e. all his attempts at (sexual)
acrobatics result only in impotence; like poulterers who often fell asleep on the
way to market. France was famous for both horsemanship and syphilis, which
could lead to impotence.
74 *cypress hat-band* cobweb lawn or crepe used as a band for the hat

for fear of breaking. He looks like the claw of a black-   75
bird, first salted and then broiled in a candle.

Exeunt

[Act III, Scene ii]

THE ARRAIGNMENT OF VITTORIA

Enter FRANCISCO, MONTICELSO, *the six lieger*
Ambassadors, BRACHIANO, VITTORIA, [ZANCHE, FLAMINEO,
MARCELLO,] LAWYER, *and a* GUARD

MONTICELSO
[*To* BRACHIANO] Forbear my lord, here is no place   ·
  assigned you,
This business by his holiness is left
To our examination.
BRACHIANO   May it thrive with you.

Lays a rich gown under him

FRANCISCO
A chair there for his lordship.

75–6 *He ... candle* an ingenious analogy, in which the wide ruffs sported by the
  Spanish are compared to the claw of the blackbird which is spread wide when
  prepared for grilling
76 s.d. Flamineo, Marcello and the lawyer exit only to re-enter immediately in the
  larger group, thus emphasizing visually their loss of dramatic control as the
  arraignment begins.
0 s.d.1 *MONTICELSO* ed. (Montcelso Q)
  s.d.2–3 *ZANCHE ... MARCELLO* ed. (Isabella Q)
  The title and mass entry signal the central importance of the arraignment for
  readers. The third act is divided into scenes for the convenience of readers, but
  may be considered a single unbroken dramatic unit on the stage. In fact, the
  stage is probably never cleared in Act III, and the ambassadors, Flamineo, Marcello and the lawyer simply take their places, while the others enter. Judging
  from a title-page woodcut depicting a courtroom scene from *Swetnam the*
  Woman Hater, a Red Bull play staged about 1619, the original staging may have
  had Monticelso seated on a throne, facing the standing Vittoria (and possibly
  Zanche), while the ambassadors, court officials and Francisco, seated on low
  stools, were symmetrically placed on either side; Brachiano probably sat
  (conspicuously) on the floor, close to the audience (NCW, pp. 101–3).
  The entry for Isabella – who has just been killed in the previous act – is usually
  dismissed as an irrational slip, but may be explained by the doubling of Isabella
  with Zanche (omitted in the stage direction but present in the scene). An actor
  who had just played Isabella may still have been identified in Webster's mind
  with that part. When Isabella reappears as a ghost in IV.i (obviously not in the
  blackface required for Zanche), she may have been shrouded (Francisco
  replaces his 'dead sister's face' with her more general 'figure' in his imagination,

BRACHIANO

Forbear your kindness; an unbidden guest   5
Should travail as Dutch women go to church:
Bear their stools with them.

MONTICELSO   At your pleasure sir.
Stand to the table gentlewomen. Now signior,
Fall to your plea.

[LAWYER]
Domine Judex converte oculos in hanc pestem mulierum   10
corruptissimam.

VITTORIA
What's he?

FRANCISCO   A lawyer that pleads against you.

VITTORIA
Pray my lord, let him speak his usual tongue.
I'll make no answer else.

FRANCISCO   Why you understand Latin.

VITTORIA
I do sir, but amongst this auditory   15

IV.i.98–101) or even played by another actor. Such a doubling would serve not
only theatrical economy but also aesthetic design, linking Vittoria with Isabella
through Zanche and further blurring the play's black/white, good/evil polarities.

1 *assigned* ed. (assing'd Q)

3 s.d. Brachiano's action may recall I.ii.202ff., where the two lovers rest on 'fair
cushions' as they embrace. If so, the lovers' adultery is recalled even as it is
about to be punished.

8 *Stand . . . gentlewomen* Though many editors emend to 'gentlewoman', Monticelso may be referring to Vittoria and Zanche in these dignified terms with
heavy irony, since the trial will reveal his contempt for both of them. The
women are condemned together (ll. 263–4). The analogies between them that
are later suggested would be strengthened by their appearing here side by side.
On the other hand, if Vittoria appeared solo (requiring emendation of the text),
that would strengthen parallels and contrasts with I.i and II.i, where Lodovico
and Brachiano face social disapproval alone. The choice is left to the director.

10 s.p. *LAWYER* ed. (not in Q). The comically ineffectual lawyer may originally
have been doubled with Camillo, 'thus failing twice to bring Vittoria to book'
(Thomson, p. 28).

10–11 *Domine . . . corruptissimam* 'Lord Judge, turn your eyes upon this plague,
the most corrupted of women.'

14 *Why . . . Latin* Probably a taunt, for in early modern England women rarely
learned Latin. While Vittoria disdains the use of Latin, however, she pointedly
uses it at l. 200.

15–16 *this . . . cause* probably a reference to the theatre audience (rather than to
the well-educated ambassadors), some of whom would also be sitting on the
stage at the Red Bull; an early indication of the metadramatic control Webster
gives Vittoria

Which come to hear my cause, the half or more
May be ignorant in't.
MONTICELSO   Go on sir.
VITTORIA   By your favour,
I will not have my accusation clouded
In a strange tongue: all this assembly
Shall hear what you can charge me with.
FRANCISCO   Signior,   20
You need not stand on't much; pray change your
    language.
MONTICELSO
O for God sake: gentlewoman, your credit
Shall be more famous by it.
LAWYER   Well then have at you.
VITTORIA
I am at the mark sir, I'll give aim to you,
And tell you how near you shoot.   25
LAWYER
Most literated judges, please your lordships,
So to connive your judgements to the view
Of this debauched and diversivolent woman
Who such a black concatenation
Of mischief hath effected, that to extirp   30
The memory of't must be the consummation
Of her and her projections –
VITTORIA   What's all this?
LAWYER
Hold your peace.
Exorbitant sins must have exulceration.
VITTORIA
Surely my lords this lawyer here hath swallowed   35
Some pothecary's bills, or proclamations.

21 *stand on't* insist on it
22 *credit* reputation
24 *give aim* in archery, to guide someone's aim by informing him of the result of
    a previous shot
27 *connive your judgements* a malapropism (for 'conduct your judgments'?) caused
    by the lawyer's pompous search for elaborate terms ('connive' means to shut
    one's eyes to, to be complicit in, injustice)
28 *diversivolent* wishing strife (a nonce-word, presumably inspired by the lawyer's
    avid search for Latinisms in place of Latin)
32 *projections* projects
34 *Exorbitant . . . exulceration* i.e. outrageous sins require punishment (ulcers must
    be lanced)
36 *pothecary's bills* medical prescriptions, often inflated and long-winded. Cf. Web-
    ster's 'Character' of a 'Quacksalver': 'a Mountebanke of a larger bill then a

And now the hard and undigestible words
Come up like stones we use give hawks for physic.
Why this is Welsh to Latin.

LAWYER   My lords, the woman
Knows not her tropes nor figures, nor is perfect   40
In the academic derivation
Of grammatical elocution.

FRANCISCO   Sir your pains
Shall be well spared, and your deep eloquence
Be worthily applauded amongst those
Which understand you.

LAWYER   My good lord.

FRANCISCO (*Speaks this as in scorn*)   Sir,   45
Put up your papers in your fustian bag –
Cry mercy sir, 'tis buckram – and accept
My notion of your learn'd verbosity.

LAWYER
I most graduatically thank your lordship.
I shall have use for them elsewhere.   [*Exit*]   50

MONTICELSO
I shall be plainer with you, and paint out
Your follies in more natural red and white

Taylor; if he can but come by names enow of Diseases, to stuffe it with, tis all
the skill hee studies for'.

proclamations formal orders issued in the name of the sovereign, often written
in inflated prose

38 *Come up* are vomited

stones . . . physic 'If your Hawke by over-flying, or too soone flying, be heated
and inflamed in her body, as they are much subject thereunto, you shall then
to coole their bodies, give them stones' (Gervase Markham, *Cheape and Good
Husbandry* (1614) S3).

39 *Welsh to Latin* Renaissance dramatists often used Welsh as the prototype of an
unintelligible language (cf. *A Chaste Maid in Cheapside* IV.i.100–65, *1 Henry IV*
III.i.187–240).

40 *tropes . . . figures* in rhetoric, the figurative use of words or phrases

42 *elocution* oratory: the art of appropriate and effective expression

45 s.d. ed. (to r. of ll. 46–7 in Q)

46 *fustian* a pun: coarse cloth made of cotton and flax; inflated, bombastic language
composed of high-sounding words and phrases

47 *buckram* coarse, stiff linen traditionally used for lawyers' bags (as Francisco
would know)

49 *graduatically* a nonce-word, meaning as a graduate should

51–3 *plainer . . . cheek* The Cardinal is invoking the misogynist stereotype of the
'painted' woman (cf. *Hamlet* III.i.143–4: 'God hath given you one face and you
make yourselves another'), and claiming he will use the 'plain' style to 'paint'
(show) Vittoria by contrast.

Than that upon your cheek.

VITTORIA   O you mistake.
You raise a blood as noble in this cheek
As ever was your mother's.   55

MONTICELSO
I must spare you till proof cry whore to that;
Observe this creature here my honoured lords,
A woman of a most prodigious spirit
In her effected.

VITTORIA   Honourable my lord,
It doth not suit a reverend cardinal   60
To play the lawyer thus.

MONTICELSO
O your trade instructs your language!
You see my lords what goodly fruit she seems,
Yet like those apples travellers report
To grow where Sodom and Gomorrah stood: 65
I will but touch her and you straight shall see
She'll fall to soot and ashes.

VITTORIA
Your envenomed pothecary should do't.

MONTICELSO
I am resolved.
Were there a second paradise to loose   70
This devil would betray it.

VITTORIA   O poor charity!
Thou art seldom found in scarlet.

MONTICELSO
Who knows not how, when several night by night
Her gates were choked with coaches and her rooms
Outbraved the stars with several kind of lights,   75

---

58 *spirit* courage; perhaps punning on the bawdy senses 'semen' or 'erection' (as in
   Romeo and Juliet II.i.23–4: ' 'Twould anger him / To raise a spirit in his mistress'
   circle')

59 *effected* brought about, produced (a weak and redundant ending to Monticelso's
   grand rhetorical flourish – here he sounds like the kind of lawyer Vittoria
   accuses him of playing); ejaculated (NCW III.ii.59 n.)

64–7 *apples . . . ashes* The original source is Deuteronomy 32:32: 'their vine is of
   the vine of Sodom, and of the fields of Gomorrah; their grapes are grapes of
   gall, their clusters are bitter'. This detail about apples turning to ashes is apo-
   cryphal, but frequently invoked by authors such as Sir John Mandeville (*Travels*,
   p. xxx), who interprets it as a sign of God's vengeance in burning up the cities.

68 *Your . . . do't* i.e. your poisonous apothecary, not you, should reduce me to
   ashes. Vittoria cleverly turns Monticelso's metaphor against him – his or his
   apothecary's touch, rather than her nature, is 'envenomed'.

72 *scarlet* colour of a cardinal's vestments and a lawyer's robes

When she did counterfeit a prince's court
In music, banquets and most riotous surfeits,
This whore, forsooth, was holy?
VITTORIA   Ha? Whore, what's that?
MONTICELSO
Shall I expound whore to you? Sure I shall;
I'll give their perfect character. They are first   80
Sweetmeats which rot the eater: in man's nostril
Poisoned perfumes. They are coz'ning alchemy,
Shipwrecks in calmest weather! What are whores?
Cold Russian winters, that appear so barren
As if that nature had forgot the spring.   85
They are the true material fire of hell,
Worse than those tributes i'th'Low Countries paid,
Exactions upon meat, drink, garments, sleep;
Ay even on man's perdition, his sin.
They are those brittle evidences of law   90
Which forfeit all a wretched man's estate
For leaving out one syllable. What are whores?
They are those flattering bells have all one tune,
At weddings, and at funerals: your rich whores
Are only treasuries by extortion filled,   95
And emptied by curs'd riot. They are worse,
Worse than dead bodies, which are begged at gallows
And wrought upon by surgeons, to teach man
Wherein he is imperfect. What's a whore?
She's like the guilty counterfeited coin   100
Which whosoe'er first stamps it brings in trouble

---

78 *holy?* ed. (holy Q)
80 *character* formal description of a character-type based on the classical models
   of Theophrastus. Webster himself contributed several to the second edition of
   Overbury's *Characters*.
82 *Poisoned perfumes* a fleeting verbal reminder of Brachiano's murder of Isabella,
   which is still undiscovered; Brachiano's unpunished crimes are recalled as Vittoria is tried simply for 'black lust' (III.i.7).
   alchemy the process of transforming baser metals into gold, often requiring the
   investment of vast sums of money by hopefuls (cf. I.ii.151)
87–9 *Worse . . . sin* At this time in the Low Countries taxes, especially those on
   wine, often equalled or exceeded the value of the commodity itself.
97–9 *dead . . . imperfect* The Barber-Surgeons were legally allowed four executed
   felons a year for the purpose of instructing students in anatomy; others may
   have been 'begged'.
100 *guilty* probably with a play on 'gilt'
100–1 *counterfeited . . . it* For counterfeiting as a metaphor for illicit intercourse, cf.
   Measure for Measure II.iv.45–6.
101 *brings* ed. (bring Q)

All that receive it.

VITTORIA   This character scapes me.

MONTICELSO
You, gentlewoman,
Take from all beasts, and from all minerals
Their deadly poison.

VITTORIA   Well what then?

MONTICELSO   I'll tell thee.   105
I'll find in thee a pothecary's shop
To sample them all.

FRENCH AMBASSADOR   She hath lived ill.

ENGLISH AMBASSADOR
True, but the cardinal's too bitter.

MONTICELSO
You know what whore is; next the devil, Adult'ry,
Enters the devil, Murder.

FRANCISCO   Your unhappy husband   110
Is dead.

VITTORIA   O he's a happy husband
Now he owes nature nothing.

FRANCISCO
And by a vaulting engine.

MONTICELSO   An active plot;
He jumped into his grave.

FRANCISCO   What a prodigy was't,
That from some two yards' height a slender man   115
Should break his neck?

MONTICELSO   I'th'rushes.

FRANCISCO   And what's more,
Upon the instant lose all use of speech,
All vital motion, like a man had lain
Wound up three days. Now mark each circumstance.

MONTICELSO
And look upon this creature was his wife.   120
She comes not like a widow: she comes armed
With scorn and impudence. Is this a mourning habit?

VITTORIA
Had I foreknown his death as you suggest,

---

109 *whore . . . Adult'ry* ed. (Whore is next the devell; Adultry. Q)
116 *rushes* commonly strewn on the floor in private houses and on the stage
117 *lose* ed. (loose Q)
119 *Wound up* wrapped in a winding-sheet or shroud
122 Vittoria is wearing a sumptuous gown.

I would have bespoke my mourning.
MONTICELSO   O you are cunning.
VITTORIA
You shame your wit and judgement   125
To call it so. What, is my just defence
By him that is my judge called impudence?
Let me appeal then from this Christian court
To the uncivil Tartar.
MONTICELSO   See my lords,
She scandals our proceedings.
VITTORIA [*Kneeling*]   Humbly thus,   130
Thus low, to the most worthy and respected
Lieger ambassadors, my modesty
And womanhood I tender; but withal
So entangled in a cursed accusation
That my defence, of force, like Perseus   135
Must personate masculine virtue to the point.
Find me but guilty, sever head from body:
We'll part good friends: I scorn to hold my life
At yours or any man's entreaty, sir.
ENGLISH AMBASSADOR
She hath a brave spirit.   140
MONTICELSO
Well, well, such counterfeit jewels
Make true ones oft suspected.
VITTORIA   You are deceived.
For know that all your strict combined heads,
Which strike against this mine of diamonds,
Shall prove but glassen hammers, they shall break;   145
These are but feigned shadows of my evils.

128 *Christian* ecclesiastical; civilized (not barbarous)
129 *uncivil* uncivilized. The Tartars were infamous for barbarism and cruelty.
130 *scandals* disgraces
     s.d. Vittoria may curtsy here; however, kneeling seems an appropriate demon-
     stration of her humility and courage (cf. *The Duchess of Malfi* IV.ii.230) and
     echoes I.ii.276.
135 *of force* of necessity
     Perseus son of Zeus and Danae. Perseus cut off the head of the Gorgon Medusa
     and saved Andromeda from the sea monster. In Jonson's *Masque of Queens*
     (1609), Perseus, 'expressing heroique and masculine Vertue', routs the anti-
     masque of witches and celebrates the virtues of twelve famous queens.
136 *personate* imitate; symbolize, emblematically represent
     virtue moral excellence; physical courage, valour
     to the point exactly, in every detail
143 *strict combined heads* literally, the joint force of your hammer-heads; figuratively,
     your closely allied military forces

Terrify babes, my lord, with painted devils,
I am past such needless palsy, for your names
Of Whore and Murd'ress, they proceed from you,
As if a man should spit against the wind,   150
The filth returns in's face.

MONTICELSO
Pray you mistress satisfy me one question:
Who lodged beneath your roof that fatal night
Your husband brake his neck?

BRACHIANO   That question
Enforceth me break silence: I was there.   155

MONTICELSO
Your business?

BRACHIANO   Why I came to comfort her,
And take some course for settling her estate,
Because I heard her husband was in debt
To you my lord.

MONTICELSO   He was.

BRACHIANO   And 'twas strangely feared
That you would cozen her.

MONTICELSO   Who made you overseer?   160

BRACHIANO
Why my charity, my charity, which should flow
From every generous and noble spirit,
To orphans and to widows.

MONTICELSO   Your lust.

BRACHIANO
Cowardly dogs bark loudest. Sirrah priest,
I'll talk with you hereafter, – Do you hear?   165
The sword you frame of such an excellent temper,
I'll sheathe in your own bowels:
There are a number of thy coat resemble
Your common post-boys.

MONTICELSO   Ha?

BRACHIANO   Your mercenary post-
boys

148 *palsy* trembling (with fear)
161 *charity* Cf. l. 71: Brachiano supplies the 'charity' which (as Vittoria remarks)
    Monticelso should show. While it targets Monticelso, the line also exposes
    Brachiano as a liar and possibly a coward, since he is providing himself with
    an alibi.
166 *sword* metaphoric weapon against Brachiano, which he declares he will use as
    a sword of justice
    temper referring to Monticelso, anger; referring to the sword, the resilient
    strength imparted to steel by tempering
168 *coat* clerical profession   169 *post-boys* letter-carriers

Your letters carry truth, but 'tis your guise   170
To fill your mouths with gross and impudent lies.

[*He makes for the door*]

SERVANT
  My lord your gown.
BRACHIANO   Thou liest, 'twas my stool.
  Bestow't upon thy master that will challenge
  The rest o'th'household stuff, for Brachiano
  Was ne'er so beggarly, to take a stool   175
  Out of another's lodging: let him make
  Valance for his bed on't, or a demi-foot-cloth,
  For his most reverent moil; Monticelso,
  Nemo me impune lacessit.   *Exit*
MONTICELSO
  Your champion's gone.
VITTORIA   The wolf may prey the better.   180
FRANCISCO
  My lord there's great suspicion of the murder,
  But no sound proof who did it: for my part
  I do not think she hath a soul so black
  To act a deed so bloody; if she have,
  As in cold countries husbandmen plant vines   185
  And with warm blood manure them, even so
  One summer she will bear unsavoury fruit,
  And ere next spring wither both branch and root.
  The act of blood let pass, only descend
  To matter of incontinence.
VITTORIA   I discern poison   190
  Under your gilded pills.
MONTICELSO
  [*Showing a letter*] Now the Duke's gone I will produce
    a letter,

---

173 *challenge* lay claim to
177 *Valance* drapes around a bed canopy
    demi-foot-cloth half-length covering for a horse, used by lesser dignitaries; an
    insult (NCW III.ii.177 n.)   178 *moil* mule (traditional mount for cardinals)
179 *Nemo me impune lacessit* 'No one wounds me with impunity.'
    lacessit ed. (lacescit Q)
    s.d. *Exit* ed. (Exit Brachiano Q)
190–1 *poison . . . pills* Apothecaries sometimes covered pills with gold in order to
    increase their prices.

Wherein 'twas plotted he and you should meet
At an apothecary's summer-house,
Down by the river Tiber: view't my lords: 195
Where after wanton bathing and the heat
Of a lascivious banquet – I pray read it,
I shame to speak the rest.

VITTORIA   Grant I was tempted,
Temptation to lust proves not the act,
Casta est quam nemo rogavit,   200
You read his hot love to me, but you want
My frosty answer.

MONTICELSO   Frost i'th'dog-days! Strange!

VITTORIA
Condemn you me for that the Duke did love me,
So may you blame some fair and crystal river
For that some melancholic distracted man   205
Hath drowned himself in't.

MONTICELSO   Truly drowned indeed.

VITTORIA

Sum up my faults I pray, and you shall find
That beauty and gay clothes, a merry heart,
And a good stomach to feast, are all,
All the poor crimes that you can charge me with: 210
In faith my lord you might go pistol flies,
The sport would be more noble.

MONTICELSO   Very good.

VITTORIA
But take you your course, it seems you have beggared
    me first
And now would fain undo me; I have houses,
Jewels, and a poor remnant of crusadoes,   215
Would those would make you charitable.

MONTICELSO   If the devil
Did ever take good shape behold his picture.

---

193 *he* ed. (her Q)

195 At several points during the scene (ll. 57, 107–8, 119–20, 130–3, 140), the
    audience's attention is drawn away from the sparring combatants to the ambas-
    sadors, allowing a more detached assessment of the scene.

200 *Casta est quam nemo rogavit* 'Chaste is she whom no man has asked' (from Ovid,
    Amores I.viii.43). The context of the line is ironic since it occurs in a speech
    designed to persuade a woman to take many lovers.

202 *dog-days* very hot and oppressive weather when Sinus the Dog-star is high, and
    when malignant influences including lust were supposed to prevail

215 *crusadoes* Portuguese coins of gold or silver bearing the figure of a cross

VITTORIA
    You have one virtue left,
    You will not flatter me.
FRANCISCO   Who brought this letter?
VITTORIA
    I am not compelled to tell you.   220
MONTICELSO
    My lord Duke sent to you a thousand ducats,
    The twelfth of August.
VITTORIA   'Twas to keep your cousin
    From prison; I paid use for't.
MONTICELSO   I rather think
    'Twas interest for his lust.
VITTORIA
    Who says so but yourself? If you be my accuser   225
    Pray cease to be my judge, come from the bench,
    Give in your evidence 'gainst me, and let these
    Be moderators; my lord cardinal,
    Were your intelligencing ears as long
    As to my thoughts, had you an honest tongue   230
    I would not care though you proclaimed them all.
MONTICELSO
    Go to, go to.
    After your goodly and vain-glorious banquet
    I'll give you a choke-pear.
VITTORIA   O' your own grafting?
MONTICELSO
    You were born in Venice, honourably descended   235
    From the Vitelli; 'twas my cousin's fate –
    Ill may I name the hour – to marry you;
    He bought you of your father.
VITTORIA   Ha?
MONTICELSO
    He spent there in six months

___

223 *use* interest
227 *these* i.e. the ambassadors, or more broadly, the theatre audience
229 *intelligencing* spying
    long ed. (louing Q)
234 *choke-pear* rough, unpalatable pear, difficult to swallow; a severe reproof
    grafting literally, with trees and plants, the action of inserting a shoot or scion
    into a groove or slit made in another stock, so as to allow the sap of the latter
    to circulate through the former; with an obvious bawdy sense (as in *The Duchess
    of Malfi* II.i.148–9)
235–6 *born . . . Vitelli* The real Vittoria was descended from the Accoramboni and
    born at Gubbio, but Webster may have wanted to associate her with Venice,
    famed for its prostitutes.

Twelve thousand ducats, and to my acquaintance   240
Received in dowry with you not one julio:
'Twas a hard penny-worth, the ware being so light.
I yet but draw the curtain now to your picture:
You came from thence a most notorious strumpet,
And so you have continued.

VITTORIA   My lord.

MONTICELSO   Nay hear me,   245
You shall have time to prate – my lord Brachiano –
Alas I make but repetition,
Of what is ordinary and Rialto talk,
And ballated, and would be played o'th'stage,
But that vice many times finds such loud friends   250
That preachers are charmed silent.
You gentlemen Flamineo and Marcello,
The court hath nothing now to charge you with,
Only you must remain upon your sureties
For your appearance.

FRANCISCO   I stand for Marcello.   255

FLAMINEO
And my lord Duke for me.

MONTICELSO
For you Vittoria, your public fault,
Joined to th'condition of the present time,
Takes from you all the fruits of noble pity.
Such a corrupted trial have you made   260
Both of your life and beauty, and been styled
No less in ominous fate than blazing stars
To princes; here's your sentence: you are confined
Unto a house of convertites and your bawd –

---

241 *julio* silver coin struck by Pope Julius II (1503–13), formerly current in Italy.
There may be an unintended ironic reference to 'Doctor Julio' (cf. II.ii.28) as
Vittoria's real 'dowry' or gift to Camillo, especially since the word is italicized
like other proper names in the copy.

242 *light* not heavy; wanton, unchaste

246 *prate . . . Brachiano* – ed. (no punctuation in Q)
prate tell or repeat to little purpose

248 *Rialto talk* talk of the Exchange, or meeting-place

249 *ballated* turned into a ballad (and thus made notorious)
would . . . stage As many contemporary scandals were in Webster's time.

254 *sureties* persons who will make themselves liable for another's appearance in
court

257 *public* Cf. III.1.19 n.

262 *blazing stars* comets, considered signs of ill omen, especially for great men

263 *To . . . here's* ed. (To Princes heares; Q)

264 *Unto* ed. (VIT. Unto Q)

FLAMINEO
  [*Aside*] Who I?
MONTICELSO   The Moor.
FLAMINEO [*Aside*]   O I am a sound man again.   265
VITTORIA
  A house of convertites, what's that?
MONTICELSO   A house
  Of penitent whores.
VITTORIA   Do the noblemen in Rome
  Erect it for their wives, that I am sent
  To lodge there?
FRANCISCO
  You must have patience.
VITTORIA   I must first have vengeance.   270
  I fain would know if you have your salvation
  By patent, that you proceed thus.
MONTICELSO   Away with her.
  Take her hence.   [GUARD *leads* VITTORIA *away*]
VITTORIA   A rape, a rape!
MONTICELSO   How?
VITTORIA
  Yes, you have ravished Justice,
  Forced her to do your pleasure.
MONTICELSO   Fie, she's mad.   275
VITTORIA
  Die with these pills in your most cursed maws,
  Should bring you health, or while you sit o'th'bench,
  Let your own spittle choke you.
MONTICELSO   She's turned fury.
VITTORIA
  That the last day of judgement may so find you,
  And leave you the same devil you were before,   280
  Instruct me some good horse-leech to speak treason,

---

house of convertites The real-life Vittoria was imprisoned in Castel Sant'Angelo in Rome, though a contemporary account, translated by John Florio, claims she was 'put into a monasterie of Nunnes'. In Jacobean London the 'house of correction' for reformed prostitutes was Bridewell.

266–7 *A ... Rome* ed. (A ... that? / MON ... whoores. / Do ... Rome, Q)
269–70 *To ... there? / You ... vengeance* ed. (To ... patience / I ... vengeance Q)
272 *patent* special licence   276 *maws* throats, gullets
276–7 *Die ... health* probably a reference to the 'gilded pills' (l. 191) or apparently pious words uttered by her enemies
281 *horse-leech* literally, blood-sucker; a cunning rhetorician (as in Erasmus, *Praise of Folly* (1509): 'the rhetoricians of our day who consider themselves as good as gods if like horse-leeches they can seem to have two tongues' (trans. Clarence Miller, 1979: p. 14))

For since you cannot take my life for deeds,
Take it for words. O woman's poor revenge
Which dwells but in the tongue; I will not weep,
No I do scorn to call up one poor tear   285
To fawn on your injustice; bear me hence,
Unto this house of – what's your mitigating title?

MONTICELSO
Of convertites.

VITTORIA
It shall not be a house of convertites.
My mind shall make it honester to me   290
Than the Pope's palace, and more peaceable
Than thy soul, though thou art a cardinal.
Know this, and let it somewhat raise your spite,
Through darkness diamonds spread their richest light.
                    Exit [*with* ZANCHE, *guarded*]

                    Enter BRACHIANO

BRACHIANO
Now you and I are friends sir, we'll shake hands,   295
In a friend's grave, together: a fit place,
Being the emblem of soft peace t'atone our hatred.

FRANCISCO
Sir, what's the matter?

BRACHIANO
I will not chase more blood from that loved cheek,
You have lost too much already; fare you well.   [*Exit*]   300

FRANCISCO
How strange these words sound? What's the interpretation?

FLAMINEO
[*Aside*] Good, this is a preface to the discovery of the
Duchess' death. He carries it well. Because now I
cannot counterfeit a whining passion for the death of   305
my lady, I will feign a mad humour for the disgrace of
my sister, and that will keep off idle questions.
Treason's tongue hath a villainous palsy in't; I will talk

288–9 ed. (one line in Q)
294 s.d. *Exit* ed. (Exit Vittoria Q)
295–339 Webster again employs the simultaneous staging which allows him to
    develop visual parallels (cf. II.i.282–322); the ambassadors silently confer with
    Monticelso (about the trial) while Francisco and Giovanni react to news of
    Isabella's death: thus Vittoria's 'disgrace' is juxtaposed with Isabella's 'death'
    (as in Flamineo's speech, ll. 304–7), and cause and effect are reversed in the
    dramatic sequence.
308 *palsy* nervous disease characterized by involuntary tremors

to any man, hear no man, and for a time appear a politic
madman.   [*Exit*] 310

Enter GIOVANNI, *Count* LODOVICO

FRANCISCO
  How now my noble cousin, what in black?
GIOVANNI
  Yes uncle, I was taught to imitate you
  In virtue, and you must imitate me
  In colours for your garments; my sweet mother
  Is –
FRANCISCO How? Where?   315
GIOVANNI
  Is there – no, yonder; indeed sir I'll not tell you,
  For I shall make you weep.
FRANCISCO   Is dead.
GIOVANNI
  Do not blame me now,
  I did not tell you so.
LODOVICO   She's dead my lord.
FRANCISCO
  Dead?   320
MONTICELSO
  Blessed lady; thou art now above thy woes.
  [*To* AMBASSADORS] Wilt please your lordships to with-
    draw a little?
GIOVANNI
  What do the dead do, uncle? Do they eat,
  Hear music, go a-hunting, and be merry,
  As we that live?   325
FRANCISCO
  No coz; they sleep.
GIOVANNI   Lord, Lord, that I were dead –
  I have not slept these six nights. When do they wake?
FRANCISCO
  When God shall please.
GIOVANNI   Good God let her sleep ever.
  For I have known her wake an hundred nights,
  When all the pillow, where she laid her head,   330
  Was brine-wet with her tears. I am to complain to you
    sir.
  I'll tell you how they have used her now she's dead:

321 *Blessed . . . woes* ed. (Dead? . . . Lady / Thou . . . woes Q)
324–5 ed. (one line in Q)
329 *For* ed. (GIO. For I Q) s.p. misplaced

They wrapped her in a cruel fold of lead,
And would not let me kiss her.
FRANCISCO   Thou didst love her.
GIOVANNI
I have often heard her say she gave me suck,   335
And it should seem by that she dearly loved me,
Since princes seldom do it.
FRANCISCO
O all of my poor sister that remains!
Take him away for God's sake –
                    [*Exeunt* GIOVANNI *and* LODOVICO]
MONTICELSO   How now my Lord?
FRANCISCO
Believe me I am nothing but her grave,   340
And I shall keep her blessed memory
Longer than thousand epitaphs.

                                        [*Exeunt*]

[Act III, Scene iii]

Enter FLAMINEO *as distracted*[, MARCELLO *and* LODOVICO]

FLAMINEO
We endure the strokes like anvils or hard steel,
Till pain itself make us no pain to feel.
Who shall do me right now? Is this the end of service?
I'd rather go weed garlic; travail through France, and
be mine own ostler; wear sheep-skin linings; or shoes   5
that stink of blacking; be entered into the list of the forty
thousand pedlars in Poland.

---

333 *fold of lead* covering made of lead (an aristocratic addition to the more per-
    meable winding sheet made of linen in which all corpses were wrapped); a
    leaden coffin moulded to the shape of the body (designed to preserve the
    corpse)

335 *she . . . suck* No mean boast among the English or Italian upper classes, whose
    infants were usually sent out to wet-nurses. Much of the domestic conduct
    literature recommended that mothers nurse their own children: 'How can a
    mother better expresse her love to her young babe, then by letting it sucke of
    her owne breasts?' (William Gouge, *Of Domesticall Duties* (1612) p. 509).

  0 s.d. *as distracted* The s.d. ('as distracted') may indicate gestures or dress befitting
    the 'distracted' person. The s.d. at V.iv.91 reads 'Cornelia doth this in several
    forms of distraction', suggesting, perhaps, such conventionalized gestures as
    wringing the hands and beating the breast.

  5 *ostler* groom, stable-boy
    linings underclothing

6–7 *forty . . . Poland* The Poles were proverbially poor.

Enter Savoy [Ambassador]

Would I had rotted in some surgeon's house at Venice,
built upon the pox as well as on piles, ere I had served
Brachiano.   10

SAVOY AMBASSADOR
You must have comfort.

FLAMINEO
Your comfortable words are like honey. They relish well
in your mouth that's whole; but in mine that's wounded
they go down as if the sting of the bee were in them.
O they have wrought their purpose cunningly, as if they   15
would not seem to do it of malice. In this a politician
imitates the devil, as the devil imitates a cannon.
Wheresoever he comes to do mischief, he comes with
his backside towards you.

Enter the French [Ambassador]

FRENCH AMBASSADOR
The proofs are evident.   20

FLAMINEO
Proof! 'Twas corruption. O Gold, what a god art thou!
And O man, what a devil art thou to be tempted by
that cursed mineral! Yon diversivolent lawyer – mark
him, knaves turn informers, as maggots turn to flies; you
may catch gudgeons with either. A cardinal – I would he   25
would hear me – there's nothing so holy but money will
corrupt and putrify it, like victual under the line.

[Enter English Ambassador]

---

9 *built . . . piles* i.e. built on a fortune made from curing syphilis, as well as haem-
   orrhoids (with a pun on 'piles' as pillars or timbers, especially necessary as
   foundations in Venice)
12–14 *They . . . them* lines borrowed from an unidentified translation of Seneca,
   Epistles 109, 7: 'Some there are to whom honey seemeth bitter in regard of their
   sickenesse' (trans. Lodge). Cf. Pierre Matthieu, *The History of Lewis the Eleventh*
   (1611): 'Honey how sweet soever it be, is sharpe and offensive to a mouth
   ulcered with passion and slander' (p. 25).
18–19 *Wheresoever . . . you* Showing one's back is not threatening but, as with a
   cannon, one has only to turn to face someone to be a threat.
23 *Yon* ed. (You Q)
   diversivolent Flamineo uses the lawyer's word against him (cf. III.ii.28).
24 *turn* turn into
25 *gudgeons* small fish much used for bait; credulous gulls
27 *victual . . . line* food at the equator
   line ed. (live Q)
27 s.d. ed. (*Enter English Ambassador* l. margin opposite l. 29 in Q)

You are happy in England, my lord; here they sell justice with those weights they press men to death with. O
horrible salary!   30

ENGLISH AMBASSADOR
Fie, fie, Flamineo.

FLAMINEO
Bells ne'er ring well till they are at their full pitch, and
I hope yon cardinal shall never have the grace to pray
well, till he come to the scaffold.
                                        [*Exeunt Ambassadors*]
If they were racked now to know the confederacy! But   35
your noblemen are privileged from the rack; and well
may. For a little thing would pull some of them a' pieces
afore they came to their arraignment. Religion; oh how
it is commeddled with policy. The first bloodshed in
the world happened about religion. Would I were a Jew.   40

MARCELLO
Oh, there are too many.

FLAMINEO
You are deceived. There are not Jews enough, priests
enough, nor gentlemen enough.

MARCELLO
How?

FLAMINEO
I'll prove it. For if there were Jews enough, so many   45
Christians would not turn usurers; if priests enough,
one should not have six benefices; and if gentlemen
enough, so many early mushrooms, whose best growth
sprang from a dunghill, should not aspire to gentility.
Farewell. Let others live by begging. Be thou one of   50
them; practise the art of Wolner in England to swallow

28–9 *here ... with* ironic, since it was English law which devised the *peine forte et
    dure*, or torture of the press, for those who remained mute when required to
    plead at trial. Prisoners who were thus starved and crushed under heavy iron
    weights died in slow agony, though their property could not be confiscated from
    their heirs because they could not be convicted.
30 *salary* reward   32 *full pitch* highest point (of a bell-tower)
36–7 *well may* with good reason
37 *pull ... pieces* dismember on the rack; reduce to a state of confusion
39 *commeddled* mixed together
   policy intrigue
39–40 *first ... religion* a reference to Cain's murder of his brother Abel, possibly
    foreshadowing Flamineo's murder of Marcello (cf. V.vi.13–14)
42 *Jews* synonymous with usurers, as in *The Merchant of Venice*
48 *early mushrooms* young upstarts
51–2 *practise ... thee* Wolner was a famous Elizabethan glutton who consumed
    iron, glass, oyster shells, raw meat and raw fish. He died of eating raw eel.

all's given thee; and yet let one purgation make thee as
hungry again as fellows that work in a sawpit. I'll go
hear the screech-owl.   *Exit*

LODOVICO
    [*Aside*] This was Brachiano's pander, and 'tis strange   55
    That in such open and apparent guilt
    Of his adulterous sister, he dare utter
    So scandalous a passion. I must wind him.

                    Enter FLAMINEO

FLAMINEO
    [*Aside*] How dares this banished count return to Rome,
    His pardon not yet purchased? I have heard   60
    The deceased Duchess gave him pension,
    And that he came along from Padua
    I'th'train of the young prince. There's somewhat in't.
    Physicians, that cure poisons, still do work
    With counterpoisons.
MARCELLO [*Aside*]   Mark this strange encounter.   65
FLAMINEO
    The god of melancholy turn thy gall to poison,
    And let the stigmatic wrinkles in thy face
    Like to the boisterous waves in a rough tide
    One still overtake another.
LODOVICO   I do thank thee
    And I do wish ingeniously for thy sake   70
    The dog-days all year long.
FLAMINEO   How croaks the raven?
    Is our good Duchess dead?
LODOVICO   Dead.
FLAMINEO   O fate!
    Misfortune comes like the crowner's business,

Flamineo is very likely reiterating his cynical view of Marcello's exploitation by
Francisco (cf. III.i.39–44).

53 *a sawpit* ed. (sawpit Q)   54 *screech-owl* bird of evil omen
58 *wind* find out about   60 *purchased* obtained
61 *pension* salary, wages
65–134 This 'strange encounter' brings the play's two tool-villains into parallel rela-
    tion: both are the miserable dependants of great men, though Lodovico does
    not share Flamineo's complex ambivalence about his position.
66 *gall* gall bladder, supposed source of bitterness and choler
67 *stigmatic* branded, deformed, ugly
70 *ingeniously* cleverly (usual sense): also used, mistakenly, to mean ingenuously,
    candidly
71 *dog-days* Cf. III.ii.202 n.
    raven another bird of ill omen   73 *crowner's* coroner's

Huddle upon huddle.
LODOVICO
Shalt thou and I join housekeeping?
FLAMINEO   Yes, content.   75
Let's be unsociably sociable.
LODOVICO
Sit some three days together, and discourse.
FLAMINEO
Only with making faces;
Lie in our clothes.
LODOVICO
With faggots for our pillows.
FLAMINEO   And be lousy.   80
LODOVICO
In taffeta linings; that's gentle melancholy;
Sleep all day.
FLAMINEO   Yes: and like your melancholic hare
Feed after midnight.

Enter ANTONELLI [*and* GASPARO, *laughing*]

We are observed: see how yon couple grieve.
LODOVICO
What a strange creature is a laughing fool,   85
As if man were created to no use
But only to show his teeth.
FLAMINEO   I'll tell thee what,
It would do well instead of looking-glasses
To set one's face each morning by a saucer

74 *Huddle upon huddle* 'tumbling in heaps one over the other' (Lucas, p. 235)
74–5 ed. (Huddle . . . housekeeping? / FLA. Yes, . . . content. Q)
79–80 ed. (Lie . . . pillowes. / FLA. And . . . lowsie. Q)
80 *faggots* bundles of sticks
    lousy full of lice; filthy, vile
81 *taffeta linings* glossy silk underclothing (supposed to protect against lice)
    gentle ed. (gentile Q)
82–3 *melancholic . . . midnight* Hares were supposed to be among the most melan-
    choly beasts, sleeping all day and feeding at night (because 'their hart and
    bloode is cold', explains Topsell in *The Historie of Four-footed Beasts* (1607)).
83 s.d. *Enter Antonelli* ed. (to r. of l. 95 in Q)
84 *We . . . grieve* Q offers no s.d., though there is space for one. The likeliest
    explanation is that Antonelli's entry has been misplaced to 11 lines later (to
    correspond with his speech), and Gasparo's entry omitted. It is less likely,
    though possible, that two ambassadors have remained on stage as witnesses to
    the comic 'flyting', or exchange of insults.
    grieve probably intended ironically, given Lodovico's subsequent remark
89 *saucer* receptacle for blood in blood-letting

Of a witch's congealed blood.

LODOVICO   Precious girn, rogue.   90
We'll never part.

FLAMINEO   Never: till the beggary of courtiers,
The discontent of churchmen, want of soldiers,
And all the creatures that hang manacled,
Worse than strappadoed, on the lowest felly
Of Fortune's wheel, be taught in our two lives   95
To scorn that world which life of means deprives.

ANTONELLI
My lord, I bring good news. The Pope on's death-bed,
At th'earnest suit of the great Duke of Florence,
Hath signed your pardon, and restored unto you –

LODOVICO
I thank you for your news. Look up again   100
Flamineo, see my pardon.

FLAMINEO   Why do you laugh?
There was no such condition in our covenant.

LODOVICO   Why?

FLAMINEO
You shall not seem a happier man than I;
You know our vow sir, if you will be merry,
Do it i'th'like posture, as if some great man   105
Sat while his enemy were executed:
Though it be very lechery unto thee,

---

90 *witch's ... blood* Witches were supposed to be melancholy (Scot, *Discoverie of
Witchcraft* (1584) p. 7), hence cold and dry, which caused their blood to congeal. (Cf. *The Taming of the Shrew* Induction ii.132: '. . . too much sadness hath
congeal'd your blood'.)

   girn, rogue ed. (gue Q) 'Girn' meant 'the act of showing the teeth; a snarl', and
Marston's *Antonio and Mellida* contains a parallel passage; after 'setting of faces'
in a looking glass, Balurdo cries: 'O that girn kills, it kills' (III.ii.125–6). Lodovico may be reacting to Flamineo distorting his visage. Altered during press correction from 'grine rouge' to 'gue', the latter (from French *gueux*, beggar),
meaning 'rogue, sharper', is rarely accepted as authoritative; 'gue' (which looks
like the end of 'rogue') may be the result of a botched attempt at correcting the
spelling of both words. Perhaps the compositor mistook the press-corrector's
transposition sign for a deletion (see NCW III.iii.82 n.).

94 *strappadoed* hoisted from the ground by the hands when tied across the back,
a torture

   felly felloe or section of the rim of a wheel

95 *Fortune's wheel* The proverbial turning of this wheel might raise one to prosperity or lower one to misfortune. For this reason it was frequently conflated, as
here, with a torture-wheel (cf. *King Lear* IV.vii.45–6: 'I am bound / Upon a
wheel of fire').

Do't with a crabbed politician's face.

LODOVICO

Your sister is a damnable whore.

FLAMINEO   Ha?

LODOVICO

Look you; I spake that laughing.   110

FLAMINEO

Dost ever think to speak again?

LODOVICO   Do you hear?

Wilt sell me forty ounces of her blood,
To water a mandrake?

FLAMINEO   Poor lord, you did vow

To live a lousy creature.

LODOVICO   Yes.

FLAMINEO   Like one

That had for ever forfeited the daylight,   115
By being in debt.

LODOVICO   Ha, ha!

FLAMINEO

I do not greatly wonder you do break:
Your lordship learnt long since. But I'll tell you –

LODOVICO

What?

FLAMINEO   And't shall stick by you.

LODOVICO   I long for it.

FLAMINEO

This laughter scurvily becomes your face;   120
If you will not be melancholy, be angry.   *Strikes him*
See, now I laugh too.

MARCELLO

[*Seizing* FLAMINEO] You are to blame, I'll force you
    hence.

LODOVICO [*To* ANTONELLI *and* GASPARO]   Unhand me.
                    Exit MAR[CELLO] *&* FLAM[INEO]

That e'er I should be forced to right myself

112–13 *forty . . . mandrake?* Cf. III.i.50 n. Lodovico implies that Vittoria will be
    executed.

115 *for ever . . . daylight* i.e. been imprisoned for life

117 *break* break your covenant (cf. l. 103); become bankrupt (as in previous line)

118 *learnt* ed. (learn't Q)

119 *stick* remain in your memory; with a suggestion of 'stab, pierce' (though Flami-
    neo clearly uses his fist, not a sword)

123 *Unhand me* Antonelli and Gasparo restrain Lodovico physically as they restrain
    him verbally in I.i.

Upon a pander.

ANTONELLI   My lord.   125

LODOVICO
H'had been as good met with his fist a thunderbolt.

GASPARO
How this shows!

LODOVICO   Ud's death, how did my sword miss
him?
These rogues that are most weary of their lives
Still scape the greatest dangers;
A pox upon him: all his reputation –   130
Nay all the goodness of his family –
Is not worth half this earthquake.
I learnt it of no fencer to shake thus;
Come, I'll forget him, and go drink some wine.

Exeunt

[Act IV, Scene i]

Enter FRANCISCO *and* MONTICELSO

MONTICELSO
Come, come my lord, untie your folded thoughts,
And let them dangle loose as a bride's hair.
Your sister's poisoned.

FRANCISCO   Far be it from my thoughts
To seek revenge.

MONTICELSO   What, are you turned all marble?

FRANCISCO
Shall I defy him, and impose a war   5
Most burdensome on my poor subjects' necks,
Which at my will I have not power to end?
You know; for all the murders, rapes, and thefts,
Committed in the horrid lust of war,
He that unjustly caused it first proceed   10
Shall find it in his grave and in his seed.

MONTICELSO
That's not the course I'd wish you: pray, observe me.
We see that undermining more prevails
Than doth the cannon. Bear your wrongs concealed,

---

127 *Ud's death* (By) God's death, an oath

  2 *loose . . . hair* Jacobean virgin brides wore their hair loose. Loose or dishevelled
    hair was also a conventional sign for distraction or grief.

And, patient as the tortoise, let this camel   15
Stalk o'er your back unbruised: sleep with the lion,
And let this brood of secure foolish mice
Play with your nostrils, till the time be ripe
For th' bloody audit and the fatal gripe:
Aim like a cunning fowler, close one eye,   20
That you the better may your game espy.
FRANCISCO
Free me my innocence from treacherous acts:
I know there's thunder yonder: and I'll stand
Like a safe valley which low bends the knee
To some aspiring mountain: since I know   25
Treason, like spiders weaving nets for flies,
By her foul work is found, and in it dies.
To pass away these thoughts, my honoured lord,
It is reported you possess a book
Wherein you have quoted, by intelligence,   30
The names of all notorious offenders
Lurking about the city.
MONTICELSO   Sir I do;
And some there are which call it my black book.
Well may the title hold: for though it teach not
The art of conjuring, yet in it lurk   35
The names of many devils.
FRANCISCO   Pray let's see it.
MONTICELSO
I'll fetch it to your lordship.   *Exit*

15–16 *patient . . . unbruised* In George Wither's *Collection of Emblems* (1635), the
   tortoise represents self-sufficient virtue: 'If any at his harmlesse person strike; /
   Himselfe hee streight contracteth, Torteis-like, / To make the Shell of Suf-
   france, his defence; / And counts it Life, to die with Innocence' (p. 86). The
   application of the image in this context is thus highly ironic.
19 *audit* searching inspection
20 *fowler* hunter of fowl
22 *from* ed. (fro Q)
23–5 *I . . . mountain* Though Francisco's words imply that he leaves vengeance to
   heaven, his actions (perhaps gesturing towards and bowing before Monticelso)
   may appeal to Monticelso himself as that 'aspiring mountain'.
30 *quoted* noted, set down
   by intelligence by secret information
33 *black book* an official register bound in black; a record of those liable to censure.
   In his *Disputation* (1592), Robert Greene promised to publish a pamphlet called
   The Blacke Booke to expose the knaves of London.
35 *conjuring* the 'black art' of calling up devils to do one's bidding (cf. *Doctor
   Faustus* I.i.154, where Faustus is advised to consult books by famed magicians
   like Bacon in order to conjure)
37 s.d. *Exit* ed. (Exit Monticelso Q)

FRANCISCO   Monticelso,
I will not trust thee, but in all my plots
I'll rest as jealous as a town besieged.
Thou canst not reach what I intend to act;   40
Your flax soon kindles, soon is out again,
But gold slow heats, and long will hot remain.

Enter MONT[ICELSO,] *presents* FRAN[CISCO] *with a book*

MONTICELSO
'Tis here my lord.
FRANCISCO
First your intelligencers, pray let's see.
MONTICELSO
Their number rises strangely,   45
And some of them
You'd take for honest men.
Next are panders.
These are your pirates: and these following leaves,
For base rogues that undo young gentlemen   50
By taking up commodities; for politic bankrupts;
For fellows that are bawds to their own wives,
Only to put off horses and slight jewels,
Clocks, defaced plate, and such commodities,
At birth of their first children.
FRANCISCO   Are there such?   55
MONTICELSO
These are for impudent bawds
That go in men's apparel; for usurers

39 *jealous* vigilant
42 *heats* ed. (heat's Q)
   s.d. ed. (to r. of ll. 43–4 in Q)
45–8 The sequence of half-lines is unusual, and may indicate pauses in Monticelso's speech as he turns the pages and points to sections of his black book
   (Brown IV.i.45–8 n.)
51 *taking up commodities* To circumvent laws against high rates of interest, swind-
   lers lent cheap commodities, at a highly inflated value, instead of money. Then
   the gullible borrower, required to repay the alleged value of the commodities,
   often ended up in debtors' prison.
   politic bankrupts those who feign bankruptcy in order to avoid creditors
53–5 *Only . . . commodities* i.e. men who prostituted their own wives in exchange
   for goods sold at an inflated price to their wives' lovers
56–7 *impudent . . . apparel* a reference to the contemporary controversy surrounding women crossdressing as men, some of whom were prostitutes, all of
   whom were attacked in antifeminist tracts
57–8 *usurers . . . reportage* i.e. moneylenders who give a 'cut' to scriveners (who
   supplied those who wanted to raise money on security) in exchange for their
   recommendation, their good report

That share with scriveners for their good reportage:
For lawyers that will antedate their writs:
And some divines you might find folded there,   60
But that I slip them o'er for conscience' sake.
Here is a general catalogue of knaves.
A man might study all the prisons o'er
Yet never attain this knowledge.
FRANCISCO   Murderers.
Fold down the leaf I pray;   65
Good my lord let me borrow this strange doctrine.
MONTICELSO
[*Handing him the book*] Pray use't my lord.
FRANCISCO   I do
    assure your lordship,
You are a worthy member of the state,
And have done infinite good in your discovery
Of these offenders.
MONTICELSO   Somewhat sir.
FRANCISCO   O God!   70
Better than tribute of wolves paid in England,
'Twill hang their skins o'th'hedge.
MONTICELSO   I must make bold
To leave your lordship.
FRANCISCO   Dearly sir, I thank you;
If any ask for me at court, report
You have left me in the company of knaves.   75
                                    Exit MONT[ICELSO]
I gather now by this, some cunning fellow
That's my lord's officer, one that lately skipped
From a clerk's desk up to a justice' chair,
Hath made this knavish summons; and intends,
As th'Irish rebels wont were to sell heads,   80
So to make prize of these. And thus it happens,
Your poor rogues pay for't, which have not the means
To present bribe in fist: the rest o'th'band
Are razed out of the knaves' record; or else
My lord he winks at them with easy will,   85
His man grows rich, the knaves are the knaves still.

59 *antedate* . . . *writs* i.e. produce a phony legal document (alleging an offence)
   antedated so as to take precedence over, and thus displace, a genuine one (cf.
   II.i.292–7)

71 *tribute* . . . *England* The Welsh were supposedly ordered by King Edgar (944–
   75) to pay a tribute of three hundred wolves a year as a means of controlling
   the wolf population in Wales.

80 *Irish* . . . *heads* A bounty was paid by Elizabeth I's officers for heads in the Irish
   rebellions.

But to the use I'll make of it; it shall serve
To point me out a list of murderers,
Agents for any villainy. Did I want
Ten leash of courtesans, it would furnish me;   90
Nay laundress three armies. That in so little paper
Should lie th'undoing of so many men!
'Tis not so big as twenty declarations.
See the corrupted use some make of books:
Divinity, wrested by some factious blood,   95
Draws swords, swells battles, and o'erthrows all good.
To fashion my revenge more seriously,
Let me remember my dead sister's face:
Call for her picture: no; I'll close mine eyes,
And in a melancholic thought I'll frame   100

Enter ISABEL[L]A's *Ghost*

Her figure 'fore me. Now I ha't – d'foot! How strong
Imagination works! How she can frame
Things which are not! Methinks she stands afore me;
And by the quick idea of my mind,
Were my skill pregnant, I could draw her picture.   105
Thought, as a subtle juggler, makes us deem
Things supernatural which have cause
Common as sickness. 'Tis my melancholy;
How cam'st thou by thy death? How idle am I

---

90 *leash* set of three (animals or birds used in hunting)
91 *laundress* furnish with laundresses (reputedly of easy virtue)
   in so ed. (so in Q)
93 *declarations* official proclamations
95 *wrested . . . blood* i.e. stirred by some violent, seditious passion
100 s.d. *Enter* ISABELLA's *Ghost* Francisco's view of the ghost as a figment of his own
   imagination is in tension with a long stage tradition of unquestioned presenta-
   tion of ghosts. This one is highly ambiguous, unlike the ghost of Brachiano
   which appears in V.iv.
101 *ha't – d'foot* ed. (– ha'te Q) The uncorrected Q reads 'Now I – d'foot' ('by
   God's foot', an oath). The editors of NCW hypothesize (IV.i.99 n.) that the
   mark of inclusion for 'ha'te' led the corrector to think that 'd'foot' was being
   struck out. If both words stand, the actor can register more effectively the shock
   of opening his eyes to find a real ghost before him.
104 *quick* active, vital
105 *pregnant* fertile, imaginative
106 *juggler* conjuror, magician
108 *melancholy* During the Renaissance, melancholy was believed to be a physiolo-
   gical disease caused by an excess of black bile which often produced visual
   hallucinations: 'From the fuming melancholy of our spleen mounteth that hot
   matter into the higher region of the brain, whereof many fearful visions are
   framed' (Thomas Nashe, *Terrors of the Night* (1594)).

To question my own idleness? Did ever   110
Man dream awake till now? Remove this object,
Out of my brain with't: what have I to do
With tombs, or death-beds, funerals, or tears,
That have to meditate upon revenge?

                                        [*Exit Ghost*]
So now 'tis ended, like an old wives' story.   115
Statesmen think often they see stranger sights
Than madmen. Come, to this weighty business.
My tragedy must have some idle mirth in't,
Else it will never pass. I am in love,
In love with Corombona, and my suit   120
Thus halts to her in verse. – *Writes*
I have done it rarely: O the fate of princes!
I am so used to frequent flattery,
That being alone I now flatter myself;
But it will serve; 'tis sealed.

                        Enter SERVANT

                        Bear this   125
To th'house of convertites; and watch your leisure
To give it to the hands of Corombona,
Or to the matron, when some followers
Of Brachiano may be by. Away.

                                        Exit SERVANT
He that deals all by strength, his wit is shallow: 130
When a man's head goes through, each limb will follow.
The engine for my business, bold Count Lodowick;
'Tis gold must such an instrument procure,
With empty fist no man doth falcons lure.
Brachiano, I am now fit for thy encounter.   135
Like the wild Irish I'll ne'er think thee dead
Till I can play at football with thy head.
Flectere si nequeo superos, Acheronta movebo.   *Exit*

110 *idleness* folly; delirium
121 *halts* is defective in rhyme and measure (like this line)
  s.d. ed. (opposite l. 123 in Q)
  s.d. *Writes* ed. (he writes Q)
131 *When . . . follow* proverbial image for a cunning fox or snake, here applied to a
  man
134 *lure* i.e. train a falcon to come to the lure (a bunch of feathers held by the
  falconer resembling its prey); hence entice, tempt
136–7 *Like . . . head* The Irish were notoriously cruel and bloodthirsty.
138 *Flectere . . . movebo* 'If I cannot prevail upon the gods above, I will move the
  gods of the infernal regions' (Virgil, *Aeneid* VII, 312). This was a stock remark
  for villains in the drama.
  s.d. *Exit* ed. (Exit Mon. Q)

[Act IV, Scene ii]

Enter the MATRON, *and* FLAMINEO

MATRON
Should it be known the Duke hath such recourse
To your imprisoned sister, I were like
T'incur much damage by it.
FLAMINEO   Not a scruple.
The Pope lies on his death-bed, and their heads
Are troubled now with other business   5
Than guarding of a lady.

Enter SERVANT

SERVANT
[*Aside*] Yonder's Flamineo in conference
With the Matrona. [*To the* MATRON] Let me speak with
    you.
I would entreat you to deliver for me
This letter to the fair Vittoria –   10
MATRON
I shall sir.

Enter BRACHIANO

SERVANT   With all care and secrecy;
Hereafter you shall know me, and receive
Thanks for this courtesy.   [*Exit*]
FLAMINEO   How now? What's that?
MATRON
A letter.
FLAMINEO To my sister: I'll see't delivered.
                    [*Takes the letter. Exit* MATRON]
BRACHIANO
What's that you read Flamineo?
FLAMINEO   Look.   15

[*Gives him the letter*]

---

3 *scruple* very small quantity; with a play on the usual modern sense, a thought
    that troubles the conscience
4 *Pope . . . death-bed* Gregory XIII, historically responsible for Vittoria's imprison-
    ment in a monastery, died on 10 April 1585.
10 *letter . . . Vittoria* Francisco's letter to Vittoria becomes an important prop in
    this scene; passed rapidly from one character to another, it triggers explosive
    feeling and reinforces gesturally the heated verbal exchanges.

BRACHIANO
  Ha? [*Reads*] 'To the most unfortunate his best respected
    Vittoria – '
  Who was the messenger?
FLAMINEO   I know not.
BRACHIANO
  No! Who sent it?
FLAMINEO   Ud's foot, you speak as if a man
  Should know what fowl is coffined in a baked meat
  Afore you cut it up.   20
BRACHIANO
  I'll open't, were't her heart. What's here subscribed –
  Florence? This juggling is gross and palpable.
  I have found out the conveyance; read it, read it.

          [*Thrusts the letter at* FLAMINEO]

FLAMINEO
  (*Reads the letter*) 'Your tears I'll turn to triumphs, be
    but mine.
  Your prop is fall'n; I pity that a vine   25
  Which princes heretofore have longed to gather,
  Wanting supporters, now should fade and wither.'
  Wine i'faith, my lord, with lees would serve his turn.
  'Your sad imprisonment I'll soon uncharm,
  And with a princely uncontrolled arm   30
  Lead you to Florence, where my love and care
  Shall hang your wishes in my silver hair.'
  A halter on his strange equivocation.
  'Nor for my years return me the sad willow:

18 *Ud's foot* (By) God's foot (see III.iii.128)
19 *coffined . . . meat* i.e. enclosed in pastry or in a pie
22 ed. (Florence? / This Q)
    juggling . . . palpable i.e. this deception is plain and manifest
23 *conveyance* means of communication; cunning contrivance; document by which
    property (i.e. Vittoria) is transferred from one person to another (NCW
    IV.ii.24 n.)
24 s.d. *Reads the letter* ed. (outer r. margin ll. 24–5 in Q)
24–7 *Your . . . wither* Cf. III.ii.185–8, where Francisco describes Vittoria as a vine
    in a much less complimentary context; cf. also II.i.396–7, where in Francisco's
    analogy Brachiano is the vine and Vittoria the withered, rotting elm.
28 *Wine . . . turn* Flamineo mockingly takes Francisco's analogy literally: wine with
    its dregs (lees) can be made by gathering vines.
30 *uncontrolled* ungoverned, not subjected to control
33 *halter . . . equivocation* Flamineo calls for a rope with a noose (a halter) to
    emphasize Francisco's 'equivocation', his possibly duplicitous use of the word
    'hang' (as a threat as well as a promise).
34 *willow* sign of a rejected lover

Who prefer blossoms before fruit that's mellow?'   35
Rotten on my knowledge with lying too long i'th'
    bed-straw.
'And all the lines of age this line convinces:
The gods never wax old, no more do princes.'
A pox on't, tear it, let's have no more atheists for God's
    sake.

BRACHIANO
Ud's death, I'll cut her into atomies   40
And let th'irregular north-wind sweep her up
And blow her int' his nostrils. Where's this whore?

FLAMINEO
That – ? What do you call her?

BRACHIANO   O, I could be mad,
Prevent the curst disease she'll bring me to,
And tear my hair off. Where's this changeable stuff?   45

FLAMINEO
O'er head and ears in water, I assure you,
She is not for your wearing.

BRACHIANO   In you pander!

FLAMINEO
[*Facing him*] What me, my lord, am I your dog?

BRACHIANO
A bloodhound: do you brave? Do you stand me?

---

36 *Rotten . . . bed-straw* Fruit was ripened in straw; people could grow melancholy
    and lousy by lying too long in bed (where straw served as a mattress); cf.
    III.iii.79–82.

37 *all . . . convinces* i.e. all the wrinkles of age this line refutes; all the maxims of
    old this maxim confutes

39 *atheists* Here, Francisco is an 'atheist' because he appears to deny the Christian
    God by invoking the classical gods. Flamineo again wittily reacts with shock
    not to Francisco's attempted seduction of Vittoria but to his stale analogies.

40 *atomies* minute particles, motes

41 *irregular* disorderly

43 *That – ?* ed. (That? Q)

44–5 *Prevent . . . off* i.e. forestall the hair loss caused by venereal disease I'll con-
    tract from her by tearing out my own hair

45 *changeable stuff* inconstant whore; material such as shot or watered silk that
    shows different colours under different aspects (a sense unintended by Brach-
    iano, played on by Flamineo)

46–7 *O'er . . . wearing* i.e. literally, in deep water, thus unfit to be worn (whereas
    watered silk would be); figuratively, absorbed in weeping, and thus unfit for
    Brachiano's offered destruction

49 *bloodhound* hunter for blood (for lifeblood and for sexual passion, as in the case
    of a pander)
    brave defy
    stand withstand

FLAMINEO

Stand you? Let those that have diseases run;   50
I need no plasters.

BRACHIANO

Would you be kicked?

FLAMINEO   Would you have your neck
    broke?
I tell you duke, I am not in Russia;
My shins must be kept whole.

BRACHIANO   Do you know me?

FLAMINEO

O my lord! Methodically.   55
As in this world there are degrees of evils:
So in this world there are degrees of devils.
You're a great Duke; I your poor secretary.
I do look now for a Spanish fig, or an Italian sallet daily.

BRACHIANO

Pander, ply your convoy, and leave your prating.   60

FLAMINEO

All your kindness to me is like that miserable courtesy
of Polyphemus to Ulysses; you reserve me to be de-
voured last. You would dig turves out of my grave to
feed your larks: that would be music to you. Come, I'll
lead you to her.   [Walks backwards]   65

BRACHIANO

Do you face me?

FLAMINEO

O sir, I would not go before a politic enemy with my

---

50 *run* as in the usual sense, move away quickly; also, ooze (as from a 'running'
    sore, requiring plasters)
51–2 *I . . . plasters* / *Would . . . broke?* ed. (I . . . kickt? / FLA. Would . . . broke? Q)
52 *Would . . . broke?* Flamineo threateningly reminds Brachiano of his expert
    murder of Camillo (II.ii.37).
53–4 *I . . . whole* The Russians reputedly punished those who refused to pay their
    debts ('politic bankrupts') by beating them on the shins.
55 *Methodically* in accordance with a prescribed method
59 *Spanish fig* insulting gesture of thrusting thumb between two closed fingers or
    into the mouth; also poison; *Italian sallet* Italian salad; poisonous concoction –
    Italians being notorious in Renaissance tragedy for clever ways to kill
60 *ply . . . convoy* i.e. get on with your business (of pandering)
61–3 *miserable . . . last* In Homer's *Odyssey* (IX, 369–70), Polyphemus, a Cyclops
    (a savage one-eyed giant), promised Ulysses a hospitable gift, which turned out
    to be the vow to eat him last. In the end, Ulysses blinded the Cyclops.
63 *turves* pl. of turf
63–4 *You . . . larks* i.e. you would dig grassy slabs from my grave to feed your
    ethereal birds; figuratively, you would mutilate my body to feed your soul
66 *face* stand facing; brave, defy

back towards him, though there were behind me a
whirlpool.

Enter VITTORIA *to* BRACHIANO *and* FLAMINEO

BRACHIANO
[*Showing the letter*] Can you read, mistress? Look upon
   that letter;   70
There are no characters nor hieroglyphics.
You need no comment, I am grown your receiver;
God's precious, you shall be a brave great lady,
A stately and advanced whore.
VITTORIA   Say, sir.
BRACHIANO
Come, come, let's see your cabinet, discover   75
Your treasury of love-letters. Death and furies,
I'll see them all.
VITTORIA   Sir, upon my soul,
I have not any. Whence was this directed?
BRACHIANO
Confusion on your politic ignorance.
You are reclaimed; are you? I'll give you the bells   80
And let you fly to the devil.   [*Gives her the letter*]
FLAMINEO   Ware hawk, my lord.
VITTORIA
Florence! This is some treacherous plot, my lord,
To me he ne'er was lovely I protest,
So much as in my sleep.

69 s.d. Flamineo offers to 'lead' Brachiano to Vittoria, but the s.d. suggests that
   Vittoria enters (perhaps via the discovery space). An unsummoned entry, imitat-
   ing the force of the 'whirlpool' (l. 69), would immediately give her dramatic
   control.
71 *characters* cabbalistic or magical signs
72 *comment* commentary, explanation (of the 'hieroglyphics')
   receiver procurer, pimp
73 *God's precious* i.e. by God's precious blood (an oath)
75 *cabinet* case for letters or jewels, casket
80 *reclaimed* redeemed from a wrong course of action; (in falconry) called back,
   tamed after being let fly
80–1 *I'll . . . devil* In falconry, bells attached to the hawk's legs aided recovery of
   the prey. In his disgust, Brachiano rejects everything associated with Vittoria.
81 *Ware hawk* either, simply, 'Watch out for what *this* hawk might do (when she
   gets angry)' or 'Beware the officer who pounces upon rogues' (warning Brachiano against Vittoria's retaliation), or an imitation of the hunting call used by
   the falconer when patiently training a hawk to enjoy the rewards of its own kill
   (Dent, pp. 124–5; implying that Brachiano should reward her with his
   attentions?)
83 *lovely* amorous, affectionate; lovable, attractive

BRACHIANO   Right: they are plots.
Your beauty! O, ten thousand curses on't.   85
How long have I beheld the devil in crystal?
Thou hast led me, like an heathen sacrifice,
With music and with fatal yokes of flowers
To my eternal ruin. Woman to man
Is either a god or a wolf.
VITTORIA   [*Weeps*]   My lord.
BRACHIANO   Away.   90
We'll be as differing as two adamants:
The one shall shun the other. What? Dost weep?
Procure but ten of thy dissembling trade,
Ye'd furnish all the Irish funerals
With howling, past wild Irish.
FLAMINEO   Fie, my lord.   95
BRACHIANO
[*Takes* VITTORIA's *hand*] That hand, that cursed hand,
     which I have wearied
With doting kisses! O my sweetest Duchess
How lovely art thou now! [*To* VITTORIA] Thy loose
     thoughts
Scatter like quicksilver. I was bewitched;
For all the world speaks ill of thee.
VITTORIA   No matter.   100
I'll live so now I'll make that world recant
And change her speeches. You did name your Duchess.
BRACHIANO
Whose death God pardon.
VITTORIA   Whose death God revenge
On thee, most godless Duke.
FLAMINEO   Now for two whirlwinds.
VITTORIA
What have I gained by thee but infamy?   105
Thou hast stained the spotless honour of my house,

86 *devil in crystal* a common expression signifying self-deception, easy credulity
89–90 *Woman . . . wolf* used proverbially for the relation of man to man, and
     applied by Montaigne to marriage (*Essays*, trans. Florio III, v)
91 *adamants* loadstones, magnets
94–5 *furnish . . . Irish* According to contemporary accounts, the Irish hired women
     to mourn the dead; 'for some small recompence given them, [they] will furnish
     the cry, with greater shriking and howling, then those that are grieved indeede'.
     'To weep Irish' thus meant 'to weepe at pleasure, without cause, or griefe'
     (Rich, *A New Description of Ireland* (1610), p. 13).
96–8 The gesture recalls Brachiano's divorce from Isabella by kissing her hand
     (II.i.192).
104 *two* ed. (tow Q)

And frighted thence noble society:
Like those which, sick o'th'palsy, and retain
Ill-scenting foxes 'bout them, are still shunned
By those of choicer nostrils. What do you call this
   house?   110
Is this your palace? Did not the judge style it
A house of penitent whores? Who sent me to it?
Who hath the honour to advance Vittoria
To this incontinent college? Is't not you?
Is't not your high preferment? Go, go brag   115
How many ladies you have undone, like me.
Fare you well sir; let me hear no more of you.
I had a limb corrupted to an ulcer,
But I have cut it off: and now I'll go
Weeping to heaven on crutches. For your gifts,   120
I will return them all; and I do wish
That I could make you full executor
To all my sins – O that I could toss myself
Into a grave as quickly: for all thou art worth
I'll not shed one tear more – I'll burst first.   125

Throws herself [face down] upon a bed [and weeps]

BRACHIANO
I have drunk Lethe. Vittoria?
My dearest happiness? Vittoria?
What do you ail my love? Why do you weep?

VITTORIA
[*Turns to him*] Yes, I now weep poniards, do you see.

---

110 *those ... nostrils* Foxes, known for their foul odour, were commonly used in
    the treatment of the palsy (a disease characterized by involuntary tremors or
    paralysis).
115 *preferment* promotion
118 *I ... ulcer* The historic Brachiano had a malignant ulcer in his leg.
119–120 *I ... crutches* An echo of St Mark 9.45: 'And if thy foot offend thee, cut
    it off: it is better for thee to enter halt into life, than having two feet to be cast
    into hell'.
125 s.d. *Throws* ed. (She throws Q)
125 s.d. *Throws ... bed* The bed may be thrust out on the stage at the beginning of
    the scene, or, perhaps, upon Vittoria's entry (l. 69). Vittoria's dramatic physical
    gesture, more than her words, seems to precipitate Brachiano's abrupt change
    of heart.
126 *Lethe* river of oblivion, forgetfulness
126–7 *I ... Vittoria?* ed. (I ... Lethe / Vittoria? ... Vittoria? Q)
129 *poniards* daggers (suggesting her anger as well as grief)

BRACHIANO
　Are not those matchless eyes mine?
VITTORIA   I had rather   130
　They were not matches.
BRACHIANO   Is not this lip mine?
VITTORIA
　[*Turning away*] Yes: thus to bite it off, rather than give
　　it thee.
FLAMINEO
　Turn to my lord, good sister.
VITTORIA   Hence you pander.
FLAMINEO
　Pander! Am I the author of your sin?
VITTORIA
　Yes: he's a base thief that a thief lets in.   135
FLAMINEO
　We're blown up, my lord –
BRACHIANO   Wilt thou hear me?
　Once to be jealous of thee is t'express
　That I will love thee everlastingly,
　And never more be jealous.
VITTORIA   O thou fool,
　Whose greatness hath by much o'ergrown thy wit!   140
　What dar'st thou do that I not dare to suffer,
　Excepting to be still thy whore? For that,
　In the sea's bottom sooner thou shalt make
　A bonfire.
FLAMINEO   O, no oaths for God's sake.
BRACHIANO
　Will you hear me?
VITTORIA   Never.   145
FLAMINEO
　What a damned imposthume is a woman's will?
　Can nothing break it? Fie, fie, my lord.
　Women are caught as you take tortoises,

130–1 *I . . . matches* a play on 'matchless' as 'not matches'. i.e. I had rather my eyes
　　were not symmetrical. Vittoria's desire to thwart an unwanted lover by mutilat-
　　ing herself recalls Celia's in *Volpone* III.vii.251–7.
136 *blown up* shattered, as by the explosion of a mine
146 *imposthume* abscess, festering sore
146–65 Flamineo is playing his part as pander by encouraging each of the lovers to
　　move towards reconciliation; it is unclear, however, whether his lines are asides
　　directed at Brachiano and Vittoria in turn or delivered openly in the hearing of
　　both. The choice is ultimately the actor's; however, given Flamineo's generally
　　open misogyny (cf. I.ii.113–18, 196–9), the latter seems more likely.
148–9 *Women . . . back* To catch tortoises one need only turn them on their backs.

She must be turned on her back. Sister, by this hand
I am on your side. Come, come, you have wronged her. 150
What a strange credulous man were you, my lord,
To think the Duke of Florence would love her?
Will any mercer take another's ware
When once 'tis toused and sullied? And yet sister,
How scurvily this frowardness becomes you!   155
Young leverets stand not long; and women's anger
Should, like their flight, procure a little sport;
A full cry for a quarter of an hour;
And then be put to th'dead quat.

BRACHIANO   Shall these eyes,
Which have so long time dwelt upon your face,   160
Be now put out?

FLAMINEO   No cruel landlady i'th'world,
Which lends forth groats to broom-men, and takes use
    for them
Would do't.
Hand her, my lord, and kiss her: be not like
A ferret to let go your hold with blowing.   165

BRACHIANO
Let us renew right hands.

VITTORIA   Hence.

BRACHIANO
Never shall rage, or the forgetful wine,
Make me commit like fault.

FLAMINEO
Now you are i'th'way on't, follow't hard.

BRACHIANO
Be thou at peace with me; let all the world   170
Threaten the cannon.

FLAMINEO   Mark his penitence.
Best natures do commit the grossest faults

---

153 *mercer* merchant dealing in silks, velvets and other costly materials
154 *toused* rumpled; (of a woman) abused, roughly handled
155 *frowardness* naughtiness, perversity
156 *leverets* young hares (once thought to be all female); mistresses
     stand hold out (in the hunt)
158 *full cry* full pursuit (of the hounds); open weeping
159 *quat* squat (position taken by a cornered hare)
162 i.e. who lends pennies to street-sweepers and earns interest on them
162 *them* ed. (the Q)
164 *Hand* fondle
164–5 *be . . . blowing* Blowing at a ferret forces it to let go of the thing its teeth are
     fixed in.
167 *forgetful* inducing forgetfulness

When they're giv'n o'er to jealousy; as best wine
Dying makes strongest vinegar. I'll tell you;
The sea's more rough and raging than calm rivers,   175
But nor so sweet nor wholesome. A quiet woman
Is a still water under a great bridge.
A man may shoot her safely.

VITTORIA
O ye dissembling men!

FLAMINEO   We sucked that, sister,
From women's breasts in our first infancy.   180

VITTORIA
To add misery to misery.

BRACHIANO   Sweetest.

VITTORIA
Am I not low enough?
Ay, ay, your good heart gathers like a snowball
Now your affection's cold.

FLAMINEO   Ud's foot, it shall melt
To a heart again, or all the wine in Rome   185
Shall run o'th'lees for't.

VITTORIA
Your dog or hawk should be rewarded better
Than I have been. I'll speak not one word more.

FLAMINEO
Stop her mouth
With a sweet kiss, my lord.   190

[BRACHIANO *embraces* VITTORIA]

So now the tide's turned the vessel's come about.
He's a sweet armful. O we curled-haired men
Are still most kind to women. This is well.

BRACHIANO
[*To* VITTORIA] That you should chide thus!

FLAMINEO   O, sir,
your little chimneys
Do ever cast most smoke. I sweat for you.   195
Couple together with as deep a silence
As did the Grecians in their wooden horse.

177 *great bridge* like London Bridge, which was impassable when tides ran high
178 *shoot* descend (a river) swiftly (in a boat or other vessel); penetrate sexually
178–81 ed. (A Man ... men! / Wee ... first / first ... Sweetest. Q)
184 *Ud's foot* ed. (Ud'foot Q)
187 *rewarded* (in hunting) given part of the prey they have helped to kill (and thus
    encouraged to continue hunting)
193 *still* always

My lord, supply your promises with deeds.
'You know that painted meat no hunger feeds.'
BRACHIANO
    Stay – ingrateful Rome.   200
FLAMINEO
    Rome! It deserves to be called Barbary, for our
        villainous usage.
BRACHIANO
    Soft; the same project which the Duke of Florence
    (Whether in love or gullery I know not)
    Laid down for her escape, will I pursue.
FLAMINEO
    And no time fitter than this night, my lord;   205
    The Pope being dead; and all the cardinals entered
    The conclave for th'electing a new Pope;
    The city in a great confusion;
    We may attire her in a page's suit,
    Lay her post-horse, take shipping, and amain   210
    For Padua.
BRACHIANO
    I'll instantly steal forth the Prince Giovanni,
    And make for Padua. You two with your old mother
    And young Marcello that attends on Florence,
    If you can work him to it, follow me.   215
    I will advance you all: for you Vittoria,
    Think of a Duchess' title.
FLAMINEO   Lo you sister.
    Stay, my lord, I'll tell you a tale. The crocodile, which
    lives in the river Nilus, hath a worm breeds i'th'teeth

197 *Grecians . . . horse* The Greeks won the Trojan war by presenting a large wooden
    horse as a gift to the Trojans. It was taken into Troy and the Greeks hidden
    inside it emerged to effect a victory.
200 *Stay . . . Rome* ed. (Stay ingratefull Rome. Q) Rome was proverbially ungrateful
    to Romans.
201 *Barbary* land of barbarians (in northern Africa)
203 *gullery* deception
210–11 *Lay . . . Padua* i.e. provide her with relays of post-horses, embark and sail
    with all speed to Padua
218–31 *Stay . . . patient* Webster borrows this tale from Topsell, *History of Serpents*
    (1608), pp. 135–6, and possibly from Africanus, *History and Description of Africa*
    (1600). He invents the crocodile's motive for wanting to swallow the bird ('that
    the bird may not talk largely of her abroad for non-payment'), adding a human
    concern for reward (clearly at stake in the scene) to a story of animal savagery.
    Brachiano and Flamineo suggest different interpretations of the tale; critics have
    found still others. Its precise meaning is less important than the symbiosis
    among the characters it illuminates: all three are locked into complex relation-
    ships in which desire and self-interest, love and cruelty, are inextricable.

of't, which puts it to extreme anguish: a little bird, no   220
bigger than a wren, is barber-surgeon to this crocodile;
flies into the jaws of't; picks out the worm; and brings
present remedy. The fish, glad of ease but ingrateful to
her that did it, that the bird may not talk largely of her
abroad for non-payment, closeth her chaps intending to   225
swallow her and so put her to perpetual silence. But
nature loathing such ingratitude, hath armed this bird
with a quill or prick on the head, top o'th'which wounds
the crocodile i'th'mouth, forceth her open her bloody
prison, and away flies the pretty tooth-picker from her   230
cruel patient.

BRACHIANO
Your application is, I have not rewarded
The service you have done me.

FLAMINEO   No my lord.
You sister are the crocodile: you are blemished in your
fame, my lord cures it. And though the comparison hold   235
not in every particle; yet observe, remember, what good
the bird with the prick i'th'head hath done you; and
scorn ingratitude.
[Aside] It may appear to some ridiculous
Thus to talk knave and madman; and sometimes   240
Come in with a dried sentence, stuffed with sage.
But this allows my varying of shapes,
'Knaves do grow great by being great men's apes'.

                                        Exeunt

[Act IV, Scene iii]

Enter LODOVICO, GASPARO, *and six Ambassadors. At
another door* [FRANCISCO] *the Duke of Florence*

FRANCISCO
[*To* LODOVICO] So, my lord, I commend your diligence –
Guard well the conclave, and, as the order is,
Let none have conference with the cardinals.

---

221 *barber-surgeon* Barbers acted as dentists in Webster's time.
241 *sentence* aphorism, maxim
        sage culinary herb; wisdom (cf. I.ii.135)
   0 s.d. ed. (Enter Francisco, Lodovico, Gasper, and sixe Embassadours Q)
        This scene is unique in the play for its indebtedness to a single source,
        Hierome Bignon's *A Briefe, but an Effectuall Treatise of the Election of Popes*. This
        eyewitness account of a papal election in Rome in 1605 (just seven years before
        the first performance of *The White Devil*) furnishes many of the details in the

LODOVICO
I shall, my lord. Room for the ambassadors –

[*The* AMBASSADORS *pass over the stage*]

GASPARO
They're wondrous brave today: why do they wear   5
These several habits?
LODOVICO   O sir, they're knights
Of several orders.
That lord i'th'black cloak with the silver cross
Is Knight of Rhodes; the next Knight of S. Michael;
That of the Golden Fleece; the Frenchman there   10
Knight of the Holy Ghost; my lord of Savoy

---

scene, and may even suggest stage action Webster had in mind but failed to
record fully in the printed text.

1–3 Webster opens the scene at a dramatic point in the papal election. Francisco
intercepts Lodovico as he guards the ambassadors' passage from the conclave
after they have solicited the cardinals on behalf of their own rulers. The conclave
must now be completely sealed off from the outside world until a new Pope is
elected (cf. ll. 27–32).

2 *conclave* place in which the cardinals meet in private for the election of a Pope.
In Rome, the conclave is in the Sistine chapel.

4 s.d. The theatrical spectacle of the passage of the ambassadors, magnificently
dressed as knights of venerable orders, allows Webster to feast the eyes of the
Red Bull audience while emphasizing by implied contrast the sinister perversion
of honour and ceremony by Monticelso and Francisco. (I am indebted to NCW
III.i.61 n. for identification of ambassadors with knights.)

4–17 Like Monticelso in III.ii.322–42, Francisco may be conversing with the
ambassadors while they are observed by Lodovico and Gasparo from a peri-
pheral position on the stage.

5 *brave* finely dressed

6 *several* various

9 *Rhodes* The order of the Knights of St John of Jerusalem, founded during the
First Crusade, moved from Jerusalem to Rhodes, and finally to Malta, granted
by Charles V in 1530. According to W. Segar's *Honour, Military and Civil*
(1602), they wore 'a white Crosse upon a blacke garment' (p. 97).

S. Michael Knights of this order (founded in 1469 by Louis XI) wore a richly
embroidered mantle and hood of cloth of silver over white doublet, hose and
shoes.

10 *Golden Fleece* Spanish ambassador. Knights of this order (founded in 1429 by
Philip Duke of Burgundy) wore a hood and mantle of crimson velvet with a
border of flames and fleeces; from their distinctive collar hung a fleece of
wrought gold ('which signifieth *Iustice uncorrupted*' (Segar, p. 80)).

11 *Holy Ghost* French ambassador. Knights of this order (founded in 1578 by
Henry III) wore mantles of black velvet embroidered with gold and silver and
decorated with capes of embroidered green cloth of silver, lined with orange
satin, over white doublet and hose.

Knight of th'Annunciation; the Englishman
Is Knight of th'honoured Garter, dedicated
Unto their saint, S. George. I could describe to you
Their several institutions, with the laws   15
Annexed to their orders, but that time
Permits not such discovery.
FRANCISCO   Where's Count Lodowick?
LODOVICO
Here my lord.
FRANCISCO   'Tis o'th'point of dinner time;
Marshall the cardinals' service.
LODOVICO   Sir, I shall.

Enter SERVANTS *with several dishes covered*

Stand, let me search your dish; who's this for?   20
SERVANT
For my Lord Cardinal Monticelso.
LODOVICO
Whose this?
SERVANT   For my Lord Cardinal of Bourbon.
FRENCH AMBASSADOR
Why doth he search the dishes? To observe
What meat is dressed?
ENGLISH AMBASSADOR   No sir, but to prevent
Lest any letters should be conveyed in   25
To bribe or to solicit the advancement
Of any cardinal; when first they enter
'Tis lawful for the ambassadors of princes
To enter with them, and to make their suit
For any man their prince affecteth best;   30
But after, till a general election
No man may speak with them.

---

12 *Annunciation* Savoy ambassador. Knights of this order (founded in 1362 by
   Amadeus VI of Savoy and the highest order of knights in Italy) wore white satin
   with a cloak of purple velvet along with the gold collar of their order.
13 *Garter* English ambassador. Knights of this order (founded in 1350 by Edward
   III) wore a mantle of purple velvet over a gown of crimson velvet; over the right
   shoulder hung a hood of crimson velvet lined with white. Around their necks
   these knights wore a pure gold chain worked in garters and knots, and enam-
   elled with white and red roses, from which hung the image of St George, worked
   in precious stones. Around their left legs they wore a garter worked in gold,
   pearl and stones, with the motto HONI SOIT QUI MAL Y PENSE ('Shame to him
   that evill thinketh').
19 s.d. ed. (to r. of ll. 19–22 in Q)
24 *meat* food
   dressed prepared

LODOVICO
    You that attend on the lord cardinals
    Open the window, and receive their viands.
A CARDINAL
    [*At the window*] You must return the service; the lord
        cardinals   35
    Are busied 'bout electing of the Pope;
    They have given o'er scrutiny, and are fallen
    To admiration.
LODOVICO   Away, away.
                              [*Exeunt* SERVANTS *with dishes*]
FRANCISCO
    I'll lay a thousand ducats you hear news
    Of a Pope presently – hark; sure he's elected –   40

    [*The*] *Cardinal* [*of* ARRAGON *appears*] *on the terrace*

Behold! My Lord of Arragon appears
On the church battlements.
ARRAGON
    [*Holding up a cross*] *Denuntio vobis gaudium magnum. Rev-*
    erendissimus Cardinalis Lorenzo de Monticelso electus est in
    sedem apostolicam, et elegit sibi nomen Paulum quartum.   45
OMNES
    Vivat Sanctus Pater Paulus Quartus.

                    [*Enter* SERVANT]

35 s.d. *window* probably a grating or wicket in a stage door, or perhaps a stage-level
    window (NCW IV.iii.35 n.)
37 *scrutiny* taking of individual votes. The cardinals voted until a two-thirds major-
    ity elected a new Pope.
38 *admiration* adoration: means of papal election by divine inspiration. The car-
    dinals turned and kneeled before the one they desired to be made Pope; when
    they saw that two-thirds had done so, the Pope was elected. Bignon comments
    that this method is not as lawful as voting, 'because by meanes of contentions,
    and partialities, there may be some fraude or violence committed therein, in
    that the weaker side may be drawne to Adoration by the example of those more
    mightie, and those fearful, induced by them more resolute' (Brown, p. 196).
    Papal elections (like that of the real Montalto) were often decided in this way.
40 s.d. ed. (to r. of ll. 39–40 in Q)
    terrace i.e. the upper stage
42 s.d. Since Webster follows Bignon closely verbally here, he may intend the
    accompanying action: 'he shewes forth a Crosse'.
43–7 *Denuntio . . . Quartus* i.e. 'I announce to you tidings of great joy. The Most
    Reverend Cardinal Lorenzo di Monticelso has been elected to the Apostolic
    See, and has chosen for himself the name of Paul IV.' ALL: 'Long live the Holy
    Father Paul IV.' In fact, the historical Cardinal Montalto became Pope
    Sixtus V.

SERVANT
  Vittoria my lord –
FRANCISCO   Well: what of her?
SERVANT
  Is fled the city –
FRANCISCO   Ha?
SERVANT   With Duke Brachiano.
FRANCISCO
  Fled? Where's the Prince Giovanni?
SERVANT   Gone with his
    father.   50
FRANCISCO
  Let the Matrona of the convertites
  Be apprehended: fled – O damnable!

                              [*Exit* SERVANT]
  How fortunate are my wishes. Why? 'Twas this
  I only laboured. I did send the letter
  T'instruct him what to do. Thy fame, fond Duke,   55
  I first have poisoned; directed thee the way
  To marry a whore; what can be worse? This follows.
  The hand must act to drown the passionate tongue,
  I scorn to wear a sword and prate of wrong.

          Enter MONTICELSO *in state* [*in pontifical robes*]

MONTICELSO
  Concedimus vobis apostolicam benedictionem et remissionem   60
  peccatorum.   [FRANCISCO *whispers to him*]
  My lord reports Vittoria Corombona
  Is stol'n from forth the house of convertites
  By Brachiano, and they're fled the city.
  Now, though this be the first day of our seat,   65
  We cannot better please the divine power
  Than to sequester from the holy church
  These cursed persons. Make it therefore known,

48–50 ed. (*Vittoria* ... Lord. / FRAN. Wel ... Ha? / SER. With ... *Giovanni* / SER.
    Gone ... father. Q)

51–3 The speech illustrates the gap between public and private. Francisco's first
    two lines are spoken for the benefit of the ambassadors; the rest are addressed
    to Lodovico and the audience (NCW IV.iii.52, 53 n.).

55 *fond* foolish; infatuated

60–1 *Concedimus* ... *peccatorum* 'We grant you the Apostolic blessing and remis-
    sion of sins.' This Latin benediction was added by Webster during press correc-
    tion, perhaps a verbal expansion of stage business already implicit in Mon-
    ticelso's entry 'in state'.

65 *seat* technical term for the throne or office of a Pope. Monticelso may be carried
    on and offstage in the 'great and high Pontificall Chayre' described by Bignon.

We do denounce excommunication
Against them both: all that are theirs in Rome   70
We likewise banish. Set on.
                Exeunt [all except FRANCISCO *and* LODOVICO]
FRANCISCO
Come dear Lodovico.
You have ta'en the sacrament to prosecute
Th'intended murder.
LODOVICO   With all constancy.
But, sir, I wonder you'll engage yourself,   75
In person, being a great prince.
FRANCISCO   Divert me not.
Most of his court are of my faction,
And some are of my counsel. Noble friend,
Our danger shall be 'like in this design;
Give leave, part of the glory may be mine.   [*Bows*]   80
                                                        Exit

            Enter MONTICELSO [LODOVICO *kneels*]

MONTICELSO
Why did the Duke of Florence with such care
Labour your pardon? Say.
LODOVICO
Italian beggars will resolve you that
Who, begging of an alms, bid those they beg of
Do good for their own sakes; or't may be   85
He spreads his bounty with a sowing hand,
Like kings, who many times give out of measure
Not for desert so much as for their pleasure.
MONTICELSO
I know you're cunning. Come, what devil was that
That you were raising?
LODOVICO   Devil, my lord?
[MONTICELSO]   I ask you   90
How doth the Duke employ you, that his bonnet
Fell with such compliment unto his knee
When he departed from you?
LODOVICO   Why, my lord,
He told me of a resty Barbary horse

---

80 *Exit* ed. (Exit Fran. Q)   81–2 Cf. III.iii.98.
86 *sowing* scattering (like seed); presumably, in hope of reaping
87 *out of measure* excessively
89 *cunning* sly, crafty; possessing magical skill (to raise or conjure devils)
90 MONTICELSO . . . *you* ed. (I aske you / MONT. How . . . bonnet Q)
94 *resty* restive, intractable, stubborn
    Barbary horse small, swift and hot-tempered horse from Barbary

Which he would fain have brought to the career,   95
The 'sault, and the ring-galliard. Now, my lord,
I have a rare French rider.
MONTICELSO   Take you heed:
Lest the jade break your neck. Do you put me off
With your wild horse-tricks? Sirrah you do lie.
O, thou'rt a foul black cloud, and thou dost threat   100
A violent storm.
LODOVICO   Storms are i'th'air, my lord;
I am too low to storm.
MONTICELSO   Wretched creature!
I know that thou art fashioned for all ill,
Like dogs that once get blood, they'll ever kill.
About some murder? Was't not?
LODOVICO   I'll not tell you;   105
And yet I care not greatly if I do;
Marry with this preparation. Holy Father,
I come not to you as an intelligencer,
But as a penitent sinner. What I utter
Is in confession merely; which you know   110
Must never be revealed.
MONTICELSO   You have o'erta'en me.
LODOVICO
Sir I did love Brachiano's Duchess dearly;
Or rather I pursued her with hot lust,
Though she ne'er knew on't. She was poisoned;
Upon my soul she was: for which I have sworn   115
T'avenge her murder.
MONTICELSO   To the Duke of Florence?
LODOVICO
To him I have.
MONTICELSO   Miserable creature!
If thou persist in this, 'tis damnable.

---

95 *career* a gallop at full speed brought up short
96 *'sault* leaps and vaults
   ring-galliard a mixture of bounding forward and lashing out with the heels
97 *French rider* The French were supposed to be excellent horsemen and promiscuous lovers (hence prone to syphilis).
98 *jade* ill-tempered horse; woman (used pejoratively)
99 *horse-tricks* exercises in the horse's manage; horseplay
102 *I . . . storm* Lodovico refers both to his social status and (perhaps) to his physical
    position as he kneels before Monticelso.
108 *intelligencer* spy, informer
111 *o'erta'en* i.e. caught, ensnared (with an unexpected event)

Dost thou imagine thou canst slide on blood
And not be tainted with a shameful fall?   120
Or, like the black, and melancholic yew-tree,
Dost think to root thyself in dead men's graves,
And yet to prosper? Instruction to thee
Comes like sweet showers to over-hard'ned ground:
They wet, but pierce not deep. And so I leave thee   125
With all the Furies hanging 'bout thy neck,
Till by thy penitence thou remove this evil,
In conjuring from thy breast that cruel devil.   *Exit*
LODOVICO
I'll give it o'er. He says 'tis damnable:
Besides I did expect his suffrage   130
By reason of Camillo's death.

Enter SERVANT *and* FRANCISCO

FRANCISCO
Do you know that count?
SERVANT   Yes, my lord.
FRANCISCO
Bear him these thousand ducats to his lodging;
Tell him the Pope hath sent them. Happily
That will confirm more than all the rest.   [*Exit*]
SERVANT   [*Giving money to* LODOVICO]   Sir.   135
LODOVICO
To me sir?
SERVANT
His Holiness hath sent you a thousand crowns,
And wills you if you travel, to make him
Your patron for intelligence.
LODOVICO   His creature
Ever to be commanded.   140
                              [*Exit* SERVANT]

119 *slide* slip
120 *tainted* injured; convicted, proven guilty
121 *yew-tree* Cf. I.ii.241. For the audience, the image may connect Lodovico with
    his victim, Brachiano (the yew/you of I.ii).
126 *Furies* Cf. I.ii.268 n.
128 s.d. ed. (to r. of l. 129 in Q)
    s.d. *Exit* ed. (Exit Mon. Q)
130 *suffrage* support, assistance; prayers, liturgical intercessory petitions
131 s.d. ed. (to r. of ll. 131–2 in Q)
135 s.d. Francisco may exit or withdraw to observe (NCW IV.iii.135 n.).
138 *wills* ed. (will Q)
139 *intelligence* secret information or news
139–40 *Your . . . commanded* ed. (one line in Q)

Why now 'tis come about. He railed upon me;
And yet these crowns were told out and laid ready
Before he knew my voyage. O the art,
The modest form of greatness! That do sit
Like brides at wedding dinners, with their looks turned   145
From the least wanton jests, their puling stomach
Sick of the modesty, when their thoughts are loose,
Even acting of those hot and lustful sports
Are to ensue about midnight: such his cunning!
He sounds my depth thus with a golden plummet;   150
I am doubly armed now. Now to th'act of blood;
There's but three Furies found in spacious hell;
But in a great man's breast three thousand dwell.

                                                  [*Exit*]

[Act V, Scene i]

A passage over the stage of BRACHIANO, FLAMINEO,
MARCELLO, HORTENSIO, [VITTORIA] COROMBONA, CORNELIA,
ZANCHE *and others*
                    [*Exeunt all but* FLAMINEO *and* HORTENSIO]

FLAMINEO
In all the weary minutes of my life
Day ne'er broke up till now. This marriage
Confirms me happy.
HORTENSIO   'Tis a good assurance.
Saw you not yet the Moor that's come to court?

142 *told out* counted out
143 *art* ed. (Art Q)
144 *form* customary method; outward appearance
145–9 Lodovico's simile anticipates the wedding that opens Act V.
146 *puling* weak, sickly
147 *loose* unchaste
150 *plummet* ball of lead attached to a line to measure depth (here, money)
152–3 *There's . . . dwell* These lines turn Monticelso's own words (ll. 125–8) back
  on himself.
  0 s.d. This is probably a wedding procession, with Brachiano and Vittoria splen-
      didly dressed (the latter with her hair flowing loose and sprinkled with arras
      powder). Though Lodovico's final speech in IV.iii, on the hypocrisy of appar-
      ently virtuous brides, must cast a shadow over this procession, the presence of
      Marcello and Cornelia – and possibly, among the 'others', the ambassadors (ll.
      58–60), still dressed in magnificent robes – emphasizes the lovers' new stature,
      despite their excommunication in the previous scene. Typically in Webster, a
      formal public moment rapidly gives way to private commentary.
  2 *up till* until

FLAMINEO
  Yes, and conferred with him i'th'Duke's closet;   5
  I have not seen a goodlier personage
  Nor ever talked with man better experienced
  In state affairs or rudiments of war.
  He hath by report served the Venetian
  In Candy these twice seven years, and been chief   10
  In many a bold design.
HORTENSIO   What are those two
  That bear him company?
FLAMINEO
  Two noblemen of Hungary, that living in the emperor's
  service as commanders, eight years since, contrary to
  the expectation of all the court entered into religion,   15
  into the strict order of Capuchins: but being not well
  settled in their undertaking they left their order and
  returned to court: for which being after troubled in con-
  science, they vowed their service against the enemies of
  Christ; went to Malta; were there knighted; and in their   20
  return back, at this great solemnity, they are resolved
  for ever to forsake the world, and settle themselves here
  in a house of Capuchins in Padua.
HORTENSIO
  'Tis strange.
FLAMINEO
  One thing makes it so. They have vowed for ever to   25
  wear next their bare bodies those coats of mail they
  served in.
HORTENSIO
  Hard penance. Is the Moor a Christian?
FLAMINEO
  He is.
HORTENSIO
  Why proffers he his service to our Duke?   30

---

10 *Candy* Crete, and, by ironic metaphoric extension, death. Flamineo's apparent
   obliviousness to the pun he himself made earlier (cf. II.i.290) suggests his new
   loss of linguistic and thus dramatic control.
16 *Capuchins* order of monks established in 1528 to restore the original austerity
   and simplicity of the Franciscans. The pun on the name of the Duke of Florence, here submerged, surfaces at V.iii.38. Capuchins derived their name from
   their long, pointed hoods, a useful disguise for Gasparo and Lodovico. This
   circular account of the career of the supposed Capuchins, with its alternation
   of militarism and religious devotion, is probably designed to arouse suspicion
   in the minds of the audience.
28–9 *Hard . . . is* ed. (ued . . . penance / Is . . . is. Q)

FLAMINEO

Because he understands there's like to grow
Some wars between us and the Duke of Florence,
In which he hopes employment.
I never saw one in a stern bold look
Wear more command, nor in a lofty phrase   35
Express more knowing, or more deep contempt
Of our slight airy courtiers. He talks
As if he had travelled all the princes' courts
Of Christendom; in all things strives t'express,
That all that should dispute with him may know: 40
Glories, like glow-worms, afar off shine bright
But looked to near, have neither heat nor light.
The Duke.

Enter BRACHIANO, [FRANCISCO, *Duke of*] *Florence
disguised like Mulinassar;* LODOVICO, ANTONELLI, GASPARO
[*all disguised*]; FERNESE *bearing their swords and
helmets;* [CARLO *and* PEDRO]

BRACHIANO

You are nobly welcome. We have heard at full
Your honourable service 'gainst the Turk.   45
To you, brave Mulinassar, we assign
A competent pension: and are inly sorrow,
The vows of those two worthy gentlemen
Make them incapable of our proffered bounty.
Your wish is you may leave your warlike swords   50

33 no s.d. ed. (Enter Duke Brachiano Q)
41-2 *Glories . . . light* Fond of this phrase (borrowed from Alexander's *Alexandrean
   Tragedy*), Webster reused it in *The Duchess of Malfi* (IV.ii.141-2). Here, Flamineo again misses the dramatic irony of his own words on the deceptiveness of
   outward appearances. Since Alexander's lines are a comment on the futility of
   princely ambition, the irony may also encompass Francisco as well as Brachiano
   (a 'glow-worm' or 'proud fool' was applied contemptuously to persons after
   1624), as they both enter while Flamineo speaks.
43 s.d. *CARLO . . . PEDRO* While it is possible (and some editors maintain) that Carlo
   and Pedro (who appear in speech prefixes at ll. 63 and 65) are names taken by
   Lodovico and Gasparo in disguise, it is more likely that they are separate characters, members of Brachiano's court who are of Francisco's faction (IV.iii.77).
   Thus the 'moles' welcome Francisco and his travelling companions at l. 65
   (with 'all things ready' for the murder), witness Marcello's death – possibly
   bearing his body to Cornelia's lodging (V.ii.71) – and appear in the final masque
   and murder to 'strike [Flamineo, Vittoria and Zanche] with a joint motion'
   (V.vi.229-30) and taste the justice of Giovanni (V.vi.290). The presence of
   conspirators inside Brachiano's own court may emphasize his self-destruction;
   in *Antony and Cleopatra*, Caesar plants defectors in the front lines 'That Antony
   may seem to spend his fury / Upon himself' (IV.vi.9-10).

For monuments in our chapel. I accept it
As a great honour done me, and must crave
Your leave to furnish out our Duchess' revels.
Only one thing, as the last vanity
You e'er shall view, deny me not to stay   55
To see a barriers prepared tonight.
You shall have private standings: it hath pleased
The great ambassadors of several princes
In their return from Rome to their own countries
To grace our marriage, and to honour me   60
With such a kind of sport.
FRANCISCO   I shall persuade them
  To stay, my lord.
[BRACHIANO]   Set on there to the presence.

          Exeunt BRACHIANO, FLAMINEO *and* [HORTENSIO]

CARLO
  Noble my lord, most fortunately welcome,

                The conspirators here embrace

You have our vows sealed with the sacrament
To second your attempts.
PEDRO   And all things ready.   65
  He could not have invented his own ruin,
  Had he despaired, with more propriety.
LODOVICO
  You would not take my way.
FRANCISCO   'Tis better ordered.
LODOVICO
  T'have poisoned his prayer book, or a pair of beads,
  The pommel of his saddle, his looking-glass,   70

---

56 *barriers* Cf I.ii.28–30. In January 1610 and again in January 1612 (probably just
   before the first performance of *The White Devil*), Prince Henry fought at barriers
   at Whitehall (carefully staged by Ben Jonson and Inigo Jones in 1610). Webster
   composed an elegy (*A Monumental Columne*) for Prince Henry after his sudden
   death in 1612, mourning the loss of this popular chivalric hero.
62 ed. (To . . . Lord / Set . . . presence Q) Most editors assign the final command
   to Brachiano, but Webster may want to suggest Francisco's control in Brachiano's court.
   presence presence chamber
   s.p. *BRACHIANO* ed. (not in Q)
   s.d. *HORTENSIO* ed. (Marcello Q). Unless Marcello remains silent, he probably
   passes over the stage and exits with the rest at the opening of the scene. The
   exit is probably intended for Hortensio, who has spoken, rather than Marcello.
63 s.d. ed. (to r. of ll. 63–5 in Q)
70 *pommel . . . saddle* Edward Squire, a Catholic conspirator, was hanged in 1598
   for poisoning the pommel of the Queen's saddle. The contemporary allusion

Or th'handle of his racket – O that, that!
That while he had been bandying at tennis,
He might have sworn himself to hell, and struck
His soul into the hazard! O my lord!
I would have our plot be ingenious,   75
And have it hereafter recorded for example
Rather than borrow example.
FRANCISCO   There's no way
More speeding than this thought on.
LODOVICO   On then.
FRANCISCO
And yet methinks that this revenge is poor,
Because it steals upon him like a thief;   80
To have ta'en him by the casque in a pitched field,
Led him to Florence!
LODOVICO   It had been rare. – And there
Have crowned him with a wreath of stinking garlic.
T'have shown the sharpness of his government,
And rankness of his lust. Flamineo comes.   85

> *Exeunt* LODOVICO, ANTONELLI [*and*
> GASPARO, FERNESE, CARLO, PEDRO]

[FRANCISCO *stands apart*]

Enter FLAMINEO, MARCELLO *and* ZANCHE

MARCELLO
Why doth this devil haunt you? Say.
FLAMINEO   I know not.
For by this light I do not conjure for her.
'Tis not so great a cunning as men think
To raise the devil: for here's one up already;
The greatest cunning were to lay him down.   90

---

strengthens Webster's association of Brachiano with legitimate power and his
enemies with popish heresy.
72–4 *bandying . . . hazard* Brachiano has earlier been identified with the aristocratic
game of tennis (II.i.53). Here Lodovico, like Hamlet, is bent on destroying his
enemy's soul as well as his body. In the image, Brachiano's soul is a tennis ball
struck into the 'hazard' (an opening in the inner wall of the royal tennis court;
also risk or peril).
81 *ta'en . . . field* i.e. seized him by the helmet in a field planned for battle; the
honorable military alternative
85 ed. (And . . . lust / Flamineo comes. Q)
   s.d. ed. (to r. of ll. 84–6 in Q)
89–90 *raise . . . down* The joke is Flamineo's bawdy attempt to defend his mistress
(cf. *Romeo and Juliet* II.i.23–9): the 'devil' is not (as first appears) Zanche, but
Flamineo's own erection, which must be laid down through his mistress's
'cunning'.

MARCELLO
  She is your shame.
FLAMINEO   I prithee pardon her.
  In faith you see, women are like to burs;
  Where their affection throws them, there they'll stick.
ZANCHE
  [*Motioning towards* FRANCISCO] That is my countryman,
    a goodly person;
  When he's at leisure I'll discourse with him   95
  In our own language.
FLAMINEO   I beseech you do –

                                        Exit ZANCHE

  How is't brave soldier? O that I had seen
  Some of your iron days! I pray relate
  Some of your service to us.
FRANCISCO
  'Tis a ridiculous thing for a man to be his own chron-   100
  icle; I did never wash my mouth with mine own praise
  for fear of getting a stinking breath.
MARCELLO
  You're too stoical. The Duke will expect other dis-
  course from you.
FRANCISCO
  I shall never flatter him, I have studied man too much   105
  to do that. What difference is between the Duke and I?
  No more than between two bricks; all made of one clay.
  Only 't may be one is placed on the top of a turret; the
  other in the bottom of a well by mere chance; if I were
  placed as high as the Duke, I should stick as fast; make   110
  as fair a show; and bear out weather equally.
FLAMINEO
  If this soldier had a patent to beg in churches, then he
  would tell them stories.
MARCELLO
  I have been a soldier too.
FRANCISCO
  How have you thrived?   115

---

  96 s.d. (to r. of l. 95 in Q)
  106–11 *What . . . equally* These apparently egalitarian remarks, borrowed from Ste-
    fano Guazzo's *Civil Conversation* (trans. Pettie 1581), mask a deeper irony: there
    is in fact no difference in class between the two dukes, and both are, literally,
    'fair' or white-skinned.
  112 *soldier . . . churches* Beggars often claimed to be soliders without employment
    (cf. ll. 135–7); without a licence, they could be arrested and whipped as
    vagabonds.

MARCELLO
Faith, poorly.

FRANCISCO
That's the misery of peace. Only outsides are then
respected: as ships seem very great upon the river, ·
which show very little upon the seas: so some men
i'th'court seem Colossuses in a chamber, who if they   120
came into the field would appear pitiful pigmies.

FLAMINEO
Give me a fair room yet hung with arras, and some great
cardinal to lug me by th'ears as his endeared minion.

FRANCISCO
And thou may'st do – the devil knows what villainy.

FLAMINEO
And safely.   125

FRANCISCO
Right; you shall see in the country in harvest time,
pigeons, though they destroy never so much corn, the
farmer dare not present the fowling-piece to them!
Why? Because they belong to the Lord of the Manor;
whilst your poor sparrows that belong to the Lord of   130
heaven, they go to the pot for't.

FLAMINEO
I will now give you some politic instruction. The Duke
says he will give you pension; that's but bare promise:
get it under his hand. For I have known men that have
come from serving against the Turk; for three or four   135
months they have had pension to buy them new wooden
legs and fresh plasters; but after 'twas not to be had.
And this miserable courtesy shows as if a tormentor
should give hot cordial drinks to one three-quarters
dead o'th'rack, only to fetch the miserable soul again to   140
endure more dog-days.

117–21 *misery . . . pigmies* a common sentiment. Cf. *Measure for Measure* I.ii.14–16:
  'There's not a soldier of us all, that in the thanksgiving before meat, do relish
  the petition well that prays for peace'.
121 *pitiful pigmies* ed. (pittifull. Pigmies. Q)
122 *arras* tapestry adorning rooms at court (behind which one might hide unsuspec-
  ted, as in *Hamlet* III.iv.7)
127–9 *pigeons . . . Manor* Pigeons, though considered pests, were raised for their
  ready value on the open market.
140 *miserable* compassionate; miserly; wretched
141 *dog-days* Cf. III.ii.202.
  s.d. Flamineo's cynical commentary on the court is punctuated by the arrival
  of the young lord, who epitomizes the sycophancy which Flamineo both desires
  and despises.

Enter HORTENSIO, *a* YOUNG LORD, ZANCHE *and two more*

How now, gallants; what, are they ready for the barriers?

[*Exit* FRANCISCO]

YOUNG LORD

Yes: the lords are putting on their armour.

[HORTENSIO *and* FLAMINEO *stand apart*]

HORTENSIO

What's he?   145

FLAMINEO

A new upstart: one that swears like a falc'ner, and will lie in the Duke's ear day by day like a maker of almanacs; and yet I knew him since he came to th'court smell worse of sweat than an under-tennis-court-keeper.

HORTENSIO

Look you, yonder's your sweet mistress.   150

FLAMINEO

Thou art my sworn brother, I'll tell thee – I do love that Moor, that witch, very constrainedly: she knows some of my villainy; I do love her, just as a man holds a wolf by the ears. But for fear of turning upon me, and pulling out my throat, I would let her go to the devil.   155

HORTENSIO

I hear she claims marriage of thee.

FLAMINEO

'Faith, I made to her some such dark promise and in seeking to fly from't I run on, like a frighted dog with a bottle at's tail that fain would bite it off and yet dares not look behind him. [*To* ZANCHE] Now my precious   160
gipsy!

ZANCHE

Ay, your love to me rather cools than heats.

---

144 s.d. All except Flamineo and Hortensio are very likely setting up the barriers on stage (NCW V.i.134.I n.).

147–8 *maker of almanacs* fortune-teller, astrologer

153–4 *holds . . . ears* common proverb. Cf. Philip Sidney, *Arcadia*, *Works* II, 12: 'like them that holde the wolfe by the eares, bitten while they hold, and slaine if they loose'.

161 *gipsy* Like Cleopatra, Zanche is 'with Phoebus' amorous pinches black' (*Antony and Cleopatra* I.v.28) – as dark-skinned as the gipsies, who arrived in England in the early sixteenth century and were thought to come from Egypt.

162 *cools* abates, declines (as used by Zanche); allays, cools down (implied by Flamineo)

FLAMINEO

Marry, I am the sounder lover – we have many wenches
about the town heat too fast.

HORTENSIO

What do you think of these perfumed gallants then?   165

FLAMINEO

Their satin cannot save them. I am confident
They have a certain spice of the disease,
For they that sleep with dogs shall rise with fleas.

ZANCHE

Believe it! A little painting and gay clothes
Make you loathe me.   170

FLAMINEO

How? Love a lady for painting or gay apparel? I'll un-
kennel one example more for thee. Aesop had a foolish
dog that let go the flesh to catch the shadow. I would
have courtiers be better diners.

ZANCHE

You remember your oaths.   175

FLAMINEO

Lovers' oaths are like mariners' prayers, uttered in
extremity; but when the tempest is o'er and that the
vessel leaves tumbling, they fall from protesting to
drinking. And yet amongst gentlemen protesting and
drinking go together, and agree as well as shoemakers   180
and Westphalia bacon. They are both drawers on: for
drink draws on protestation and protestation draws on
more drink. Is not this discourse better now than the
morality of your sunburnt gentleman?

163 *sounder lover* ed. (sounder, lover Q)
164 *heat* become sexually aroused; contract venereal disease
166 *satin* with a pun on 'Satan'
169–70 *A little . . . me* i.e. women who wear makeup and dress well attract you, and
     lead you to reject me
172–4 *Aesop . . . diners* i.e. a bird in the hand is worth two in the bush; only a fool
     gives up what he has for what he desires
174 *diners* ed. (*Diuers.* Q)
178 *tumbling* tossing and rolling about (as a ship in a storm; as in sexual intercourse)
180–1 *agree . . . bacon* Bacon draws men on to drink, and shoemakers draw shoes
     on to feet.
184 *morality* ed. (mortality Q)
     s.d. *Enter CORNELIA* Flamineo's complacent misogyny is abruptly and dramatic-
     ally disturbed by Cornelia's violent entrance, which recalls her interruption at
     I.ii.269 and signals the disruption of the apparent harmony of the wedding
     procession, in which Cornelia and Zanche appeared together.

Enter CORNELIA

CORNELIA

    Is this your perch, you haggard? [*Strikes* ZANCHE] Fly to

      th'stews.   185

FLAMINEO

    You should be clapped by th'heels now: strike

    i'th'court!

                                               [*Exit* CORNELIA]

ZANCHE

    She's good for nothing but to make her maids

    Catch cold o'nights; they dare not use a bedstaff

    For fear of her light fingers.

MARCELLO   You're a strumpet.

    An impudent one.   [*Kicks* ZANCHE]

FLAMINEO   Why do you kick her? Say,   190

    Do you think that she's like a walnut-tree?

    Must she be cudgelled ere she bear good fruit?

MARCELLO

    She brags that you shall marry her.

FLAMINEO   What then?

MARCELLO

    I had rather she were pitched upon a stake

    In some new-seeded garden, to affright   195

    Her fellow crows thence.

FLAMINEO   You're a boy, a fool,

    Be guardian to your hound, I am of age.

MARCELLO

    If I take her near you I'll cut her throat.

---

185 *haggard* wild female hawk, often applied to a promiscuous, intractable woman

    stews brothel

186 *clapped . . . heels* put in irons or in the stocks

    strike . . . court Striking and drawing blood at court was severely punished:
    offenders might be imprisoned for life or have their right hands chopped off.

188–9 *they . . . fingers* Bed-staves were either slats supporting the bedding or sticks
    used in making beds, well known as ready weapons; Zanche's bed-staff is a
    potential weapon or a warm male companion. She dare not use either because
    (she implies) Cornelia covets both.

191–2 *Do . . . fruit?* The source from which Webster lifted this common proverb
    reads: 'A woman, an asse, and a walnut tree / Bring the more fruit, the more
    beaten they bee' (Pettie III.39). The same text counters it with this: 'He God
    offendes, and holy love undoes / Which on his wife doth fasten churlish bloes'.

194–6 *pitched . . . thence* Marcello conflates images of Zanche as a witch ('upon a
    stake') and a crow (the black scavenger so hated by English farmers).

195 *new-seeded garden* Cf. I.ii.275.

196 *You're* ed. (Your Q)

FLAMINEO
  With a fan of feathers?
MARCELLO   And for you, I'll whip
  This folly from you.
FLAMINEO   Are you choleric?   200
  I'll purge't with rhubarb.
HORTENSIO   O your brother –
FLAMINEO   Hang him.
  He wrongs me most that ought t'offend me least.
  [*To* MARCELLO] I do suspect my mother played foul play
  When she conceived thee.
MARCELLO   Now by all my hopes,
  Like the two slaughtered sons of Oedipus,   205
  The very flames of our affection
  Shall turn two ways. Those words I'll make thee answer
  With thy heart blood.
FLAMINEO   Do like the geese in the progress;
  You know where you shall find me –   [*Exit*]
MARCELLO   Very good.
  And thou beest a noble friend, bear him my sword,   210
  And bid him fit the length on't.
YOUNG LORD   Sir I shall.

                  [*Exeunt all but* ZANCHE]

    Enter FRANCISCO *the Duke of Florence* [*disguised*]

ZANCHE
  [*Aside*] He comes. Hence petty thought of my disgrace –
  I ne'er loved my complexion till now,
  Cause I may boldly say without a blush

199 *fan of feathers* appropriate to the courtier Marcello has become, not the soldier
    he has been
200 *choleric* Choler was one of the four humours of early physiology, hot and dry,
    and supposed to cause irascibility. Flamineo here treats it as a digestive malady,
    attended with bilious diarrhoea and vomiting, remedied by purging. Rhubarb
    was a commonly prescribed purgative (cf. *The Duchess of Malfi* II.v.12–13,
    'Rhubarb, O for rhubarb / To purge this choler').
205–7 *two . . . ways* After the two sons of Oedipus, Eteocles and Polinices, were
    killed in combat for their father's throne, their bodies were burnt together; the
    flames miraculously parted, showing that death did not end their mutual hatred.
208 *geese* ed. (gesse Q) prostitutes. The word 'gesses' is a technical term for the
    stopping places on a royal progress, and may be intended (Lucas, p. 251). But
    prostitutes plied their trade during progresses, and Flamineo's bawdy remark
    is typical. The syntax is ambiguous, however, and so the line may read 'Do as
    the prostitutes do in a progress, who know where their victims are to be found',
    or 'Do – I shall be found as easily as prostitutes in a progress'.
211 s.d.   ed. (to r. of ll. 213–14 in Q)

I love you.

[FRANCISCO] Your love is untimely sown;   215
    There's a spring at Michaelmas, but 'tis but a faint
      one –
    I am sunk in years, and I have vowed never to marry.

ZANCHE
    Alas! Poor maids get more lovers than husbands. Yet
    you may mistake my wealth. For, as when ambassadors
    are sent to congratulate princes, there's commonly sent   220
    along with them a rich present; so that though the
    prince like not the ambassador's person nor words, yet
    he likes well of the presentment. So I may come to you
    in the same manner, and be better loved for my dowry
    than my virtue.   225

[FRANCISCO]
    I'll think on the motion.

ZANCHE
    Do, I'll now detain you no longer. At your better leisure
    I'll tell you things shall startle your blood.
    Nor blame me that this passion I reveal;
    Lovers die inward that their flames conceal.   230

[FRANCISCO]
    [*Aside*] Of all intelligence this may prove the best,
    Sure I shall draw strange fowl, from this foul nest.

                            Exeunt

[Act V, Scene ii]

Enter MARCELLO *and* CORNELIA [*and a* PAGE]

CORNELIA
    I hear a whispering all about the court,
    You are to fight; who is your opposite?
    What is the quarrel?

MARCELLO   'Tis an idle rumour.

CORNELIA
    Will you dissemble? Sure you do not well
    To fright me thus – you never look thus pale,   5
    But when you are most angry. I do charge you
    Upon my blessing; nay I'll call the Duke,

215, 226, 231 s.p. *FRANCISCO* ed. (FLA Q)
216–17 ed. (Ther's . . . sunck / In . . . marry. Q)
216 *spring . . . one* Michaelmas is 29 September.
226 *motion* offer, proposal
  2 *You* ed. (Your Q)

And he shall school you.

MARCELLO   Publish not a fear
Which would convert to laughter; 'tis not so –
Was not this crucifix my father's?

CORNELIA   Yes.   10

MARCELLO
I have heard you say, giving my brother suck,
He took the crucifix between his hands,
And broke a limb off.

CORNELIA   Yes: but 'tis mended.

Enter FLAMINEO

FLAMINEO
I have brought your weapon back.

FLAMINEO *runs* MARCELLO *through*

CORNELIA   Ha, O my horror!

MARCELLO
You have brought it home indeed.

CORNELIA   Help – O he's
    murdered.   15

FLAMINEO
Do you turn your gall up? I'll to sanctuary,
And send a surgeon to you.   [*Exit*]

Enter CARL[O,] HORT[ENSIO,] PEDRO

HORTENSIO   How? O'th'ground?

MARCELLO
O mother now remember what I told
Of breaking off the crucifix: farewell –

---

10 *crucifix* Cornelia wears this around her neck, probably from the beginning of
the play, immediately identifying her (along with the Cardinal) as a guardian
of traditional Christian values.

13 s.d. ed. (to r. of l. 12 in Q). The sudden violence of Flamineo's entrance and
subsequent assault imitates precisely Cornelia's attack on Zanche (V.i.185).
Thus Flamineo makes clear that his action is a direct response to his mother's
rigid morality.

16 *turn . . . up* probably a witty extension of Flamineo's earlier remark about pur-
ging Marcello's choler (supposed to have its seat in the gall). Since bloodletting
was a remedy for choler (like purgation), Flamineo may be humorously
expressing surprise that Marcello's irascibility is increased by being stabbed. He
then offers to send a doctor to complete the cure.

17 s.d. ed. (to r. of ll. 19–20 in Q). The entrance of Carlo and Pedro, 'moles'
in league with Francisco, as witnesses to Flamineo's fratricide emphasizes the
self-determination of Brachiano and his allies; the revenge plot is unexpectedly
superseded in the final act.

There are some sins which heaven doth duly punish   20
In a whole family. This it is to rise
By all dishonest means. Let all men know
That tree shall long time keep a steady foot
Whose branches spread no wider than the root.

CORNELIA
O my perpetual sorrow!

HORTENSIO   Virtuous Marcello.   25
He's dead: pray leave him lady; come, you shall.

CORNELIA
Alas he is not dead: he's in a trance.
Why here's nobody shall get anything by his death. Let
me call him again for God's sake.

CARLO
I would you were deceived.   30

CORNELIA
O you abuse me, you abuse me, you abuse me. How
many have gone away thus for lack of tendance; rear
up's head, rear up's head; his bleeding inward will kill
him.

HORTENSIO
You see he is departed.   35

CORNELIA
Let me come to him; give me him as he is, if he be
turned to earth; let me but give him one hearty kiss,
and you shall put us both into one coffin. Fetch a looking-glass, see if his breath will not stain it; or pull out
some feathers from my pillow, and lay them to his lips –   40
will you lose him for a little pains-taking?

HORTENSIO
Your kindest office is to pray for him.

CORNELIA
Alas! I would not pray for him yet. He may live to lay
me i'th'ground, and pray for me, if you'll let me come
to him.   45

23–4 *That ... root* Cf. I.ii.249–53, where the 'yew' of Vittoria's dream strikes
   Isabella and Camillo dead with one of its branches.
24 *wider* ed. (wilder Q)
26 Carlo, Pedro and Hortensio force Cornelia away from the body of Marcello,
   and she struggles to free herself.
37–40 *earth ... lips* Webster is borrowing from *King Lear* (V.iii.262–6): 'She's dead
   as earth. Lend me a looking-glass, / If that her breath will mist or stain the
   stone, / Why then she lives ... This feather stirs; she lives!'
41 *lose* ed. (loose Q)
45 s.d. ed. (to r. of ll. 45–7 in Q)

Enter BRACHIANO *all armed, save the beaver, with*
FLAMINEO, [LODOVICO *disguised and* FRANCISCO
disguised as MULINASSAR]

BRACHIANO
Was this your handiwork?
FLAMINEO
It was my misfortune.
CORNELIA
He lies, he lies, he did not kill him: these have killed
him, that would not let him be better looked to.
BRACHIANO
Have comfort my grieved mother.

[*Rushing at* FLAMINEO]

CORNELIA
O you screech-owl.
HORTENSIO
[*Restraining her*] Forbear, good madam.
CORNELIA
[*Shaking him off*] Let me go, let me go.

She runs to FLAMINEO *with her knife drawn and*
coming to him lets it fall

The God of heaven forgive thee. Dost not wonder
I pray for thee? I'll tell thee what's the reason –   55
I have scarce breath to number twenty minutes;
I'd not spend that in cursing. Fare thee well –
Half of thyself lies there: and may'st thou live
To fill an hour-glass with his mouldered ashes,
To tell how thou shouldst spend the time to come   60
In blest repentance.
BRACHIANO   Mother, pray tell me
How came he by his death? What was the quarrel?
CORNELIA
Indeed my younger boy presumed too much
Upon his manhood; gave him bitter words;
Drew his sword first; and so I know not how,   65

---

51 *screech-owl* bird of ill-omen. The line is addressed either to Brachiano, who has
   attempted to comfort her, or to Flamineo.
53 s.d. ed. (to r. of ll. 53–7 in Q)
63 *younger boy* Marcello. Younger brothers were frequently angry about their dis-
   enfranchised position (cf. Orlando in *As You Like It*); Cornelia may be capitaliz-
   ing on the choleric reputation of younger brothers.

For I was out of my wits, he fell with's head
Just in my bosom.
PAGE   This is not true madam.
CORNELIA
I pray thee peace.
One arrow's grazed already; it were vain
T'lose this: for that will ne'er be found again.   70
BRACHIANO
Go, bear the body to Cornelia's lodging:
And we command that none acquaint our Duchess
With this sad accident: for you Flamineo,
Hark you, I will not grant your pardon.
FRANCISCO   No?
BRACHIANO
Only a lease of your life. And that shall last   75
But for one day. Thou shalt be forced each evening
To renew it, or be hanged.
FLAMINEO   At your pleasure.

> LODOVICO *sprinkles* BRACHIANO*'s beaver with a poison*

Your will is law now, I'll not meddle with it.
BRACHIANO
You once did brave me in your sister's lodging;
I'll now keep you in awe for't. Where's our beaver?   80
FRANCISCO
[*Aside*] He calls for his destruction. Noble youth,
I pity thy sad fate. Now to the barriers.
This shall his passage to the black lake further,
The last good deed he did, he pardoned murder.

> *Exeunt*

---

69 *grazed* probably 'grassed' (lost in the grass) with the secondary meaning 'grazed'
(to cut the surface of, as in a wound). The idea of shooting a second arrow to
find the first was a common metaphor for ambition.
76–7 *But . . . pleasure* ed. (But . . . it, / or . . . pleasure Q)
77 s.d. *beaver* lower portion of the face-guard of a helmet. The poisoning of Brachiano's mouthpiece recalls the dumb show in II.ii.23, when Dr Julio washed the
lips of Brachiano's picture in order to poison Isabella when she kissed it.
79 *You . . . lodging* Cf. IV.ii.48–9.
83 *black lake* probably Acheron, black river of the underworld

[Act V, Scene iii]

*Charges and shouts. They fight at barriers; first
single pairs, then three to three*

Enter BRACHIANO *and* FLAMINEO *with others*
[GIOVANNI, VITTORIA, *and* FRANCISCO
disguised as MULINASSAR]

BRACHIANO
An armourer! Ud's death, an armourer!
FLAMINEO
Armourer; where's the armourer?
BRACHIANO
Tear off my beaver.
FLAMINEO   Are you hurt, my lord?
BRACHIANO
O my brain's on fire,

Enter ARMOURER

the helmet is poisoned.

ARMOURER
My lord upon my soul –   5
BRACHIANO
Away with him to torture.

                         [*Exit* ARMOURER, *guarded*]
There are some great ones that have hand in this,
And near about me.
VITTORIA   O my loved lord, poisoned?
FLAMINEO
Remove the bar: here's unfortunate revels –
Call the physicians;

Ent[er] 2 PHYSICIANS

a plague upon you;   10
We have too much of your cunning here already.
I fear the ambassadors are likewise poisoned.

0 s.d. The fight at barriers, a spectacle for the Red Bull stage, was a highly formal
  ceremonial combat (frequently allegorized as, for example, Truth vs. Opinion)
  rapidly disappearing from courtly life. Here, it gives Webster the opportunity
  to juxtapose chivalric courtly ideals with the Machiavellian revenge plot. The
  scene opens with six combatants jousting in full armour (probably Brachiano
  and five of the ambassadors; cf. l. 12); they may be observed (perhaps, from
  the upper stage) by an audience which includes Francisco, Lodovico, Gasparo,
  Vittoria, Zanche, Giovanni and Flamineo (so NCW V.iii.0.1–2 n.).
4 *O . . . poisoned* ed. (O . . . fire / The . . . soule Q)
9 *bar* probably the barrier, still on the stage

BRACHIANO
    O I am gone already: the infection
    Flies to the brain and heart. O thou strong heart!
    There's such a covenant 'tween the world and it,   15
    They're loth to break.
GIOVANNI   O my most loved father!
BRACHIANO
    Remove the boy away.

                              [GIOVANNI *is led offstage*]
    Where's this good woman? Had I infinite worlds
    They were too little for thee. Must I leave thee?
    What say yon screech-owls, is the venom mortal?   20
PHYSICIANS
    Most deadly.
BRACHIANO   Most corrupted politic hangman!
    You kill without book; but your art to save
    Fails you as oft as great men's needy friends.
    I that have given life to offending slaves
    And wretched murderers, have I not power   25
    To lengthen mine own a twelvemonth?
    [*To* VITTORIA] Do not kiss me, for I shall poison thee.
    This unction is sent from the great Duke of Florence.
FRANCISCO
    Sir be of comfort.
BRACHIANO
    O thou soft natural death, that art joint-twin   30
    To sweetest slumber: no rough-bearded comet
    Stares on thy mild departure: the dull owl
    Beats not against thy casement: the hoarse wolf
    Scents not thy carrion. Pity winds thy corse,
    Whilst horror waits on princes.   35

---

20 *screech-owls* the physicians, who can foretell, but not prevent, death
21–3 *Most . . . friends* This is addressed to Death, here envisaged as a schemer who
    kills by rote (without book), but lacks the ability to save life as great men lack
    friends. This speech reveals that, while Brachiano knows he is Francisco's victim
    (in a revenge tragedy), he nonetheless sees himself as the great victim of Fate
    (in a *de casibus* tragedy) and thus ignores the disguised Duke of Florence to
    focus on larger forces.
24–5 *I . . . murderers* Cf. V.ii.84.
27 *Do . . . me* Brachiano protects Vittoria from the poisoned kiss which, in picture,
    killed Isabella (II.ii.23).
30–1 *death . . . slumber* Sleep is 'death's second self, that seals up all in rest'
    (Shakespeare, Sonnet 73).
31–3 *rough-bearded . . . casement* a series of prodigies associated with the fall of
    kings
35–6 ed. (one line in Q)

VITTORIA

[*Wailing*] I am lost for ever.

BRACHIANO

How miserable a thing it is to die,
'Mongst women howling!

[*Enter* LODOVICO *and* GASPARO *disguised as Capuchins*]

               What are those?

FLAMINEO   Franciscans.

They have brought the extreme unction.

BRACHIANO

On pain of death, let no man name death to me,   40
It is a word infinitely terrible.
Withdraw into our cabinet.

             Exeunt [*all*] *but* FRANCISCO *and* FLAMINEO

FLAMINEO

To see what solitariness is about dying princes. As heretofore they have unpeopled towns, divorced friends, and
made great houses unhospitable, so now, O justice!   45
where are their flatterers now? Flatterers are but the
shadows of princes' bodies, the least thick cloud makes
them invisible.

FLAMINEO

There's great moan made for him.

FLAMINEO

'Faith, for some few hours salt water will run most plen-   50
tifully in every office o'th'court. But believe it; most of
them do but weep over their stepmothers' graves.

FRANCISCO

How mean you?

FLAMINEO

Why? They dissemble, as some men do that live within
compass o'th'verge.   55

FRANCISCO

Come, you have thrived well under him.

---

38 *Franciscans* a wonderful pun: the murderers are both disguised Franciscan friars
and servants to Francisco.

39 *extreme unction* both the anointment of the faithful before death and the most
powerful poison of the murderers

42 *Withdraw . . . cabinet* Brachiano, Vittoria and the disguised assassins may retreat
into the curtained discovery space at the rear of the stage, where they are discovered at l. 83.

55 *compass . . . verge* within twelve miles of the king's court, under the jurisdiction
of the Lord High Steward

FLAMINEO
'Faith, like a wolf in a woman's breast; I have been fed
with poultry; but for money, understand me, I had as
good a will to cozen him, as e'er an officer of them all.
But I had not cunning enough to do it.   60
FRANCISCO
What did'st thou think of him? 'Faith speak freely.
FLAMINEO
He was a kind of statesman that would sooner have
reckoned how many cannon bullets he had discharged
against a town, to count his expense that way, than how
many of his valiant and deserving subjects he lost   65
before it.
FRANCISCO
O, speak well of the Duke.
FLAMINEO
I have done. Wilt hear some of my court wisdom?

Enter LODOVICO [*disguised*]

To reprehend princes is dangerous: and to over-
commend some of them is palpable lying.   70
FRANCISCO
How is it with the Duke?
LODOVICO   Most deadly ill.
He's fall'n into a strange distraction.
He talks of battles and monopolies,
Levying of taxes, and from that descends
To the most brain-sick language. His mind fastens   75
On twenty several objects, which confound
Deep sense with folly. Such a fearful end
May teach some men that bear too lofty crest,
Though they live happiest, yet they die not best.
He hath conferred the whole state of the dukedom   80
Upon your sister, till the Prince arrive
At mature age.
FLAMINEO   There's some good luck in that yet.
FRANCISCO
See here he comes.

57-8 *wolf . . . poultry* The 'ulcerous wolf' (*The Duchess of Malfi* II.i.57), common
    parlance for a cancerous ulcer, was fed with fresh meat so that it would not
    consume human flesh. The ulcer in the thigh of the real-life Brachiano was
    treated with raw meat. There may also be a pun on 'poultry' and 'paltry'
    (rubbish, trash).
83 *See . . . already* ed. (See . . . comes / There's . . . allready Q)

Enter BRACHIANO, *presented in a bed,* VITTORIA *and
others* [*including* GASPARO, *disguised*]

There's death in's face already.

VITTORIA
    O my good lord!

*These speeches are several kinds of distractions
and in the action should appear so*

BRACHIANO   Away, you have abused me.
    You have conveyed coin forth our territories,   85
    Bought and sold offices, oppressed the poor,
    And I ne'er dreamt on't. Make up your accounts;
    I'll now be mine own steward.
FLAMINEO   Sir, have patience.
BRACHIANO
    Indeed I am too blame.
    For did you ever hear the dusky raven   90
    Chide blackness? Or was't ever known the devil
    Railed against cloven creatures?
VITTORIA   O my lord!
BRACHIANO
    Let me have some quails to supper.
FLAMINEO   Sir, you shall.
BRACHIANO
    No: some fried dog-fish. Your quails feed on poison –
    That old dog-fox, that politician Florence –   95
    I'll forswear hunting and turn dog-killer.
    Rare! I'll be friends with him: for mark you sir, one
        dog

83 s.d. ed. (to r. of l. 83 in Q) The bed recalls that in the house of convertites in
    IV.ii.125, upon which Vittoria threw herself earlier; now Brachiano, like Vittoria
    in the earlier scene, is the accuser. The bed may have been thrust out onto the
    main stage and remained for the rest of the scene.
84 s.d. ed. (to l. of ll. 85–92 in Q). This s.d. suggests that distraction was signalled
    by conventionalized gestures (cf. V.iv.91 s.d.): perhaps beating the breast or
    wringing the hands (see Thomson, p. 31). Brachiano is clearly feeling the effects
    of the poison.
85 *conveyed . . . territories* The export of money was a serious offence; Henry VIII
    published a statute forbidding it.
90–1 *raven . . . blackness* 'The raven chides blackness' is proverbial, like the pot
    calling the kettle black. Ravens were considered malignant: Brachiano may refer
    either to the dark-haired Vittoria or the dark-skinned Zanche. Francisco, dis-
    guised as Mulinassar, is a more appropriate, though unintended, target for this
    remark.
93 *quails* birds supposed to feed on venomous seeds, and considered a culinary
    delicacy; courtesans
94 *dog-fish* a small shark; applied opprobriously to persons
95 *dog-fox* male fox (symbol of sly cunning and craft)

    Still sets another a-barking: peace, peace,
    Yonder's a fine slave come in now.

FLAMINEO   Where?

BRACHIANO   Why, there.
    In a blue bonnet, and a pair of breeches   100
    With a great codpiece. Ha, ha, ha,
    Look you his codpiece is stuck full of pins
    With pearls o'th'head of them. Do not you know him?

FLAMINEO
    No my lord.

BRACHIANO   Why 'tis the devil.
    I know him by a great rose he wears on's shoe   105
    To hide his cloven foot. I'll dispute with him.
    He's a rare linguist.

VITTORIA   My lord here's nothing.

BRACHIANO
    Nothing? Rare! Nothing! When I want money,
    Our treasury is empty; there is nothing, –
    I'll not be used thus.

VITTORIA   O! Lie still my lord –   110

BRACHIANO
    See, see, Flamineo that killed his brother
    Is dancing on the ropes there: and he carries
    A money-bag in each hand, to keep him even,
    For fear of breaking's neck. And there's a lawyer
    In a gown whipt with velvet, stares and gapes   115
    When the money will fall. How the rogue cuts capers!
    It should have been in a halter.
    'Tis there; what's she?   [*Points to* VITTORIA]

FLAMINEO   Vittoria, my lord.

BRACHIANO
    Ha, ha, ha. Her hair is sprinkled with arras powder, that
    makes her look as if she had sinned in the pastry. What's   120
    he?   [*Points to* GASPARO *or* LODOVICO]

97–8 *one . . . a-barking* It is proverbial that if one dog barks, they all do.

101–3 *codpiece . . . them* Codpieces, out of fashion in 1612, were in Henry VIII's
    time very prominent and highly decorated.

105–6 *rose . . . foot* Large, expensive silk rosettes on shoes became fashionable at the
    end of the sixteenth century.

107 *linguist* polyglot; eloquent speaker

112 *ropes* tightropes

115 *whipt* trimmed

116–17 *rogue . . . halter* Flamineo is the rogue cutting capers, or dancing; the rope
    on which he dances should have gone around his neck.

119 *hair . . . powder* As a new bride, Vittoria's hair would have been sprinkled with
    powdered orris, or iris root, commonly used for whitening and perfuming hair.

120 *pastry* place where pastry is made

FLAMINEO

A divine my lord.

BRACHIANO

He will be drunk: avoid him: th'argument is fearful
when churchmen stagger in't. Look you; six gray rats
that have lost their tails crawl up the pillow; send for a   125
rat-catcher.
I'll do a miracle: I'll free the court
From all foul vermin. Where's Flamineo?

FLAMINEO

I do not like that he names me so often,
Especially on's death-bed: 'tis a sign   130
I shall not live long: see he's near his end.

> BRACHIANO *seems here near his end.* LODOVICO *and*
> GASPARO *in the habit of Capuchins present him in*
> *his bed with a crucifix and hallowed candle*

LODOVICO

Pray give us leave; *Attende Domine Brachiane* –

FLAMINEO

See, see, how firmly he doth fix his eye
Upon the crucifix.

VITTORIA   O hold it constant.

It settles his wild spirits; and so his eyes   135
Melt into tears.

LODOVICO

(By the crucifix) Domine Brachiane, solebas in bello tutus
esse tuo clypeo, nunc hunc clypeum hosti tuo opponas
infernali.

124–5 *six . . . pillow* possibly a reference to witches, who often turned themselves
    into animals, like the witch in *Macbeth,* who promises 'Like a rat without a
    tail, / I'll do, I'll do, and I'll do' (I.iii.9–10)
125–8 *send . . . vermin* a possible allusion to the Pied Piper of Hamelin
131 s.d. ed. (to r. of ll. 123–34 in Q). For the crucifix as a significant property cf.
    V.ii.10. The 'hallowed candle' may recall the dumb show (II.ii.23) when Dr
    Julio and his assistant burned perfumes in the 'fire' before Brachiano's picture.
132 *Attende . . . Brachiane* 'Listen, Lord Brachiano.' The fraudulent capuchins
    begin the *Commendatio Animae,* the commending of the soul to God, which
    follows the extreme unction in Roman ritual: in this ritual, candle and crucifix
    are symbols of hope and comfort to the dying (McLeod, *Dramatic Imagery,* p.
    66).
137 s.d. ed. (to l. of ll. 137–9 in Q)
137–48 i.e. LODOVICO 'Lord Brachiano, you were accustomed to be guarded in
    battle by your shield; now this shield [the crucifix] you shall oppose against
    your infernal enemy.' – GASPARO 'Once with your spear you prevailed in battle;
    now this holy spear [the hallowed taper] you shall wield against the enemy of

GASPARO

(By the hallowed taper) Olim hasta valuisti in bello; nunc   140
hanc sacram hastam vibrabis contra hostem animarum.

LODOVICO

Attende Domine Brachiane si nunc quoque probas ea quae
acta sunt inter nos, flecte caput in dextrum.

GASPARO

Esto securus Domine Brachiane: cogita quantum habeas
meritorum – denique memineris meam animam pro tua   145
oppignoratam si quid esset periculi.

LODOVICO

Si nunc quoque probas ea quae acta sunt inter nos, flecte
caput in loevum.

He is departing: pray stand all apart,
And let us only whisper in his ears   150
Some private meditations which our order
Permits you not to hear.

> *Here the rest being departed* LODOVICO *and* GASPARO
> *discover themselves*

GASPARO   Brachiano.

LODOVICO

Devil Brachiano. Thou art damned.

GASPARO   Perpetually.

LODOVICO

A slave condemned and given up to the gallows

---

souls.' – LODOVICO 'Listen, Lord Brachiano, if you now also approve what has
been done between us, turn your head to the right.' – GASPARO 'Rest assured
Lord Brachiano: think how many good deeds you have done – lastly remember
that my soul is pledged for yours if there should be any peril.' – LODOVICO 'If
you now also approve what has been done between us, turn your head to the
left.'

   The whole passage is based on Erasmus, *Funus*, an account of the death of
Georgius Balearicus, a corrupt and wealthy man, whose death is described by
Erasmus as 'the last acte of the comedy'. After purchasing papal remission of
sins (and justifying all his goods 'goten by extorcyon and robbery'), Georgius
himself, 'lyke a man of warre', delivers the first two speeches which Webster
gives to the assassins. Erasmus emphasizes the corruption and hypocrisy of the
dying man; Webster uses the same ceremony to highlight the villainy and hypocrisy of the dying man's assassins.

140 s.d. ed. (to l. of ll. 140–2 in Q)

149–70 The revengers parody the *Commendatio*, by dismissing witnesses (who normally participated in prayers for the dying one's soul), and by commending
   Brachiano not to God but to the devil (NCW V.iii.144–7, 148–64 n.).

152 s.d. ed. (to r. of ll. 151–3 in Q)

Is thy great lord and master.
GASPARO   True: for thou   155
Art given up to the devil.
LODOVICO   O you slave!
You that were held the famous politician;
Whose art was poison.
GASPARO   And whose conscience murder.
LODOVICO
That would have broke your wife's neck down the stairs
Ere she was poisoned.   160
GASPARO
That had your villainous sallets –
LODOVICO
And fine embroidered bottles, and perfumes
Equally mortal with a winter plague –
GASPARO
Now there's mercury –
LODOVICO   And copperas –
GASPARO   And quicksilver –
LODOVICO
With other devilish pothecary stuff   165
A-melting in your politic brains; dost hear?
GASPARO
This is Count Lodovico.
LODOVICO   This Gasparo.
And thou shalt die like a poor rogue.
GASPARO   And stink
Like a dead fly-blown dog.
LODOVICO   And be forgotten
Before thy funeral sermon.   170

158 *conscience* inmost thought
159–60 ed. (prose in Q)
    broke . . . poisoned probably an allusion to the notorious Earl of Leicester's
    alleged attempt to poison his wife, Amy Robsart, before having her thrown
    down the stairs at Cumnor Place in 1560, when she finally died. Leicester
    wanted to be free to marry Queen Elizabeth; according to the 1584 pamphlet
    Leicester's Commonwealth, the Earl employed a poisoner named Dr Julio as well
    as two 'atheists' for 'figuring and conjuring'. Renaissance Italy was thus not so
    different from Renaissance England.   161 *sallets* salads
162 *And . . . perfumes* ed. (And . . . bottles / And perfumes Q)
163 *winter plague* A plague which flourished during the cold months was considered
    most pernicious.
164 *mercury . . . quicksilver* Mercury *is* quicksilver (unless the poisonous plant, *Mer-
    curialis perennis*, or wild mercury, is meant); Gasparo is trying to 'terrify him at
    the last gasp' (l. 215) through sheer emphasis. Copperas (sulphate of copper,
    iron or zinc) is fatal only when taken in quantity.
169–70 ed. (one line in Q)

BRACHIANO
  Vittoria! Vittoria!
LODOVICO   O the cursed devil,
  Come to himself again. We are undone.

Enter VITTORIA *and the* ATTEND[ANTS]

GASPARO
  [*Aside to* LODOVICO] Strangle him in private. [*Aloud*]
    What? Will you call him again
  To live in treble torments? For charity,
  For Christian charity, avoid the chamber.   175
                    [*Exeunt* VITTORIA *and* ATTENDANTS]
LODOVICO
  You would prate, sir. This is a true-love knot
  Sent from the Duke of Florence.

BRACHIANO *is strangled*

GASPARO   What, is it done?
LODOVICO
  The snuff is out. No woman-keeper i'th'world,
  Though she had practised seven year at the pest-house,
  Could have done't quaintlier.

[*Enter* VITTORIA, FRANCISCO, FLAMINEO, *and*
                    ATTENDANTS]

                              My lords he's dead.   180
OMNES
  Rest to his soul.
VITTORIA   O me! This place is hell.
                    Exit [*with* ATTENDANTS *and* GASPARO]
[FRANCISCO]
  How heavily she takes it.
FLAMINEO   O yes, yes;
  Had women navigable rivers in their eyes

172–81 Thomson (pp. 33–4) argues that the bustle of mass entries and exits risks
    bringing the scene close to farce on the stage; the visual movement of Vittoria
    with her attendants on and off the stage certainly emphasizes by contrast Brach-
    iano's isolation and stillness in death.
175 *charity* a word that echoes throughout the arraignment (cf. III.ii.71, 161)
176 *true-love knot* the noose used to strangle Brachiano (perhaps Lodovico's
    waistcord or rosary: so NCW V.iii.171 n.). The word-play links Brachiano's
    death with his love affair, and recalls Francisco's feigned courtship of Vittoria.
178 *snuff* proverbial: to die is to go out like a candle in a snuff (possibly punctuated
    by Lodovico snuffing out the hallowed taper)
    woman-keeper female nurse, often suspected of killing off patients
179 *pest-house* a hospice for those sick of the plague. One was erected in London
    in 1594.   180 *quaintlier* more skilfully
181 s.d. *Exit* ed. (Exit Vittoria Q)   182–209, 221 s.p. FRANCISCO ed. (FLO Q)

They would dispend them all; surely I wonder
Why we should wish more rivers to the city   185
When they sell water so good cheap. I'll tell thee,
These are but moonish shades of griefs or fears,
There's nothing sooner dry than women's tears.
Why here's an end of all my harvest, he has given me
     nothing –
Court promises! Let wise men count them cursed   190
For while you live he that scores best pays worst.
[FRANCISCO]
Sure, this was Florence' doing.
FLAMINEO   Very likely.
Those are found weighty strokes which come from
     th'hand,
But those are killing strokes which come from th'head.
O the rare tricks of a Machiavellian!   195
He doth not come like a gross plodding slave
And buffet you to death: no, my quaint knave,
He tickles you to death, makes you die laughing
As if you had swallowed down a pound of saffron.
You see the feat, 'tis practised in a trice –   200
To teach court-honesty it jumps on ice.
[FRANCISCO]
Now have the people liberty to talk
And descant on his vices.
FLAMINEO   Misery of princes,
That must of force be censured by their slaves!
Not only blamed for doing things are ill,   205
But for not doing all that all men will.

185–6 *Why ... cheap* Sir Hugh Middleton's artificial New River, which was
     designed to supply London with water, was begun in 1608 and under way at
     the time of the play's first performance.
187 *moonish* changeable (like the moon)
191 *he ... worst* i.e. he who runs up a score or debt on credit (like him who depends
     on promises) pays dearly for it
195 *Machiavellian* ed. (Machivillian Q, with a pun on 'villain')
197 *buffet* strike, beat
     quaint ingenious
199 *saffron* in moderation, supposed to quicken the senses and make men merry;
     fatal when taken in excess
201 *To ... ice* i.e. to teach court intrigue that it is precarious and dangerous. In the
     The Duchess of Malfi, courts are 'slippery ice-pavements' on which 'men may
     break their necks' (V.ii.328–9).
     court-honesty honesty as practised at court – deception, intrigue
203 *descant* comment, enlarge

One were better be a thresher.
Ud's death, I would fain speak with this Duke yet.
[FRANCISCO]
    Now he's dead?
FLAMINEO
    I cannot conjure, but if prayers or oaths   210
    Will get to th'speech of him, though forty devils
    Wait on him in his livery of flames,
    I'll speak to him and shake him by the hand,
    Though I be blasted.   *Exit*
FRANCISCO   Excellent Lodovico!
    What? Did you terrify him at the last gasp?   215
LODOVICO
    Yes; and so idly, that the Duke had like
    T'have terrified us.
FRANCISCO   How?

                Enter [ZANCHE] *the Moor*

LODOVICO   You shall hear that hereafter.
    See! Yon's the infernal that would make up sport.
    Now to the revelation of that secret
    She promised when she fell in love with you.   220
[FRANCISCO]
    You're passionately met in this sad world.
[ZANCHE]
    I would have you look up, sir; these court tears
    Claim not your tribute to them. Let those weep
    That guiltily partake in the sad cause.
    I knew last night by a sad dream I had   225
    Some mischief would ensue, yet to say truth

---

214 *blasted* stricken by supernatural agency
    s.d. *Exit* ed. (Exit Flamineo Q)
    s.d. ed. (to r. of l. 215 in Q)
    Lodovico, in his hooded Capuchins' robe, has been a silent witness to the pre-
    ceding dialogue; his presence on the stage is a constant visual reminder of Fran-
    cisco's hypocrisy.
218 *infernal* Zanche is considered devilish because she is black (the s.p. 'Moor'
    draws attention to her colour); Francisco, here in blackface as Mulinassar, may
    exemplify the proverb 'The white devil is worse than the black' (Tilley D310).
218 *make up sport* make our fun complete
222–68 s.p. *ZANCHE* ed. (MOO or MOORE. Q)
225–40 This scene both illustrates visually Flamineo's words about the Machiavel-
    lian (here, Francisco) who 'tickles you to death' (l.198) and clearly recalls
    I.ii.228ff., where two lovers embrace and Vittoria recounts her dream, which
    is to lead to murder.

My dream most concerned you.
LODOVICO   Shall's fall a-dreaming?
FRANCISCO
    Yes, and for fashion sake I'll dream with her.
[ZANCHE]
    Methought, sir, you came stealing to my bed.
FRANCISCO
    Wilt thou believe me sweeting? By this light   230
    I was a-dreamt on thee too, for methought
    I saw thee naked.
[ZANCHE]   Fie, sir! As I told you,
    Methought you lay down by me.
FRANCISCO   So dreamt I,
    And lest thou shouldst take cold, I covered thee
    With this Irish mantle.
[ZANCHE]   Verily I did dream   235
    You were somewhat bold with me; but to come to't.
LODOVICO
    How? How? I hope you will not go to't here.
FRANCISCO
    Nay, you must hear my dream out.
[ZANCHE]   Well, sir, forth.
FRANCISCO
    When I threw the mantle o'er thee, thou didst laugh
    Exceedingly methought.
[ZANCHE]   Laugh?
FRANCISCO   And cried'st out,   240
    The hair did tickle thee.
[ZANCHE]   There was a dream indeed.
LODOVICO
    Mark her, I prithee: she simpers like the suds
    A collier hath been washed in.
[ZANCHE]
    Come, sir; good fortune tends you; I did tell you
    I would reveal a secret – Isabella   245
    The Duke of Florence' sister was empoisoned
    By a fumed picture and Camillo's neck
    Was broke by damned Flamineo, the mischance

---

235 *Irish mantle* blanket worn by rustic Irish in all weathers as the only covering
    over their naked bodies
242 *simpers* with a play on 'simmers'
243 *collier* coal-carrier or coal-miner (blackened by coal dust, which would then
    appear in the soap suds)
247 *fumed* perfumed

Laid on a vaulting-horse.

FRANCISCO   Most strange!

[ZANCHE]   Most true.

LODOVICO

The bed of snakes is broke.   250

[ZANCHE]

I sadly do confess I had a hand
In the black deed.

FRANCISCO   Thou kept'st their counsel.

[ZANCHE]   Right.

For which, urged with contrition, I intend
This night to rob Vittoria.

LODOVICO   Excellent penitence!

Usurers dream on't while they sleep out sermons.   255

[ZANCHE]

To further our escape, I have entreated
Leave to retire me, till the funeral,
Unto a friend i'th'country. That excuse
Will further our escape. In coin and jewels
I shall, at least, make good unto your use   260
An hundred thousand crowns.

FRANCISCO   O noble wench!

LODOVICO

Those crowns we'll share.

[ZANCHE]   It is a dowry,

Methinks, should make that sunburnt proverb false,
'And wash the Ethiop white'.

FRANCISCO   It shall, away –

[ZANCHE]

Be ready for our flight.

FRANCISCO   An hour 'fore day.   265

Exit [ZANCHE] *the Moor*

O strange discovery! Why till now we knew not
The circumstance of either of their deaths.

Enter [ZANCHE *the*] *Moor*

249–50 ed. (Laid . . . strange! / MOO. Most . . . broke. Q)

250 *bed . . . broke* literally, the intertwined nest of snakes is untangled; figuratively,
the mystery is revealed

263–4 *sunburnt . . . white* The proverb is based on Jeremiah 13:23: 'Can the Ethio-
pian change his skin, or the leopard his spots?'

265 s.d. ed. (to r. of l. 266 in Q). Zanche's exit and immediate re-entry realistically
suggest her anxious over-insistence, as well as the precarious position of the
villains in Brachiano's court (cf. l. 172).

[ZANCHE]
  You'll wait about midnight in the chapel.
FRANCISCO   There.
                                      [*Exit* ZANCHE]

LODOVICO
  Why, now our action's justified.
FRANCISCO   Tush for justice.
  What harms it justice? We now, like the partridge,   270
  Purge the disease with laurel, for the fame
  Shall crown the enterprise and quit the shame.

                                            Exeunt

[Act V, Scene iv]

Enter FLAM[INEO] *and* GASP[ARO] *at one door, another*
                way GIOVANNI *attended*

GASPARO
  The young Duke. Did you e'er see a sweeter prince?
FLAMINEO
  I have known a poor woman's bastard better favoured.
  This is behind him. Now to his face – all comparisons
  were hateful. Wise was the courtly peacock, that being
  a great minion and being compared for beauty, by some   5
  dottrels that stood by, to the kingly eagle, said the eagle
  was a far fairer bird than herself, not in respect of her
  feathers, but in respect of her long tallants. His will
  grow out in time – My gracious lord.
GIOVANNI
  I pray leave me, sir.   10
FLAMINEO
  Your Grace must be merry: 'tis I have cause to mourn,
  for wot you what said the little boy that rode behind his
  father on horseback?
GIOVANNI
  Why, what said he?

268 *You'll ... There* ed. (You'le ... midnight / In ... There. Q)
270–2 *like ... shame* According to Pliny, partridges purged themselves by eating
      laurel (or bay leaves), also a symbol of fame; Francisco declares that they will
      rid their crimes of any taint by the glory they will achieve.
272 *quit* clear, pay off
  6 *dottrels* a variety of plover, supposed to be easy game because of their stupidity;
      term often applied to simpletons
  8 *tallants* talons (with a possible pun on 'talents', natural disposition or abilities,
      as in *Love's Labour's Lost* IV.ii.63–4)

FLAMINEO

'When you are dead, father' (said he) 'I hope then I   15
shall ride in the saddle.' O, 'tis a brave thing for a man
to sit by himself: he may stretch himself in the stirrups,
look about, and see the whole compass of the hemi-
sphere. You're now, my lord, i'th'saddle.

GIOVANNI

Study your prayers, sir, and be penitent.   20
'Twere fit you'd think on what hath former bin,
I have heard grief named the eldest child of sin.

Exit [with others]

FLAMINEO

Study my prayers? He threatens me divinely. I am
falling to pieces already – I care not, though, like
Anacharsis, I were pounded to death in a mortar. And   25
yet that death were fitter for usurers' gold and themselves to be beaten together to make a most cordial
cullis for the devil.
He hath his uncle's villainous look already,
In *decimo-sexto*.

Enter COURTIER

Now, sir, what are you?   30

COURTIER

It is the pleasure, sir, of the young Duke
That you forbear the presence, and all rooms
That owe him reverence.

FLAMINEO

So, the wolf and the raven are very pretty fools when
they are young. Is it your office, sir, to keep me out?   35

---

22 *grief . . . sin* Cf. cardinal in *The Duchess of Malfi* (V.v.53–4): 'I suffer now for
what hath former bin / *Sorrow is held the eldest child of sin*'.
s.d. *Exit [with others]* ed. (Exit Giou. Q)

25 *Anacharsis* Scythian philosopher noted for his wisdom, actually killed by his
brother with an arrow. Webster's source confuses him with Anaxarchus,
pounded to death in a mortar with iron pestles because he challenged the
authority of Nicocreon, tyrant of Cyprus. Anaxarchus was famous for jesting
at death.

26–8 *usurers' . . . devil* A cullis, or fortifying broth, could be made by simmering
together bruised chicken bones and pieces of gold (supposed to have medicinal
value).

30 *decimo-sexto* a very small book, in which a page is one-sixteenth of a full sheet;
a diminutive person
s.d. ed. (to r. of l. 29 in Q)

32 *presence* presence-chamber

COURTIER

So the Duke wills.

FLAMINEO

Verily, master courtier, extremity is not to be used in
all offices. Say that a gentlewoman were taken out of her
bed about midnight and committed to Castle Angelo, to
the tower yonder, with nothing about her but her   40
smock. Would it not show a cruel part in the gentleman
porter to lay claim to her upper garment, pull it o'er
her head and ears, and put her in naked?

COURTIER

Very good: you are merry.   [*Exit*]

FLAMINEO

Doth he make a court ejectment of me? A flaming fire-   45
brand casts more smoke without a chimney than
within't. I'll smoor some of them.

    Enter [FRANCISCO, *Duke of*] *Florence*
     [*disguised as* MULINASSAR]

How now? Thou art sad.

FRANCISCO

I met even now with the most piteous sight.

FLAMINEO

Thou met'st another here, a pitiful   50
Degraded courtier.

FRANCISCO   Your reverend mother
Is grown a very old woman in two hours.
I found them winding of Marcello's corse,
And there is such a solemn melody
'Tween doleful songs, tears, and sad elegies,   55
Such as old grandames watching by the dead
Were wont t'outwear the nights with, that believe me
I had no eyes to guide me forth the room,

---

39 *Castle Angelo* i.e. the Castel Sant'Angelo at Rome, in which the real-life Vittoria
  was imprisoned

40 *tower yonder* The Red Bull audience would doubtless have understood by this
  the Tower of London, where King James had recently imprisoned Arbella
  Stuart, his cousin, for marrying for love without royal permission.

45–6 *flaming firebrand* a piece of wood kindled at the fire; one who kindles strife
  or mischief; one who deserves to burn in hell. Flamineo is playing on his own
  name.

47 *smoor* smother, suffocate

53 *winding of . . . corse* wrapping Marcello's corpse in a shroud or winding-sheet
  (the face was usually left uncovered)

56–7 *old . . . with* The practice of watching all night over the deceased, with candles
  burning, was increasingly disappearing in seventeenth-century England, but
  persisted in rural Ireland until the twentieth century.

They were so o'ercharged with water.
FLAMINEO   I will see them.
FRANCISCO
   'Twere much uncharity in you, for your sight   60
   Will add unto their tears.
FLAMINEO   I will see them.
FRANCISCO
   They are behind the traverse. I'll discover
   Their superstitious howling.   [*Draws the traverse*]

> CORNELIA, [ZANCHE] *the Moor and three other Ladies*
> *discovered, winding* MARCELLO's *corse. A song*

CORNELIA
   This rosemary is withered, pray get fresh:
   I would have these herbs grow up in his grave   65
   When I am dead and rotten. Reach the bays;
   I'll tie a garland here about his head:
   'Twill keep my boy from lightning. This sheet
   I have kept this twenty year, and every day
   Hallowed it with my prayers – I did not think   70
   He should have wore it.
[ZANCHE] [*Seeing* FLAMINEO] Look you; who are yon-
   der?
CORNELIA
   O, reach me the flowers.
[ZANCHE]
   Her ladyship's foolish.
WOMAN   Alas! Her grief
   Hath turned her child again.
CORNELIA (*To* FLAMINEO)   You're very welcome.
   There's rosemary for you and rue for you,   75

62 *traverse* a curtain at the rear of the stage. The tableau thus discovered has almost
   emblematic visual significance (recalling, perhaps, as at *King Lear* V.iii.257 s.d.,
   the pieta); it is held in place during the 'song'.
64 *rosemary* evergreen herb, symbol of immortality and remembrance, customary
   at weddings and funerals
66–8 *bays . . . lightning* Laurel wreaths were both tokens of fame and glory, and
   reputed to protect one from lightning.
68 *sheet* i.e. winding sheet
71–9 s.p. ZANCHE ed. (MOO. Q)
72–6 Cornelia may distribute real flowers, or be sufficiently unhinged to use ima-
   ginary ones (NCW IV.iv.60 ff. n.).
74 s.d. ed. (to r. of l. 75 in Q)
75–6 *rue . . . Heart's-ease* Rue, a perennial evergreen shrub, symbolized sorrow,
   repentance or compassion; the heart's-ease, or pansy, represented tranquillity.
75–7 *There's . . . myself* an obvious echo of Ophelia in *Hamlet* IV.v.175 ff.: 'There's
   rosemary, that's for remembrance; pray you, love, remember. And there is pan-
   sies, that's for thoughts . . . There's rue for you, and here's some for me.'

Heart's-ease for you. I pray make much of it.
I have left more for myself.
FRANCISCO   Lady, who's this?
CORNELIA
[*To* FLAMINEO] You are, I take it, the grave-maker.
FLAMINEO   So.
[ZANCHE]
'Tis Flamineo.
CORNELIA
Will you make me such a fool? [*Takes his hand*] Here's
   a white hand: 80
Can blood so soon be washed out? Let me see:
When screech-owls croak upon the chimney tops
And the strange cricket i'th'oven sings and hops,
When yellow spots do on your hands appear,
Be certain then you of a corse shall hear.   85
Out upon't, how 'tis speckled! H'as handled a toad
   sure.
Cowslip-water is good for the memory: pray buy me
   three ounces of't.
FLAMINEO
I would I were from hence.
CORNELIA   Do you hear, sir?
I'll give you a saying which my grandmother
Was wont, when she heard the bell toll, to sing o'er   90
Unto her lute –
FLAMINEO   Do, and you will, do.

   CORNELIA *doth this in several forms of distraction*

78 *grave-maker* grave-digger. In this case, Flamineo, as Marcello's murderer, is literally his 'grave-maker'.
80–1 *Here's . . . out?* Cf. Lady Macbeth in *Macbeth* V.i.43: 'What, will these hands
   ne'er be clean?'
82–5 *When . . . hear* In popular superstition, these were all signs that a death was
   imminent.
86 *how . . . speckled* Thomas Adams, author of *The White Devil or the Hypocrite
   Uncas'd* (1612), a sermon, praises his patron for being 'free from the aspersion
   of these speckled stains' – the sins which he is about to expose.
87 *Cowslip-water* medicinal extract from the cowslip flower, reputed to be good for
   the head and sinews
87–8 ed. (Couslep . . . oun / ces . . . sir? Q)
90–1 ed. (Was . . . lute / Doe . . . doe. Q)
91 *lute* Ophelia is playing on the lute when she enters in a distracted state in Q1
   of *Hamlet* IV.v.20; perhaps Cornelia has one too.
   s.d. ed. (to r. of ll. 93–5 in Q). The gestures of madness called for by the stage
   direction are in tension with the elegiac, melodic strain of the dirge itself; the
   discordant effect is appropriate to the play's increasing fragmentation and
   despair.

CORNELIA

    'Call for the robin-red-breast and the wren,
    Since o'er shady groves they hover,
    And with leaves and flow'rs do cover
    The friendless bodies of unburied men.   95
    Call unto his funeral dole
    The ant, the field-mouse, and the mole
    To rear him hillocks that shall keep him warm
    And (when gay tombs are robbed) sustain no harm,
    But keep the wolf far thence that's foe to men,   100
    For with his nails he'll dig them up again.'
    They would not bury him 'cause he died in a quarrel
    But I have an answer for them.
    'Let holy church receive him duly
    Since he paid the church tithes truly.'   105
    His wealth is summed, and this is all his store:
    This poor men get and great men get no more.
    Now the wares are gone, we may shut up shop.
    Bless you all good people.

              Exeunt CORNELIA[, ZANCHE] *and Ladies*

FLAMINEO

    I have a strange thing in me, to th'which   110
    I cannot give a name, without it be
    Compassion. I pray leave me.

                   Exit FRANCISCO

    This night I'll know the utmost of my fate:
    I'll be resolved what my rich sister means
    T'assign me for my service. I have lived   115
    Riotously ill, like some that live in court;
    And sometimes, when my face was full of smiles
    Have felt the maze of conscience in my breast.

---

92 *robin-red-breast . . . wren* allusion to the widespread belief that robins (and wrens, believed to be female robins) covered up and tended dead bodies

96 *dole* rites of funeral

100–1 *keep . . . again* According to popular superstition, the wolf was a minister of God's revenge, sent to dig up the corpses of those who had been murdered; cf. *The Duchess of Malfi* IV.ii.303–5: 'The wolf shall find her grave, and scrape it up; / Not to devour the corpse, but to discover / The horrid murther'.

106 *summed* reckoned
    this . . . store Cornelia may indicate the area of the stage on which Marcello lies or the winding sheet itself.

108 *shut . . . shop* Having perhaps retreated into the discovery space to sing her dirge (after talking to Flamineo), Cornelia now closes the curtains.

112 Flamineo's request that Francisco leave the stage is visual confirmation of his new interiority.

118 *maze* labyrinth; state of confusion

Oft gay and honoured robes those tortures try:
'We think caged birds sing, when indeed they cry'.   120

Enter BRACHIA[NO's] *Ghost. In his leather cassock and*
breeches, boots, a cowl [and in his hand] a
pot of lily-flowers with a skull in't

Ha! I can stand thee. [*The ghost approaches*] Nearer,
     nearer yet.
What a mockery hath death made of thee? Thou
     look'st sad.
In what place art thou? In yon starry gallery
Or in the cursed dungeon? No? Not speak?
Pray, sir, resolve me, what religion's best   125
For a man to die in? Or is it in your knowledge
To answer me how long I have to live?
That's the most necessary question.
Not answer? Are you still like some great men
That only walk like shadows up and down   130
And to no purpose? Say –

          The ghost throws earth upon him and
               shows him the skull

What's that? O fatal! He throws earth upon me.
A dead man's skull beneath the roots of flowers.
I pray speak, sir. Our Italian churchmen

---

119 i.e. often those who wear gay and honoured robes (i.e. courtiers) experience
     those tortures
120 s.d. ed. (to r. of ll. 121–7 in Q). This spectacular vision fulfils Flamineo's earlier
     vow to shake Brachiano 'by the hand' (V.iii.213), and confirms his private vision
     of the truth underlying appearances. It is highly emblematic: the lily symbolizes
     that which is fair in show but foul in smell, beneath which is buried the horrible
     symbol of mortality, the skull (revealed at l. 131).
     s.d.1 *leather cassock* A cassock was a long coat or cloak worn by soldiers; a
     leather cassock was worn by ghosts in tragedies.
     s.d.2 *cowl* monastic hood or robe. In Renaissance Italy, men were commonly
     buried in the habit of a Franciscan friar, in the hope that it would procure a
     remission of their sins.
121 *stand thee* Flamineo's defiance of Brachiano here recalls IV.ii.49–50.
122 *mockery* counterfeit, shadow; object of ridicule
123–4 *starry . . . dungeon* probably theatrical terms: the gallery or upper stage; the
     dungeon or the area below the stage, accessible by trapdoor, from which, in
     other plays, devils ascended
124, 129 The ghost's silence and ominous gestures are a powerful contrast (and
     perhaps rebuke) to Flamineo's rapid and desperate speech (cf. ghost in *Hamlet*
     I.i.50, whose silence suggests that 'it is offended').
130 *shadows* insubstantial persons
131 s.d. ed. (to r. of ll. 131–5 in Q)

Make us believe dead men hold conference   135
With their familiars, and many times
Will come to bed to them and eat with them.

                                        Exit Ghost

He's gone; and see, the skull and earth are vanished.
This is beyond melancholy. I do dare my fate
To do its worst. Now to my sister's lodging   140
And sum up all these horrors: the disgrace
The Prince threw on me; next the piteous sight
Of my dead brother; and my mother's dotage;
And last this terrible vision. All these
Shall with Vittoria's bounty turn to good,   145
Or I will drown this weapon in her blood.   *Exit*

[Act V, Scene v]

Enter FRANCISCO, LODOVICO, *and* HORTENSIO
[*overhearing them*]

LODOVICO
My lord upon my soul you shall no further:
You have most ridiculously engaged yourself
Too far already. For my part, I have paid
All my debts, so if I should chance to fall
My creditors fall not with me; and I vow   5
To quite all in this bold assembly
To the meanest follower. My lord, leave the city
Or I'll forswear the murder.

FRANCISCO   Farewell Lodovico.
If thou dost perish in this glorious act,
I'll rear unto thy memory that fame   10
Shall in the ashes keep alive thy name.

                    [*Exeunt* FRANCISCO *and* LODOVICO]

HORTENSIO
There's some black deed on foot. I'll presently

---

139 *This . . . melancholy* i.e. this ghost is more than a figment of imagination (unlike
   Isabella's ghost in IV.i.100, which Francisco believes is produced by his
   melancholy). According to contemporary theories, beyond melancholy lay spiritual despair (NCW V.iv.136 n.).
146 *this weapon* Flamineo rushes off the stage waving, probably, a poniard.
   6 *quite* repay, requite
  11 s.d. Lodovico and Francisco probably enter through the same door (while Hort-
     ensio enters through the other); here, they exit through opposite doors, having
     said their farewells. The staging thus anticipates the fracturing of the villains'
     plot.
  12 *presently* immediately

Down to the citadel and raise some force.
These strong court factions that do brook no checks
In the career oft break the riders' necks.   [*Exit*]   15

[Act V, Scene vi]

Enter VITTORIA *with a book in her hand,* ZANCHE;
FLAMINEO *following them*

FLAMINEO

What, are you at your prayers? Give o'er.

VITTORIA   How ruffin?

FLAMINEO

I come to you 'bout worldly business:
Sit down, sit down. Nay stay, blouze, you may hear it,
The doors are fast enough.

VITTORIA   Ha, are you drunk?

FLAMINEO

Yes, yes, with wormwood water – you shall taste   5
Some of it presently.

VITTORIA   What intends the fury?

FLAMINEO

You are my lord's executrix and I claim
Reward for my long service.

VITTORIA   For your service?

FLAMINEO

Come therefore, here is pen and ink, set down
What you will give me.   10

---

15 *career* short gallop at full speed; charge in tournament or battle
    oft ed. (of't Q)

0 s.d. ed. (to l. of ll. 1–6 in Q). Flamineo's first line indicates that the 'book' is
    devotional (perhaps a bible). One of Webster's sources claims that the mur-
    derers 'stabbed her where they found her at prayer'. On the stage, the reading
    of a book was a conventional sign of melancholy or guilt (cf. *The Duchess of
    Malfi* V.v.0 s.d.). Flamineo probably brandishes his poniard threateningly here,
    or otherwise menaces the women.

1 *ruffin* devil

3 *stay . . . it* Flamineo's words suggest that Zanche attempts to flee, a gesture of
    open rejection from his former 'sweet mistress' (V.i.150), and yet another rebuff
    in a series.
    blouze fat, red-faced wench (here ironic)

5 *wormwood* plant with a bitter taste; emblem of what is bitter and grievous to
    the soul

6 *fury* Cf. I.ii.268, II.i.244 and III.ii.278; normally used of an angry woman, here
    used ironically by Vittoria, perhaps turning Flamineo's description of Cornelia
    and general misogyny back on himself.

8 *service?* ed. (service Q)   10 s.d. ed. (outer margin, l. of l. 11 in Q)

She writes

VITTORIA
  There.
FLAMINEO Ha! Have you done already?
  'Tis a most short conveyance.
VITTORIA   I will read it.
  [*Reads*] 'I give that portion to thee and no other
  Which Cain groaned under having slain his brother.'
FLAMINEO
  A most courtly patent to beg by.
VITTORIA   You are a villain.   15
FLAMINEO
  Is't come to this? They say affrights cure agues.
  Thou hast a devil in thee: I will try
  If I can scare him from thee. Nay, sit still:
  My lord hath left me yet two case of jewels
  Shall make me scorn your bounty; you shall see them.   20
                                    [*Exit*]

VITTORIA
  Sure he's distracted.
ZANCHE   O he's desperate –
  For your own safety give him gentle language.

He enters with two case of pistols

FLAMINEO
  Look, these are better far at a dead lift
  Than all your jewel house.
VITTORIA   And yet methinks
  These stones have no fair lustre, they are ill set.   25
FLAMINEO
  I'll turn the right side towards you: you shall see
  How they will sparkle.
VITTORIA   Turn this horror from me!
  What do you want? What would you have me do?

---

11 *already?* ed. (already, Q)
13–14 *I . . . brother* Cf. Genesis 4:11–12: to Cain who slew his brother Abel, the
  Lord said: 'And now art thou cursed from the earth, which hath opened her
  mouth to receive thy brother's blood from thy hand; when thou tillest the
  ground, it shall not henceforth yield unto thee her strength; a fugitive and a
  vagabond shalt thou be in the earth'.
15 *courtly . . . by* Cf. V.i.112.   16 *They* ed. (the Q)
19 *case* pair (two pairs of pistols or four pistols: cf. ll. 94–5)
22 ed. (to r. of ll. 21–3 in Q)
23 *at . . . lift* in a sudden emergency (derived from pulling a heavy, or 'dead'
  weight), with an obvious play on 'dead'
27 *they* ed. (the Q)

Is not all mine yours? Have I any children?

FLAMINEO
Pray thee good woman, do not trouble me   30
With this vain worldly business; say your prayers.
I made a vow to my deceased lord
Neither yourself nor I should outlive him
The numb'ring of four hours.

VITTORIA   Did he enjoin it?

FLAMINEO
He did, and 'twas a deadly jealousy   35
Lest any should enjoy thee after him
That urged him vow me to it. For my death,
I did propound it voluntarily, knowing
If he could not be safe in his own court
Being a great Duke, what hope then for us?   40

VITTORIA
This is your melancholy and despair.

FLAMINEO   Away!
Fool thou art to think that politicians
Do use to kill the effects of injuries
And let the cause live. Shall we groan in irons
Or be a shameful and a weighty burden   45
To a public scaffold? This is my resolve:
I would not live at any man's entreaty
Nor die at any's bidding.

VITTORIA   Will you hear me?

FLAMINEO
My life hath done service to other men;
My death shall serve mine own turn. Make you ready.   50

VITTORIA
Do you mean to die indeed?

FLAMINEO   With as much pleasure
As e'er my father gat me.

VITTORIA [*Aside to* ZANCHE] Are the doors locked?

ZANCHE
Yes madam.

---

31 *worldly* ed. (wordly Q)

35–7 A possible reference to King Herod, who ordered that his adored wife Mariam
be killed upon his death; Lady Elizabeth Cary, the first woman playwright in
England, dramatized the story from Mariam's point of view in *The Tragedy
of Mariam, Fair Queen of Jewry*. Cary's play, published in 1613, circulated in
manuscript, and may be Webster's source here.

42 *Fool* ed. (Foole, Q)

47–8 *I . . . bidding* An echo of Vittoria's lines during her arraignment (III.ii.138–
9): 'I scorn to hold my life / At yours or any man's entreaty, sir'.

VITTORIA
Are you grown an atheist? Will you turn your body,
Which is the goodly palace of the soul,   55
To the soul's slaughter house? O the cursed devil,
Which doth present us with all other sins
Thrice candied o'er: despair with gall and stibium,
Yet we carouse it off – [Aside to ZANCHE] cry out for
   help –
Makes us forsake that which was made for man,   60
The world, to sink to that was made for devils,
Eternal darkness.
ZANCHE   Help, help!
FLAMINEO   I'll stop your throat
With winter plums –
VITTORIA   I prithee yet remember
Millions are now in graves, which at last day
Like mandrakes shall rise shrieking.
FLAMINEO   Leave your prating,   65
For these are but grammatical laments,
Feminine arguments, and they move me
As some in pulpits move their auditory
More with their exclamation than sense
Of reason or sound doctrine.
ZANCHE [Aside]   Gentle madam   70
Seem to consent, only persuade him teach
The way to death; let him die first.
VITTORIA
[Aside] 'Tis good, I apprehend it.
[Aloud] To kill oneself is meat that we must take
Like pills, not chew't, but quickly swallow it –   75
The smart o'th'wound or weakness of the hand

54–5 *body . . . soul* Perhaps revealing her sensual nature, Vittoria inverts the usual
   image of the body as the soul's *prison* (cf. *The Duchess of Malfi* IV.ii.127–31:
   'didst thou ever see a lark in a cage? such is the soul in the body: this world is
   like her little turf of grass, and the heaven o'er our heads, like her looking-glass,
   only gives us a miserable knowledge of the small compass of our prison'.)

58 *candied o'er* sugared over

58–9 *despair . . . off* i.e. despair (unlike other sins) is flavoured with gall (bile;
   venom) and stibium (the poison antimony), yet we drink it down (commit
   suicide)

62–3 *stop . . . plums* i.e. gag you with hard fruit (stop your mouth with bullets); so
   NCW V.vi.63–4 n.

65 *mandrakes* Cf. III.i.50 n.

66–7 *grammatical . . . arguments* i.e. laments composed according to formal rules,
   weak arguments

69 *exclamation* formal declamation; emphatic speech

May else bring treble torments.

FLAMINEO   I have held it
A wretched and most miserable life,
Which is not able to die.

VITTORIA   O but frailty!
Yet I am now resolved: farewell, affliction!   80
Behold Brachiano, I, that while you lived
Did make a flaming altar of my heart
To sacrifice unto you, now am ready
To sacrifice heart and all. Farewell, Zanche.

ZANCHE
How, madam! Do you think that I'll outlive you?   85
Especially when my best self Flamineo
Goes the same voyage?

FLAMINEO   O most loved Moor!

ZANCHE
Only by all my love let me entreat you:
Since it is most necessary none of us
Do violence on ourselves, let you or I   90
Be her sad taster, teach her how to die.

FLAMINEO
Thou dost instruct me nobly. Take these pistols,
Because my hand is stained with blood already;
Two of these you shall level at my breast,
Th'other 'gainst your own, and so we'll die,   95
Most equally contented. But first swear
Not to outlive me.

VITTORIA and [ZANCHE]   Most religiously.

FLAMINEO
Then here's an end of me. Farewell daylight
And O contemptible physic! That dost take
So long a study only to preserve   100
So short a life, I take my leave of thee.
These are two cupping-glasses that shall draw
All my infected blood out –

82–3 *flaming ... you* A continental emblem book (Rollenhagen's *Nucleus Emblematum*, Cologne, 1611–13) shows a flaming heart on an altar as an image of sacrifice to God.

91 *taster* a servant whose duty it is to taste food and drink before they are served to his master, in order to ascertain their quality or detect poison

92–5 Flamineo offers each woman a case or pair of pistols; each of them points one at Flamineo, one at the other woman.

97 s.p. ed. (VIT. & MOO. Q)

102 *cupping-glasses* cup-shaped surgical vessels applied to the body, then heated to create a vacuum and thus draw off blood

Are you ready?

VITTORIA *and* ZANCHE   Ready.   *Showing the pistols*

FLAMINEO

Whither shall I go now? O Lucian thy ridiculous purga- 105
tory! To find Alexander the Great cobbling shoes,
Pompey tagging points, and Julius Caesar making hair
buttons, Hannibal selling blacking, and Augustus crying
garlic, Charlemagne selling lists by the dozen, and King
Pippin crying apples in a cart drawn with one horse.   110
Whether I resolve to fire, earth, water, air,
Or all the elements by scruples, I know not
Nor greatly care – Shoot, shoot,
Of all deaths the violent death is best,
For from ourselves it steals ourselves so fast   115
The pain once apprehended is quite past.

They shoot and run to him and tread upon him

VITTORIA

What, are you dropped?

FLAMINEO

I am mixed with earth already: as you are noble
Perform your vows and bravely follow me.

VITTORIA

Whither – to hell?

ZANCHE   To most assured damnation.   120

VITTORIA

O, thou most cursed devil.

ZANCHE   Thou art caught –

VITTORIA

In thine own engine. I tread the fire out

104 s.d. ed. (to r. of ll. 102–3 in Q)
    VITTORIA *and* ZANCHE ed. (BOTH Q)
105–6 *Lucian . . . purgatory* Lucian's *Menippos* includes different examples of the
    ignominious fates of great men, such as King Philip of Macedon cobbling shoes.
106 *purgatory!* ed. (Purgatory Q)
    Alexander . . . shoes Cf. Hamlet's different musing on the fate of Alexander
    (V.i.203–4): 'Why may not imagination trace the noble dust of Alexander, till
    'a find it stopping a bunghole?'
107 *tagging points* fixing metal tags on the laces or points which held together Elizab-
    ethan clothing
107–10 *Julius . . . horse* Flamineo increases the absurdity of his examples by giving
    them wittily appropriate activities: bald Caesar makes hair buttons, black Han-
    nibal sells black polish, King Pippin (also a variety of apple) calls out the price
    of his apples, etc. (Dent, p. 165).
109 *lists* strips of cloth   112 *by scruples* by small degrees or portions
116 s.d. ed. (to r. of ll. 115–18 in Q)
120 ed. (Whither to hell, Q)   122 *engine* device

That would have been my ruin.
FLAMINEO
Will you be perjured? What a religious oath was Styx
that the gods never durst swear by and violate? O that   125
we had such an oath to minister, and to be so well kept
in our courts of justice.
VITTORIA
Think whither thou art going.
ZANCHE   And remember
What villanies thou hast acted.
VITTORIA   This thy death
Shall make me like a blazing ominous star –   130
Look up and tremble.
FLAMINEO   O I am caught with a springe!
VITTORIA
You see the fox comes many times short home,
'Tis here proved true.
FLAMINEO   Killed with a couple of braches.
VITTORIA
No fitter offering for the infernal Furies
Than one in whom they reigned while he was living.   135
FLAMINEO
O, the way's dark and horrid! I cannot see –
Shall I have no company?
VITTORIA   O yes, thy sins
Do run before thee to fetch fire from hell
To light thee thither.
FLAMINEO   O I smell soot,
Most stinking soot, the chimney is a-fire –   140
My liver's parboiled like Scotch holy-bread;

124 *Styx* in Greek myth, a river in the underworld. The gods swore their oaths upon
    its honoured waters (*Iliad* XV, 36 ff.).
128 *Think . . . remember* ed. (Iustice . . . remeber Q)
130 *blazing . . . star* an ominous prodigy foreshadowing the fall of princes (cf. the
    'rough-bearded comet' of V.iii.31). Using light imagery (cf. the 'diamonds' of
    III.ii.294), Vittoria prophesies her own triumphant revenge.
131 *springe* snare for trapping small game and birds
132 *fox . . . home* i.e. even the cunning fox can come home without his tail (i.e.
    dead)
133 *with . . . braches* i.e. by a couple of bitches
134 *Furies* Cf. IV.iii.126, 152, where first Lodovico, then Monticelso, is supposed
    to be inhabited by the Furies.
139–40 *O . . . a-fire* ed. (one line in Q)   140 *stinking* ed. (sinking Q)
                                                        chimney is ed. (chimneis Q)
141 *liver* seat of the passions
    Scotch holy-bread according to Cotgrave's *Dictionarie of the French and English
    Tongues* (1611), a sodden sheep's liver

There's a plumber laying pipes in my guts, it scalds;
Wilt thou outlive me?
ZANCHE   Yes, and drive a stake
Through thy body; for we'll give it out
Thou didst this violence upon thyself.   145
FLAMINEO
O cunning devils! Now I have tried your love
And doubled all your reaches.

Riseth

                           I am not wounded:
The pistols held no bullets: 'twas a plot
To prove your kindness to me and I live
To punish your ingratitude. I knew   150
One time or other you would find a way
To give me a strong potion. O men
That lie upon your death-beds and are haunted
With howling wives, ne'er trust them – they'll remarry
Ere the worm pierce your winding sheet, ere the spider   155
Make a thin curtain for your epitaphs.
How cunning you were to discharge! Do you practise
at the Artillery Yard? Trust a woman? Never, never.
Brachiano be my precedent: we lay our souls to pawn
to the devil for a little pleasure and a woman makes   160
the bill of sale. That ever man should marry! For one
Hypermnestra that saved her lord and husband, forty-
nine of her sisters cut their husbands' throats all in one

143–4 *drive . . . body* traditional treatment of suicides, who were then buried at
     crossroads
147 *doubled . . . reaches* i.e. matched your plots or contrivances
     s.d. ed. (to r. of ll. 147–8 in Q)
     s.d. *Riseth* ed. (Flamineo riseth Q)
148 A metatheatrical joke; as Flamineo rises, Webster makes his audience (which
     has shared the women's illusions) conscious of the reality of the theatre, in
     which death is always feigned.
152–4 *men . . . wives* possibly a deliberate allusion to Brachiano's cry at V.iii.37–8:
     'How miserable a thing it is to die / 'Mongst women howling!'
158 *Artillery Yard* In 1610 the weekly exercise of arms and military discipline for
     citizens and merchants was revived in the Artillery Gardens at Bishopsgate.
159 *precedent* ed. (president Q)
161–4 *For . . . night* Hypermnestra's father, Danaus, was warned by an oracle that
     he would be killed by one of his brother's sons. He then persuaded his fifty
     daughters to marry his brother's fifty sons, and instructed them to murder their
     husbands on the wedding night. Only Hypermnestra disobeyed her father and
     spared her husband.

night. There was a shoal of virtuous horse-leeches.
Here are two other instruments.

Enter LOD[OVICO], GASP[ARO], PEDRO, CARLO

VITTORIA   Help, help!   165
FLAMINEO
What noise is that? Hah? False keys i'th'court!
LODOVICO
We have brought you a masque.
FLAMINEO   A matachin it seems
By your drawn swords. Churchmen turned revellers.
CONSPIRATORS
Isabella, Isabella!

[*They throw off their disguises*]

LODOVICO
Do you know us now?
FLAMINEO   Lodovico and Gasparo.   170
LODOVICO
Yes, and that Moor the Duke gave pension to
Was the great Duke of Florence.
VITTORIA   O we are lost.
FLAMINEO
You shall not take justice from forth my hands –
O let me kill her! I'll cut my safety
Through your coats of steel. Fate's a spaniel,   175
We cannot beat it from us: what remains now?
Let all that do ill take this precedent:

---

164 *horse-leeches* bloodsuckers; double-tongued rhetoricians (cf. III.ii.281)
165 *two ... instruments* i.e. two more weapons (perhaps poniard and sword, with
    which he may have intended to attack Vittoria and Zanche) probably wrested
    from his grasp by the four assassins. Alternatively, this could be a contemptuous
    reference to Vittoria and Zanche as 'instruments' of death like Hypermnestra's
    sisters.
    Help, help! Vittoria may be appealing to the masked conspirators to save her
    from Flamineo (NCW V.vi.163–4 n.).
167 *masque* ritualistic dance of masked revellers, who invited those already present
    to participate; often used by Jacobean dramatists as a means to bring on dis-
    guised conspirators for a final massacre, to which the formality of the masque
    offers a striking contrast (cf. *The Revenger's Tragedy* V.iii)
    matachin sword-dance in masks and fantastic costumes
168–9 ed. (By ... swords. / Church-men ... Isabella, Q)
175–6 *Fate's ... us* Webster probably borrows this phrase from Nashe's *Lenten
    Stuffe* (1599), which explains: 'the more you thinke to crosse it, the more you
    blesse and further it'. Spaniels were reputed to fawn on those who beat them.
177 *precedent* ed. (president Q)

'Man may his fate foresee, but not prevent'.
And of all axioms this shall win the prize:
' 'Tis better to be fortunate than wise'.   180

GASPARO
Bind him to the pillar.

VITTORIA   O your gentle pity!
I have seen a blackbird that would sooner fly
To a man's bosom, than to stay the gripe
Of the fierce sparrow-hawk.

GASPARO   Your hope deceives you.

VITTORIA
If Florence be i'th'court, would he would kill me.   185

GASPARO
Fool! Princes give rewards with their own hands,
But death or punishment by the hands of others.

LODOVICO
Sirrah you once did strike me – I'll strike you
Into the centre.

FLAMINEO
Thou'lt do it like a hangman, a base hangman,   190
Not like a noble fellow, for thou seest
I cannot strike again.

LODOVICO   Dost laugh?

FLAMINEO
Wouldst have me die, as I was born, in whining?

GASPARO
Recommend yourself to heaven.

FLAMINEO
No, I will carry mine own commendations thither.   195

LODOVICO
O, could I kill you forty times a day
And use't four year together 'twere too little:
Nought grieves but that you are too few to feed
The famine of our vengeance. What dost think on?

FLAMINEO
Nothing, of nothing: leave thy idle questions;   200
I am i'th'way to study a long silence.

181 *Bind ... pillar* either a freestanding stage post or one of the two pillars sup-
    porting the heavens
183 *stay* wait for
189 *centre* i.e. heart or soul
190 *hangman* executioner
198 *grieves* ed. (greeu's Q)
200 *Nothing ... nothing* This secular response is later echoed by the Duchess in *The
    Duchess of Malfi* before her death (IV.ii.16).
    idle foolish, useless

To prate were idle – I remember nothing.
There's nothing of so infinite vexation
As man's own thoughts.
LODOVICO   O thou glorious strumpet,
Could I divide thy breath from this pure air   205
When't leaves thy body, I would suck it up
And breathe't upon some dunghill.
VITTORIA   You, my death's-man;
Methinks thou dost not look horrid enough,
Thou hast too good a face to be a hangman;
If thou be, do thy office in right form: 210
Fall down upon thy knees and ask forgiveness.
LODOVICO
O thou hast been a most prodigious comet
But I'll cut off your train: kill the Moor first.
VITTORIA
You shall not kill her first. Behold my breast.
I will be waited on in death; my servant   215
Shall never go before me.
GASPARO
Are you so brave?
VITTORIA   Yes, I shall welcome death
As princes do some great ambassadors:
I'll meet thy weapon halfway.
LODOVICO   Thou dost tremble –
Methinks fear should dissolve thee into air.   220
VITTORIA
O thou art deceived, I am too true a woman:
Conceit can never kill me. I'll tell thee what –
I will not in my death shed one base tear,
Or if look pale, for want of blood, not fear.
CARLO
Thou art my task, black fury.
ZANCHE   I have blood   225
As red as either of theirs; wilt drink some?

210–11 It was conventional for executioners to beg a perfunctory pardon before
    going to work: cf. *Measure for Measure* IV.ii.49–51: 'I do find your hangman is
    a more penitent trade than your bawd; he doth oft'ner ask forgiveness'.
213 *train* tail of a comet, with a pun on 'attendants' (Zanche)
216–19 ed. (Shall ... brave. / Yes ... death / As ... weapon / halfe ... tremble Q)
222 *Conceit* idea or imaginative apprehension (of death); vanity or pride
    (proverbially feminine); physical conception of a child
223 An echo of Vittoria during the arraignment (III.ii.284–6): 'I will not weep, / No
    I do scorn to call up one poor tear / To fawn on your injustice'.
225–6 *I ... theirs* Red blood was a sign of courage.

'Tis good for the falling sickness: I am proud
Death cannot alter my complexion,
For I shall ne'er look pale.
LODOVICO   Strike, strike
With a joint motion.

[*They strike*]

VITTORIA   'Twas a manly blow.   230
The next thou giv'st, murder some sucking infant
And then thou wilt be famous.
FLAMINEO   O what blade is't?
A Toledo or an English fox?
I ever thought a cutler should distinguish
The cause of my death rather than a doctor.   235
Search my wound deeper: tent it with the steel
That made it.
VITTORIA
O my greatest sin lay in my blood.
Now my blood pays for't.
FLAMINEO   Th'art a noble sister –
I love thee now. If woman do breed man   240
She ought to teach him manhood: fare thee well.
Know many glorious women that are famed

227 *falling sickness* epilepsy
229–30 *Strike . . . motion* This is group tragedy, as the three are stabbed simultan-
eously: Flamineo by Lodovico, Vittoria by Gasparo, and Zanche by Carlo.
230–2 In the 1991 National Theatre production, Josette Simon as Vittoria met
Lodovico's dagger thrusts 'as though they represented a tempestuously flattering act of copulation', and completed the bitter self-parody with a 'cool pre-
tence that she is congratulating him on his sexual prowess [which] ironically
deflates his vengeful achievement' (Paul Taylor, *The Independent*, 20 June
1991).
233 *Toledo . . . fox* different types of short swords (the latter inscribed with a wolf,
commonly mistaken for a fox)
234 *cutler* one who deals in knives and cutting utensils
236 *tent* i.e. use a tent or plug to search or clean my wound; with a pun on tend,
care for (with a possible reference to miraculous cures effected by wounds)
236–7 ed. (one line in Q)
238–9 *blood . . . blood* Cf. I.ii.290. Usually interpreted as conventional penitence,
however uncharacteristic: 'My greatest sin lay in my sexual passion; now my
life-blood pays for it'. (An actor, of course, could deliver even this meaning
ironically.) However, the first 'blood' could also mean simply 'high temper,
mettle', so Vittoria maintains her spirited self-defence; it could also mean
'kindred, family', so Vittoria targets Flamineo.
240 *woman*; 242 *women* (woemen Q) The unusual spelling here may just indicate
a pun: woman as 'woe-to-man'.

For masculine virtue have been vicious
Only a happier silence did betide them.
She hath no faults, who hath the art to hide them.   245

VITTORIA

My soul, like to a ship in a black storm,
Is driven I know not whither.

FLAMINEO   Then cast anchor.
'Prosperity doth bewitch men seeming clear,
But seas do laugh, show white, when rocks are near.
We cease to grieve, cease to be Fortune's slaves,   250
Nay cease to die by dying.' [*To* ZANCHE] Art thou gone?
[*To* VITTORIA] And thou so near the bottom? False report
Which says that women vie with the nine Muses
For nine tough durable lives. I do not look
Who went before, nor who shall follow me;   255
No, at myself I will begin and end:
'While we look up to heaven we confound
Knowledge with knowledge'. O, I am in a mist.

VITTORIA

O happy they that never saw the court,
'Nor ever knew great man but by report'.   260

Dies

FLAMINEO

I recover like a spent taper for a flash,
And instantly go out.
Let all that belong to great men remember th'old wives'
tradition, to be like the lions i'th'Tower on Candlemas
day, to mourn if the sun shine for fear of the pitiful   265
remainder of winter to come.
'Tis well yet there's some goodness in my death,
My life was a black charnel. I have caught

---

247 *I . . . whither* Sinners proverbially died not knowing where they were going.

248–9 Webster's source (Alexander's *Croesus* I.i.65–73) clarifies this image: 'Vaine
    foole, that thinkes soliditie to find / . . . The fome is whitest, where the Rock is
    neare / . . . The greatest danger oft doth least appeare'.

252–4 *False . . . lives* Proverbially, nine lives are attributed to women and *cats*, not
    Muses.

260 s.d. *Dies* ed. (Vittoria dies Q)   263 *wives'* ed. (wides Q)

263–6 *Let . . . come* Proverbially, 'If Candlemas day [2 February] be fair and bright,
    winter will have another flight'. Like the lions (kept in a small zoo in the Tower),
    the courtier who anticipates gloomy weather even in bright sunshine 'will keepe
    him in such humilitie and lowlynesse as Princes like of' (Pettie II.211).

268–70 *I . . . irrecoverably* another metatheatrical joke, since an actor with a long
    part like Flamineo's might well be in danger of losing his voice at the end of
    the play

An everlasting cold. I have lost my voice
Most irrecoverably. Farewell, glorious villains.   270
'This busy trade of life appears most vain,
Since rest breeds rest where all seek pain by pain.'
Let no harsh flattering bells resound my knell,
Strike thunder and strike loud to my farewell.   *Dies*

ENGLISH AMBASSADOR
[*Within*] This way, this way, break ope the doors, this
    way.   275

LODOVICO
Ha, are we betrayed?
Why then let's constantly die all together,
And having finished this most noble deed,
Defy the worst of fate, not fear to bleed.

Enter AMBASSAD[ORS] *and* GIOVANNI [GUARDS *follow*]

ENGLISH AMBASSADOR
Keep back the Prince – shoot, shoot –

[GUARDS *shoot at conspirators*]

LODOVICO   O I am wounded.   280
I fear I shall be ta'en.
GIOVANNI   You bloody villains,
By what authority have you committed
This massacre?
LODOVICO   By thine.
GIOVANNI   Mine?
LODOVICO   Yes, thy uncle,
Which is a part of thee, enjoined us to't.
Thou know'st me I am sure, I am Count Lodowick,   285
And thy most noble uncle in disguise
Was last night in thy court.
GIOVANNI   Ha!
GASPARO   Yes, that Moor
Thy father chose his pensioner.
GIOVANNI   He turned murderer!

271 *trade* habitual course of action; passage to and fro; profession practised as a
    means of livelihood
274 *Strike thunder* a prodigious sign associated with the fall of great men (cf. *The
    Revenger's Tragedy* V.iii.44: 'Duke's groans are thunder's watchwords'); also, of
    course, a theatrical directive (or a reference to the offstage pounding of the
    doors by the ambassadors: NCW V.vi.270 n.)
277 *constantly* resolutely
279 s.d. ed. (following l. 274 in Q)
283 *This ... uncle* ed. (This ... Mine? / LOD. Yes, Q)
287–8 ed. (Was ... Ha! / Yes, ... pentioner. Q)

Away with them to prison and to torture.
All that have hands in this shall taste our justice,   290
As I hope heaven.
LODOVICO   I do glory yet
That I can call this act mine own: for my part,
The rack, the gallows, and the torturing wheel
Shall be but sound sleeps to me. Here's my rest –
'I limbed this night-piece and it was my best'.   295
GIOVANNI
Remove the bodies. See, my honoured lord,
What use you ought make of their punishment.
'Let guilty men remember their black deeds
Do lean on crutches, made of slender reeds.'

                                        [Exeunt]

Instead of an Epilogue only this of Martial supplies me: 300
Haec fuerint nobis praemia si placui.
For the action of the play, 'twas generally well, and I
dare affirm, with the joint testimony of some of their
own quality (for the true imitation of life, without striv-
ing to make nature a monster), the best that ever 305
became them: whereof as I make a general acknowl-
edgement, so in particular I must remember the well
approved industry of my friend Master Perkins, and
confess the worth of his action did crown both the
beginning and end.   310

FINIS

294 rest peace of mind; final resolution; remaining hope
295 limbed limned (painted, portrayed) with a possible pun on 'limbed' as 'pulled
    limb from limb, dismembered' (though the OED records the earliest use of this
    verb in 1674)
    night-piece painting representing a night-scene; tragic composition (used later
    by Webster himself to describe his elegy upon the death of Prince Henry (A
    Monumental Column, dedication))
297 ought make i.e. ought to make
301 Haec . . . placui 'These things will be our reward, if I have pleased' (Martial II,
    xci, 8).
304 quality profession
308 Master Perkins Richard Perkins was the leading player of Queen Anne's Men,
    well known for both his experience and his versatility; he probably played the
    part of Flamineo.